Lucy Ellen Guernsey

Lady Betty's Governess

Or the Corbet Chronicles

Lucy Ellen Guernsey

Lady Betty's Governess
Or the Corbet Chronicles

ISBN/EAN: 9783337107147

Printed in Europe, USA, Canada, Australia, Japan

Cover: Foto ©ninafisch / pixelio.de

More available books at **www.hansebooks.com**

Lady Betty's Governess;

OR,

THE CORBET CHRONICLES.

BY

LUCY ELLEN GUERNSEY,

AUTHOR OF "IRISH AMY," "WINIFRED," "CHRISTMAS AT CEDAR HILL,"
"SCHOOL-GIRL'S TREASURY," "CHILD'S TREASURE," ETC.

NEW-YORK:
T. WHITTAKER,
No. 2 BIBLE HOUSE.

THE PREAMBLE.

WHEN I was a young maid and just about to be married to my excellent husband, with whom I have lived so long and so happily, my dear and honored mother-in-law gave me as a wedding present, a chronicle (if I may so call it) which she herself had received in like manner, from her grandame, who brought her up. She said it had for some generations been the custom in her family to keep such annals, and in this way had many facts and circumstances been preserved which would otherwise have been lost.

I have always preserved this chronicle with great care, and shall make a copy of it (if time and opportunity present) for the use of my daughters, feeling that my dear and honored cousin, Lord Stanton, hath the best right to the original manuscript.

Thinking upon doing the same put it into my

mind to make a similar chronicle for the use of mine own daughters. I feel that it will interest them (especially when I am dead and gone, as I soon shall be) to know what their mother was at their age. I am able to make this account the more full and particular, as during the year or two before I was married, and specially while I was living in the family of my dear and honored lady at Stanton Court, it was my habit to keep a journal, in which I wrote down not only what most concerned me, but a vast deal besides.

In these pages I have transcribed a part of that journal, sometimes supplementing the text with my present recollections of events in those days.

It hath been my lot to see many and sad changes. The Archbishop who was so great with king and court when these pages were written, I saw mobbed, insulted, and finally thrust into prison, from which he was delivered only by death. In him was fulfilled those words of the prophet, "When thou shalt cease to oppress, then shall they oppress thee; and when thou shalt cease to deal treacherously, then shall they deal treacherously with thee!" I could never get over the way Mr. Prynne treated the old man. 'Twas not like a Christian nor a gentleman, however great had been his wrongs, and no one can deny that they were bitter enough.

Then came that terrible event, the death of the king. My husband never approved of Cromwell's course in that matter, though he said, and as I believe truly, that there was a time when Cromwell would have saved him, had the king only been true to himself. But there alas! was his great failing—sorrowfully acknowledged by friends as well as foes. With all his virtues, the king knew neither truth nor gratitude. His want of the first he called kingcraft, like his father before him: and as for the last, I do believe he felt himself raised too far above ordinary mortals to owe them anything. If they served him, even to the laying down of their lives, it was well—they did no more than their duty. If they did not, then were they rebels and traitors. But he hath gone to his account, and I will not judge him. My lord adhered to him always, and afterward went abroad to the court of the young king; Walter taking the charge of his estates and sending him money.

Since the Restoration my husband has lived in retirement, though he has had more than one offer of office and preferment; but he loves this quiet country life, and so do I.

My lord is back at the hall with the second

lady and her children and his own boys, and we are all good friends. She is an excellent woman, but no more like my own dear lady than a cabbage is like a lily. Yet we are good friends always, and she is very kind to me and my children.

I feel that my time is short, and that I must soon leave my dear husband and children. I pray my precious girls to receive this volume as a legacy from their mother, and to remember her last words—that the path of duty, though its way be hard and thorny, is always the path of safety—the path which leads to honor here and happiness hereafter. "To do his duty in that state of life to which it hath pleased God to call him," is the sum and substance of a Christian's work. A poor plowman or milk-maid can do as much with God's help, and the greatest king on earth can do no more.

MARGARET CORBET.

LADY BETTY'S GOVERNESS.

CHAPTER I.

March 1, 1637.

SO it is really all settled, and I am to leave this little parsonage, where I have spent all my days hitherto, and go to Stanton Court to live among lords and ladies and to be companion or governess to a poor little hunchbacked girl. I wonder how I shall like it? However, as Felicia says, that is the least part of the matter. Felicia need not have put it so bluntly, I think. That is always her way, but it does not help to make matters easier. As old Esther says, if she wanted to hammer a nail into a board, she would begin head foremost. She thinks, forsooth, it is all because she is so very sincere; but I don't see that she is any more so than other folks. I am sure, when she tells mother, after she and I have had a quarrel, she manages to turn things to her own advantage as well as anybody I ever saw. Mother understands her pretty well, that is one comfort.

It really does not matter much, however, whether I like it or not. We cannot all stay at home, that is clear, especially now that my dear father is gone, and we must leave the dear old parsonage for the cottage at the other end of the village, which will hardly hold us all. I don't mind leaving home so much, now that *home* no longer means this queer old pile of stone, all angles and corners and outside stairs, and all overgrown with ivy and traveller's joy, and what not. I don't think I can ever take root in any place again, even though it were far finer than this; and the cottage is by no means so pleasant, though very good for a cottage.

But some of us must earn our own bread, that is plain. Poor Dick is doing so already, with all the cheerfulness in the world, as clerk to old Master Smith, the great stationer in Chester. He never complains, though all his hopes and projects are disappointed, and why should I? Felicia is older and stronger than I am, 'tis true; but then, as mother says to me: "Who would ever live with her that could help it? She has such an unhappy temper!" So they all say. When *I* get vexed and in a fury, I have a *bad* temper. That is all the difference. As long as I can remember, every one in the house has given way to Felicia, on account of her "unhappy temper," but I don't see that it makes her any happier.

"Felicia!" Never was any one more completely misnamed. That is the worst of these significant names which people are so fond of giving now-a-days. A child is named Grace, Mercy, or Peace, and Grace grows up more awkward than a cow, Mercy takes delight in tormenting, and Peace keeps the whole house in an uproar from morning till night.

I would not for the world say anything to reflect upon my honored father, especially now that he is gone from us; but it does seem a pity that he should have risked all his savings for so many years, and all mother's little fortune, in such an adventure as that ship to the Spice Islands. 'Tis true, no doubt, that some great fortunes have been made in that way, like that of Mr Gunning, in Bristol; but I believe it is also true, that for one ship that comes home laden with pepper, mace, and nutmegs, at least four go to the bottom or are taken by pirates.

Master Smith says, however, that no such wild scheme is got up, but the foremost to rush into it, and risk their little alls, are masters and fellows in colleges, country clergymen, and widows with a little property—just the people who have the least chance of understanding the matter. I will say that dear mother was as much against it as she could ever be against any scheme of my father's; but he was so sanguine, and he ever thought little of the opinion of women on any subject.

But there is no use in going over all that now. What is done is done. What is *to do*, is to make the best struggle we can to live decently and honestly, keep out of debt, and—I don't know what else, I am sure.

March 3.

Dick is come home, by favor of Master Smith, to spend my last Sunday with us. I must say he is very kind to Dick. Indeed, every one has been very kind to us so far, even the new rector. 'Twas he got me my place at Stanton Court, where I am to go the day after to-morrow. To-day we have a new instance of his goodness. He allows mother to take what furniture she chooses from the parsonage, as he means to replenish it entirely. That will be a great help toward fitting up the cottage. Indeed, I hardly know what we should have done without it, for mother hath but little of her own, and most of the furniture here belongs to the house, though my father had it all refitted and repaired more than once. I wish I could stay here to help them move, but that is impossible. I am to go southward with the new rector and his servants, and I may not have such a good opportunity again in a long time.

I have showed Dick what I have written. I do so sometimes, though no one else knows that I keep a journal. Dick has known of it from the first. It was he that put me upon keeping it and gave me this large fair blank book. Before that I used to write upon such scraps as I could find.

When he came to that—"I don't know what else,"—Dick demurred. "You have left out the gist of the whole matter Peggy," said he. "Your summing up is like the playbill Master Smith told me of—'The play of Hamlet with the part of Hamlet omitted.'"

"What have I left out?" I asked.

"Tell me, Peggy, what do you suppose we were made for?" said he. "Why were we put into this world, and assigned certain parts and duties therein? Who has put us here, and for what?"

"Our Heavenly Father has put us here, of course;" I replied: "but Dick, if you ask me why, I am not sure that I have an answer ready."

"Do you remember when our Lord shall come in His glory and all the holy angels with Him, what will be the invitation to those on His right hand?"

"'Come, ye blessed of my Father, inherit the kingdom prepared for you from the foundation of the world,'" I repeated.

"Then, sweetheart, since such a kingdom is prepared for us—a kingdom of Everlasting Life—does it not seem likely that we are placed here as a school of preparation for that glorious heritage? And looking at it in that light, may it not give us a key whereby to understand at least some of the tasks and exercises which are set us in that same school?"

"I suppose it may," said I.

Dick said no more. It is not his way to say a great deal, and perhaps that may be one reason why his words dwell in my mind and I cannot get rid of them if I would. I wish I could think and feel as he does on these subjects. It is the only point on which we do not fully sympathize. Of course I believe in the Christian religion, and say my prayers night and morning. I *fear* God, and I wish I could honestly say that I *love* Him; but I cannot think of Him as Dick does, as a loving Father, ever watching over us for good, ordering all things for the best, and always ready to hear our requests and sympathize with our troubles. It does seem to me as though He were very far off— too far to see or care for all the little joys and sorrows which make up the lives of every-day people.

To-day we are beginning to pull up and pull down, and the house puts on an aspect of mourning. I had been working as hard as I could all the morning at mending the old tapestry hanging (and dusty, disagreeable work it is), when mother came in, and I called her to see the new head I had added to Goliah.

"You have made him as good as new," says my mother.

Dick, who had been helping us, came and looked over my shoulder to admire the truculent aspect of my giant.

"Your work gives one a new notion of the courage of David," said he. "You have made Goliah a regular Cornish giant, like Cormoran and Blunderbore in Jack's story-book."

"Unluckily David himself is not very much handsomer," I rejoined. " I must say I do not much like this fashion of putting pictures from Holy Scripture upon tapestry and Dutch tiles, and the like. One gets odd notions from them. I shall all my life have no other idea of Saint Peter than that I gained, before I can clearly remember, from the painted window in the church."

" Peggy is growing quite a Puritan lately," said Felicia, who was working upon another part of the hangings. "She objects to the painted windows in the church."

"Not to all of them," said I. "Only to the chancel window, and I do think that is profane. I cannot bear to look at it, since I knew for whom that old man in the clouds was intended. Surely if the second commandment means anything"—

"Don't you suppose the good man who gave that window to the church ever so many hundred years ago, knew as much about the meaning of the commandments as you do?" interrupted Felicia.

" Probably not," said Dick, as I did not answer. "It is very likely the poor man had never seen, in all his life, a perfect copy of the Holy Scripture."

" And, moreover, I do not think that anything painted upon a window can be so beautiful as the sky and the clouds seen through it," said I. "I admit that the colors in the old window are very wonderful and beautiful, but I think the sky more beautiful still, and besides I like to see out."

" Every one does not care to be staring abroad

in service time," retorted Felicia. "But you are a regular Puritan. I advise you to keep your notions to yourself at Stanton Court, or you will soon get into trouble. The lady will not care to have her daughter's head filled with such fancies."

"I trust my daughter will have sufficient modesty to prevent her intruding her opinions on anybody, whether at home or abroad," said my mother, not without emphasis.

"I dare say she will soon learn it," said Felicia, who is the only one in the family that ever answers mother back. "Poor relations and waiting gentlewomen get plenty of snubbing."

Whenever any one checks Felicia in the least, she always begins to talk about poor relations. I do honestly think that she presumes upon her position as a dependent, knowing that mother will never utterly lose patience with her, because she is my dear father's youngest sister. She has been in one of her worst moods all day, and nothing pleases her. She found fault with the dinner, and snubbed me and the children, till mother at last roused herself and gave her such a setting down as reduced her to silence and sulks for the rest of the meal.

After dinner I was going to sit down to my work again, but mother stopped me.

"No, my dear. This is your last Saturday at home, perhaps for a long time, and you shall not spend it all over the needle. Do you and Dick go out together and have a fine long walk. 'Tis a pleasant afternoon, and you can visit all your old haunts before dark."

"But then you and Felicia will have all the work to do," I objected, though my heart leaped at the thought of one more long solitary walk with Dick—a thing I had hardly dared to hope for.

"Oh, never mind *me*," said Felicia, in a voice which trembled with rage. *I* am nobody—only fit for a drudge and slave. Nobody cares for me, or thinks of me, now that my poor dear brother is gone." And with that she began to cry.

Mother checked me as I began to speak, and sent me for my hood and cloak. When I came back, she met me at the door.

"It is best not to answer Felicia when she is in one of these moods," said she. "Poor thing, she suffers more than any one else from her unhappy temper."

I am not so sure of that. I do think she finds a certain enjoyment in being miserable and making others so. It is rather too bad in her, thus to try to spoil Dick's holiday, but she was always jealous of his fondness for me. However, I said nothing, of course, and Dick and I were soon out in the lane. We meant to go and see the old people at the almshouses, and then across the deer-park to the spring, and so home by the church.

We found Goody Crump sitting up reading her Bible, as usual, with everything tidy and pleasant about her; but she complained sadly of the weather.

"Why, Goody, I thought it seasonable weather for March!" said I. "You know they say a peck of dust in March is worth a king's ransom."

"And so it is to the farmers, especially since the winter hath been so wet," replied the old woman; "but these east winds rack my poor old bones sadly. However," she added, with her pleasant smile, "I reckon, children, 'tis the old bones which are in fault more than the weather. I dare say the east wind doesn't trouble you."

"How old are you, Goody?" I ventured to ask.

"I was ninety-eight my last birthday, my dear. I was a good big girl when the great Queen Elizabeth came to the throne, and I well remember when I was a little thing, like your Jacky, seeing the fires lighted which were to burn two poor men at the stake, for reading their English Bibles. Ah! children, you don't know what it is to live in troublous times. But those were grand days, too—grand days!" she repeated, and her old face did so light up as she spoke. "'Twas a new world, as it might be, what with the discoveries by sea and land, and fighting the Spaniards, and the spread of the True Gospel all over the land. Why, children, I remember when a copy of Holy Scripture was like treasure hid in a field. They that had it, kept it with jealous care, and resorted to it with fear and trembling, yet with heart-felt joy, knowing that it as good as sealed their death-warrant if found in their hands. Then came the days of Queen Elizabeth, when we dwelt under our own vines and fig-trees, as it were, and none to make us afraid. Then the ships went away beyond seas. My master he sailed with Captain Drake, as was the first Englishman who went round the world—sailed away, and left me a six months wife, to tend his widowed mother, that was ever the best of mothers to me. Eh dear! 'Twas weary waiting and never knowing whether he were dead or alive. My oldest child was two years old and more, before it ever saw its father's face. But back he came at last, and brought what kept us comfortable for many a long year. But all is gone now—the gold, and the brave sailor lad, and all my fair children—and I shall soon follow. These be good and quiet times, children, but not like those days."

"None so quiet, either; what with star-chamber prosecutions, and fines, and the ship-money, and the troubles in Ireland," said Dick, who hears all the news, being as it were at head-quarters in Master Smith's shop. "There is trouble enough, both at home and abroad, and many even fear a civil war."

"I trust I shall not live to see it," said Goody Crump. "Few and evil—no, but I'll not say that, either!" said she, catching herself up. "'Tis true, I have seen many and sad changes, but I've had my share of happiness, too; and 'tis no small thing to have such a snug harbor in which to end my days at last, with the church near by, and kind friends to close my eyes and see me decently laid under ground. No! no! I've naught to complain of. Little I thought once to end my days in an almshouse, and now I am thankful for the almshouse itself."

"Then it does not make you unhappy to be dependent, as some folks say?" said I, thinking of Felicia. The old woman smiled again.

"Bless your dear heart, no! We are all dependent, child. One almost as much as another, for that matter."

"You mean upon God," said I.

"Aye, and upon one another. If not for bread yet for pleasant looks, and kind words, and little acts of service, such as go to make our lives happy. I have done for others in my time, and now others do for me. I did not grudge my service, and no more do they grudge theirs. And all comes from God, first and last, and may be given again to Him if we will. When I lived with my mistress down in Devonshire, and up to London, I had many times to put up with whims and fancies, and hard words. Not from her, though—she was ever a sweet-tempered lady—but from others of the family. But I said to myself, ' 'Tis all in the day's work,' and strove to take all cheerfully."

"Aye, that is it!" said Dick. " ' 'Tis all in the day's work,' and what matter, so we but serve our Master faithfully, and are rewarded of Him at the last."

"How cheerful Dame Crump is," said I, when we had finished our walk, and were lingering in the church, looking at our father's pulpit, and his tablet on the chancel wall. "I wish I were like her."

"You do not wish you were ninety-eight years' old, do you?" asked my brother.

"Why, I don't know—yes! If I were as ready to go as she, I think I would like to be as old. I always do envy good old people, they are so near home."

"We none of us know how near home we may be," said Richard.

I assented, thinking of my poor father. Never had he seemed stronger or more sanguine than on the very day he had that fatal seizure.

"But, Peggy, my love, why not take the old woman's motto for your own?" continued Richard. "Is it not a good one? ''Tis all in the day's work!'"

"Can *you* take it, Dick?" I asked, in wonder. "Standing here before my father's pulpit, in which you so ardently hoped to preach, can you be content to say—'It is all in the day's work'?"

"Yes, I can, Peggy!" replied Richard, firmly, though I saw his eyelash twinkle. "Standing here—even here—I can say, 'God's will be done!'"

"Well, I can't!" said I, passionately enough. "It does seem very hard to me, and I can't help it!"

"That is because you do not consider well the

nature of the service, Peggy. Have I not vowed to fight manfully under Christ's banner against sin, the world, and the devil, and continue His faithful soldier and servant unto my life's end? A soldier does not choose the nature of his service. 'Tis the very essence of a good soldier that he hath no will of his own, but goes cheerfully wherever he is sent by his commander, whether to lead a forlorn hope, or to stand sentinel at a distance from the field, or to work at an entrenchment, — whether to die in a place where all men shall see and honor him, or in some obscure service, where no man shall so much as hear of him. It is all the same to him, so he does his work well. But Christ's soldier hath this advantage, that he never can perish forgotten and unknown. He fights, conquers, and dies, if need be, under the eye of the Captain of his salvation, and when that Captain shall appear, he will receive a crown which fadeth not away. And so I say I can serve Him as well in Master Smith's shop, as here in my father's pulpit; and though I don't deny that it is a great cross to give up the thought of taking orders, yet I mean to try to bear it cheerfully, and say, through all, 'God's will be done!'"

"Amen!" said a deep and sweet voice behind us, which sounded so like my father's that both Dick and I started and turned round in a hurry. There stood a grave and comely gentleman, a dignified clergyman, by his dress. He had a most reverend and noble air, but his face was full of kindliness, not without a shrewd suspicion of humor and even of sarcasm.

"I crave your pardon, my young ones, for listening to your conversation," said he, with a courteous air; "but I caught a few words, and was really too much interested to interrupt you. I conclude," he added, glancing at my mourning dress, "that you are the children of the late excelent rector of this parish. I knew him at college, and can see some resemblance in your faces. But may I ask you, my young friend," he said, turning to Richard, "why you give up the thought of taking orders?"

"Surely, sir," answered Dick, "it is no secret. My father died poor, and I have no means of gaining the necessary education."

"But there are places—however, we will not talk longer here, since the air is something damp," said the strange gentleman, interrupting himself. "My friend Mr. Carey hath made me free of his study, where there is a fire, and we can talk there with more comfort and propriety."

As he spoke, he opened the door of the little vaulted room next the vestry, which my father had caused to be fitted up as a study. He had spent a great deal of money upon it, for dear father knew not how to save when he had the gold to spend.

The stranger invited us to sit, and placed a chair for me, as if I had been some great lady.

"I was about to say," he went on, "that there are positions at both the universities at which a scholar can get on with little or no expense. I have some little interest, and I doubt not I could use it for your advantage, if on trial it should appear that you have a true call to preach the gospel."

I saw Dick's cheek flush, and something seemed to swell in his throat. As for me, I did not know whether I were dreaming or awake, so bright a ray of hope seemed to beam from this door which the strange gentleman had opened. It was but for a moment, and then Dick answered, quietly:

"I thank you, honored sir, from the bottom of my heart, for your kind offer, but I must not accept it, at least not now. My mother is poor, and hath younger children to educate. She needs all the help which both my sister and I can give her, and for that reason we must both go into the world to earn our own living. If the call I feel is indeed from above, I doubt not that He who gives it will find a way to accomplish His own ends; and I should be disposed gravely to doubt its reality, should it lead me away from my duty toward my mother."

So here was my door closed again, and that by the very person for whom it had been opened. The tears came into my eyes, and I had much ado to keep myself from sobbing. The stranger rose and walked to the window in silence, and I feared that Dick had given him great offence; but he presently came back again, and his face was calm and benign as ever.

"What you say hath much reason in it," said he, addressing himself to Richard; "but would not your mother be willing to make the sacrifice?'

"She would, without doubt; and therefore it must not be so much as mentioned to her," answered Dick, decidedly. "No, Margaret," for he read the entreaty in my face: "not so much as mentioned. My dear mother is growing old, and it is no longer fit that she should sacrifice to her children. Wherefore, pardon me, honored sir, if I decline, with many thanks, your generous offer."

"No pardon is needed when no offence hath been committed or taken," said the stranger. "But, my son, I am loth that such an one as you seem to be should be lost to the Church, which now, as much as at any time in her history, needs zealous and faithful ministers. Therefore I would entreat you not to dismiss the thought of taking orders, but, as it were, to put it away in your mind for some future time. Believe me, you may still be preparing for the sacred office. In your master's shop, in the street, and at the fireside, you may be gaining a knowledge of men. 'Tis a kind of knowledge which is worth more to a pastor than any which can be learned out of books, and one in which we college fellows are apt to be deficient. Do you have any time to yourself to read or study?"

"Yes sir," replied Dick. "My master is very

kind in that respect, as in every other. I have the most of my evenings."

"I will, if you please, set down a list of books for your reading. Many of them, no doubt, will be found in your master's shop, and for the others, I dare say you may find them here," he said, looking round on my dear father's books, which have not yet been removed. "On my word, my friend has a fine collection."

"These are my father's books," said Richard. He seemed as if he would have added more, but paused and gazed steadfastly at the fire. The stranger glanced at him for a moment, and then, taking a sheet of paper from the table, he began to write, now and then glancing up at Dick or me. For myself, I sat as mum as a mouse, wondering more and more what was to be the end of it all. The stranger was no common man, I felt sure, but I would not even give a guess as to who he might be. Presently he folded the paper and gave it to Dick.

"There," said he, "I have written down a list of books, according to the best of my judgment, which you can study at your leisure. Meantime let me impress upon you the importance of a close daily walk with God, which is the best preparation of all. Drink daily and deeply of the fountain of all grace, by resorting to God in humble prayer. Be diligent in your daily calling, and you may be sure that a blessing will rest upon you!"

"And you, my fair maiden," said he, turning to

me with a kindly smile. "So you are to make your first flight from the nest, and go out into the world to seek your fortune!"

"I suppose so, sir," I replied.

"'Tis a hard necessity," said he, gravely. "The best place for a girl is by her mother's side till she hath a household of her own. But where are you going? Tell me all about it." His manner was so kind, and made me think so of my dear father, that I choked for a moment; but recovering myself, I told him that I was going to wait upon, and be in some sort, I supposed, a governess to my Lady Elizabeth Stanton of Stanton Court in Devonshire.

He looked very grave.

"A hard place—a hard place!" he muttered. "An honest service would have been better."

Then, catching my eye: "My child, you are going to a place where both your temper and your principles are likely to be put to the test. I would not discourage you, but 'forewarned is forearmed,' they say, though I have not always found it so. Are you, like your brother, furnished with the armor of a soldier of Christ?"

"I am afraid not," said I.

"But why not, sweetheart? Do you not need it as much?"

"I need it even more, if that were possible," said I; "for my temper is not naturally as good as Richard's; but I know not how it is, these things are not as real to me as to him. I have not the faith which he has."

"Well, well. You are but young. But, my child, you are now going among strangers, into the midst of trials, vexations, and temptations of which you know nothing. Let me beg of you to pray your Heavenly Father to give you that perfect trust in Him, and that consecration to His service, which alone can preserve you in the perils of the way. Remember that you are Christ's vowed servant and soldier, as well as your brother; and must fight manfully under his banner. 'Tis the Christian parodox that peace is found only in warfare!" he added, smiling.

"I cannot make Peggy understand that," said Richard; and I saw by his using my pet name, how much he felt at ease with the strange clergyman, for he seldom called me anything but Margaret before strangers. "Her only notion of peace consists in having nothing to disturb her."

"Aye, but that is peace never to be found in this world. I am glad your sister is going into Devonshire. I am sometimes at Stanton Court myself, and may be able to befriend her. My dear child," said he, turning to me, "will you make me one promise?"

"Yes sir," I replied, feeling that I might safely do so.

"Then promise me solemnly that you will never let a day pass without reading some portion of Holy Scripture, be it never so short, and praying for God's blessing on yourself and all that you do. Bring all to this test, and permit yourself no employment that will not endure it. Will you promise me this?"

I did so.

"That is well!" said he. "I will send you a little book which will perhaps help you to understand better what you read. Remember now that you have promised."

"And she will keep her word, I am sure," said Richard. "But may we venture to ask who it is that hath been so kind?"

The stranger smiled. "My name is Joseph Hall, and I live in Exeter," said he, simply, yet with the air of being mightily diverted at something.

I saw Dick rise up hastily with a deep blush, and while I was trying to think what could be the matter, the door opened.

"I crave your pardon, my Lord, for leaving you so long alone," said Mr. Carey, and then he stopped, as if he were amazed at seeing us in such company. For myself, I felt as if all the blood in my body rushed to my face, when it flashed across me that the stranger was no other than Bishop Hall of Exeter, one of the most learned men in England. I might have guessed before, for I had heard that Mr. Carey the new rector was nephew to the Bishop of Exeter.

"I have not been alone, as you see, nephew," said the Bishop. "I encountered these young people in the church, and having played the eavesdropper to a part of their discourse, I could do no less than ask them in here to finish it. Go now, my children! I shall perhaps see you again; and you, Margaret, since that is your name, remember what you have promised."

I was not likely to forget it. It is not every day that one talks freely with so great a man. When we got outside, we were startled to see how low the sun was, and hastened home with little talk by the way. At another time I should have met a reproof for being out of bounds so late; but dear mother is one who knows when to relax the reins and when to draw them tightly. She had even kept our supper hot by the fire.

"Have you heard who is to preach for us to-morrow?" asked Felicia. "No less a person than the Bishop of Exeter, Mr. Carey's uncle."

"We have seen him," I replied, not without a mischievous enjoyment of the amazement in her face and mother's. "It was he who kept us talking so long in the vault room."

Felicia looked from one to the other as if she suspected a plan to mystify her. Dick hastened to relate a part of what had passed at the church. Dear mother was much pleased, especially when Dick said that the Bishop had advised him not to give up the thought of being a minister, but to continue his studies as he had opportunity.

Felicia smiled scornfully.

"I do not see anything either very great or very good in that," said she. "I dare say the Bishop, if he were so minded, might easily procure Dick some place, where he might earn thrice as much as he is ever like to do with Master Smith, and without the work. Court favor can do a great deal more than that."

"If all tales be true, my Lord does not enjoy much of court favor," said Richard. "I have heard that he is no favorite with the archbishop who rules all about the king now-a-days."

"I cannot help feeling, however, as though the children had made a valuable friend," said my mother.

"And do you really suppose he will ever think of them again, or that he will even know Peggy, if by chance he meets her at Stanton Court?" asked Felicia, with her exasperating superior smile, as if she pitied my mother's weakness. "That is not the way with great people, I fancy."

"I suppose there may be a difference in great people as well as in little ones," observed my mother.

"I fancy they are much alike in that respect," said Felicia.

"Do you judge others by yourself, Felicia?" I could not help asking. "Suppose you were suddenly to make a great match, or to inherit a great fortune, would you forget all about us, and never come near us?"

"If I did, I should have a good excuse," returned Felicia, sharply. "To you at least, Peggy, I should owe no debt of kindness."

I might have said more, but I saw Dick look at

me, so I bit my lip and was silent. I dare say she would, though.

When I went to my room I remembered my promise, and took my Bible to read. The first words my eye fell upon were these: "Take my yoke upon you, and learn of me; for I am meek and lowly of heart, and ye shall find rest to your souls."

I wonder if it is a want of meekness and lowliness which makes me so easily disturbed? I should not wonder.

CHAPTER II.

March 6.

HERE I am at home, if the cottage can be called home. I have not written a word for a week, and how many things have happened! In the first place, Felicia has left us for good. My words to her were like a prophecy, for if she hath not the great fortune already, she is like to have it. An aunt of my father's, passing through Chester, came to see us, and she hath carried Felicia off with her to London, where she is to make her home henceforth, and be as a daughter to Mrs. Willson—such is the lady's name. She is a widow, childless, and very rich; so if Felicia can but please her aunt, her fortune is secure. I have my doubts whether Felicia can keep her temper in check, even when her interest is concerned; but a change may do much for her. At any rate she is gone, and it is wonderful what a vacancy she leaves behind her, and how freely we all seem to breathe without her. I can't help thinking that dear mother has grown younger; and for my own part, I feel much more comfortable about leaving home, now that mother hath only Jacky and the twins to keep in order and provide for.

I must say Mrs. Willson has been very liberal to us. When she heard that I was going to Stanton Court, nothing would serve but she must look over my clothes; and having done so, she insisted on taking me with her to Chester, and furnishing me with two new gowns and petticoats complete, with shoes, gloves, kerchiefs, and hoods, and all things answerable, the finest I ever had, though all black, of course. I would have remonstrated at the expense, but she shortly, though kindly, too, bid me hold my tongue.

"May I not do what I will with mine own?" said she; "and if I choose to bestow a little of my superfluity on my brother's grandchildren, why should you grudge me the pleasure? Learn to be obliged with grace and humility, chick, and so oblige others in your turn."

I held my tongue, but I was pleased too with the words, and the thought passed across my mind: "If this good woman should adopt me, I could make her much happier than Felicia is like to do."

Aunt Willson did not confine her bounty to me. She bought mother a gown and cloak, which she needs, and new frocks, beside toys and sweets for the little ones. We then went to Master Smith's shop, where she purchased for me what I value more than all the fine clothes, namely, a handsome Bible. I have never possessed one of my own before, and this is truly splendid, being bound in red with silver clasps. Aunt Willson had a deal of talk with good Master Smith and his wife, and before we left, she took Dick and me aside.

"I want to see you young ones together," said she. "I desire to explain somewhat to you, for though young folks should not sit in judgment on their elders, I can see that you both have sharp wits, and I have a mind you should understand me. I dare say you, Richard, are wondering why I should choose Felicia for my companion, instead of one of the little girls, or Peggy here."

"I confess I did think of it," said Richard, as Aunt Willson seemed to pause for a reply.

"Well, then, I'll tell you," said she. "I can see as far into a mill-stone as another, and I can see that Felicia—plague take the name, it sounds like a stage-play—is one by herself among you and is no help to any one. She hath just the disposition of her father, my poor brother, who was wont all his life long to take the poker by the hot end."

I could not help laughing. It was such an apt illustration.

"I see plainly that she is no help to your poor mother, and also that she could never go out and earn her living like you and Peggy here," continued Aunt Willson. "The fact is, children, she is just one of those who seem born to exercise the forbearance and patience of their friends. The best we can do is to make a means of grace of them."

"That don't seem to be a very flattering use to which to put our fellow-creatures!" said I.

"'Tis all we are any of us fit for, at times, chick."

"But do you really think," I asked, "that we have any right to think so—to think that people are made bad only for means of grace to us?"

"By no means, child!" replied my aunt. "That were spiritual pride, and presumption worse than that of the Pharisees. But we must be either better or worse for the faults of the people we live with. If we learn from them patience, forbearance, and watchfulness not to give any just offence, we are the better; and whatsoever makes us better, is a means of grace, is it not, sweetheart?"

I confessed that she was right; thinking at the same time that Felicia had been anything but a means of grace to me.

"Well, as I was saying," continued my Aunt Willson, "as I have no children to be plagued by her, and as I have a pretty even temper of my own, besides a good strong will, and plenty of money—why I will even take the poor thing in hand, and do the best I can with her. But mind, children, not a word of this to Felicia herself. Let her think, if she will, that she is doing me a great favor. I am glad I came this way, though it was a toilsome journey. I shall think of you all with pleasure; and though we may never meet again, you will hear from me. You are going into a hard place, Peggy, but keep up a good heart, put your trust above, be faithful to God and your mother, avoid all mean and little practises of tattling, eavesdropping, and the like, mind your own business, be kind to all, but beware of intimacies,— and when troubles and vexations come, as doubtless they will, keep a brave heart, put a good face on it, and be not discouraged. ' 'Tis all in the day's work!'"

"That is Richard's motto!" said I.

"And do you make it yours; though mind, chick, all depends on the master for whom the work is done. But we must soon be jogging. Dick, this is for thine own pocket," and she slipped into his hand a purse I had seen her buy, and in which she had put some gold and silver pieces out of her own. "Now do you two gossip a bit while I say farewell to our good host and hostess!"

"Is she not a good old woman?" I said to Dick, after we had looked into the purse, and I had told him of aunt's kindness to us all.

"She is indeed, and I thank her with all my heart, specially for all she has done for you and mother. 'Tis curious, is it not, that we should have made two such powerful friends in one week —the very week to which we have looked forward with such dread?"

"Felicia does not think that the Bishop will

ever remember us again," said I; "but, as I tell her, she judges every one by herself."

"Oh, Felicia—always Felicia!" said Dick, with some impatience, for him. "It was one of my comforts about your going away, Peggy, that you would be out of the influence of Felicia."

"I don't think she influences me!" said I, rather testily.

"Why then do you always refer everything to her? Why are you always thinking about what she will say, and fretting over what she does say? I tell you, Peggy, we are perhaps as much influenced by those we dislike and even hate, as by those we love."

Hate is a hard word. I wonder if I do hate Felicia? I am afraid I do, sometimes.

"At any rate, I am glad she is going away, for dear mother's sake," said I; "though I do not think Aunt Willson quite knows what she is undertaking. But she may do better in a new place, at least for a time."

And then we fell into discourse concerning my journey, and our future plans. Dick told me he had already begun to act upon the Bishop's advice, and that Master Smith was willing, and commended his plan; and he showed me the big book on which he was engaged. It was all in Latin, so I was not much the wiser, for though I know a little Latin, which I learned to please dear father, yet I cannot read without a Lexicon, as Dick can. Before we had half finished our talk, Aunt Willson was ready to start, and we set off homeward, followed by my aunt's serving man, carrying our bundles, and well loaded he was, indeed, poor man.

Felicia did not look over well pleased at my aunt's bounty to my mother and the children. She is already disposed to appropriate Aunt Willson as her own property, and shut out the rest of us. If she only knew—but of course 'tis best she should not. Mother said something about wishing that I also were going with Aunt Willson instead of among strangers—not of course expecting any such thing—when Felicia took her up quite sharply.

"That is out of the question, sister! I am surprised that you should think of such a thing. It is not reasonable to expect my aunt to burden herself with the whole family. I am sure you might be satisfied with what she has done already."

"Heighty-tighty!" said my aunt. "In London we don't suffer young folks to check and reprove their elders in that kind of fashion, especially those who have been kind to them!"

Felicia looked a good deal taken aback, and muttered something about not liking to see goodness imposed upon; whereupon my aunt said something sharply.

"Take care you don't impose upon it, then! As for me, I am able to answer for myself, and I don't fancy having words either taken out of my mouth or put into it!"

It was Felicia's cue to seem all amiability before my aunt; so she made no reply, but as we went to supper she took an opportunity to say to me, 'You have used your time well, Peggy, and played your cards cleverly. You have set my aunt against me already, I see."

I would not answer her, for I was determined not to quarrel on the last day, and I suppose she thought it would not be very good policy for herself, for she put on a very dignified and resentful air, and went to bed without speaking to me again. I was not sorry, for I was afraid of one of her outbursts, which somehow put me beside myself. The next day they went away, and before they left, Felicia told me, with great solemnity, that she forgave me for all my ill offices to her, and she hoped I should do well in my new station. She thought I might, if I would only curb my temper, and learn to forbear mischief-making and tale-bearing. All this she said before Aunt Willson. I was very angry, but I was determined to keep the peace, so I only laughed and thanked her for her good advice. Aunt Willson kissed me most kindly, and put a little purse into my hand, whispering, as she did so:

"This is for thine own pocket, chick. Never mind Felicia. I understand all about it. Keep a ood heart, and remember that, as long as I live, you have a friend at need. I will never see your good mother want, I promise you that."

So they rode away, and it has seemed, ever

since, as though some heavy oppressive vapor had cleared away out of the air. Nobody laments but Jacky, who was her special pet, and whom she upheld against everybody, mother herself included. I wish we could have hit it off together a little better. It seemed as if we ought to have been friends, growing up together as we did, and being so nearly related; but I don't know how it was, somehow every painful passage in my life almost has been connected with her. I might have been to blame too—indeed I know I have often been so; but I cannot help being glad that our paths have separated, at least for a time. Then I am quite sure mother will be happier without her. Not that Felicia could not be a great help when she chose, and a pleasant companion as well; but the least thing put her out of humor, and then she made the house simply intolerable. She has been much worse since the death of my father, who alone could control her in her bad moods.

The next great event is, that the Bishop hath bought my father's library for a good round sum—Master Smith valuing the books. They are to remain in their places in the vaulted room, and form a sort of permanent library for the use of future rectors, and my Lord has stipulated with Mr. Carey that Dick shall have the use of such books as he needs—only the great vellum covered Saint Augustine and one or two others my Lord has purchased for himself. The price of the books, and my aunt Willson's bounty, makes my mother very comfortable.

Mr. Carey made up his mind to remain a week longer, which I did not regret, as it gave me just so much more time at home, and enabled me to help mother move and settle herself in the cottage. 'Tis a pleasant little nest enough, with a fair look out over the fields, and a nice garden, well-stocked with herbs and common flowers, and some fruit as well. In this we reap the advantage of my father's careful habits, who would never let the least thing belonging to him go out of order. 'Twas not his way to anticipate, else I might think that he had stocked the garden and kept the little orchard in good bearing order, looking forward to the time when it might become a kind of humble jointure house for his widow. Be that as it may, now that the place is all put to rights, with the hangings up, the old furniture put in place, and dear mother's piled up work-basket in the window, I must say it looks very much like home. The children are pleased, of course, with any change, but dear mother looks very sad at times. Oh, if I could but stay! I said once that I should not so much mind leaving home, now that *home* no longer meant the rectory; but I find, as the time draws nigh, that home means the place where the dear ones are.

March 13.

'Tis settled now that we go on Monday. My clothes and other possessions are all packed, and I have naught to do but to enjoy my last Sunday as well as I can. I have already bid good-by to the old folks at the almshouse. Goody Crump was very solemn as she kissed and blessed me, and prayed that I might be kept from every snare. She would needs give me a keepsake also—a little gilded glass bottle which her son brought home from foreign parts on his last voyage. It is no bigger than my little finger, and is all but empty, but it still exhales a sweet odor of roses. Dame Higgins would give me a token too, in the shape of a little tarnished silver medal, having, as near as I can make out, the figure of the Virgin or some female saint, and a Latin legend, of which I can make out nothing but "*Ave.*" Dame Higgins is a Roman Catholic.

"Take it and wear it—take it and wear it!" said she. "It has the pope's blessing. An' it does you no good, it can do no harm."

That I fully believe, and I would not hurt the poor old creature by refusing her gift. When I showed it to old Esther, however, she was not well pleased, called it a Popish trinket, and bade me beware of the sin of idolatry. I could not but laugh, at which she was yet more displeased; but I coaxed her round at last to say, that after all it might do me no great harm. She herself has given me a charm—a stone with a hole in it, sovereign against witches—so I am like to have charms enow. The Bishop hath also given me a token—namely the book he promised me. It is called "Contemplations on the Old and New Testaments," and is a considerable volume. I hope to get much good from it, for 'tis writ in a plain and simple style, much like his sermons—not what one would expect from such a deeply learned man. I am glad to have it, and glad too that my Lord remembered me, though Felicia said he would never think of me again.

March 14.

The last Sunday! The very last, for Heaven only knows how long! My heart would break if I dared think about it. Mother and all of us went to church. Mr. Carey preached a very learned and fine sermon, but not so much to my mind as that of Bishop Hall. Last Sunday my Lord's text was, "Enoch walked with God;" and there was not a sentence that any poor person could not understand. Mr. Carey's had a great many quotations from the Father's and from learned authors, yet the end was simple and plain enough, and I was much pleased at his kindly ways after church, and his courtesy to my mother. 'Tis a great comfort to think that so good a man is come in dear father's room.

Well, I must needs put away my book and pen. When I take them again I shall be far enough from here.

CHAPTER III.

March 19.

STANTON COURT, DEVONSHIRE.

HAVE been here three days, and have not been able before to write in my journal. I will say naught of the leave-taking at home. It was bad enough, and I don't want to live it over again. Oh, how weary I was when I arrived here, though I enjoyed the journey, too. I rode part of the way on horseback by myself, and sometimes on a pillion behind Mr. Carey's servant, as far as Exeter, and from thence I came in the wagon. They were all very kind to me, and at Exeter, where I stayed two days, Mrs. Carey made me most kindly welcome; so that it was like a new grief to part with her. She asked me many questions about the parish, and specially about the poor people. She would know something of the gentry and farmers as well, but here Mr. Carey checked her.

"Don't tempt the child to gossip, my love," said he.

Mrs. Carey blushed and laughed, but took all in good part. For my part I was not sorry, for I know my tongue sometimes runs too fast, and I hardly ever talk about *people* without saying something I am sorry for afterwards.

I saw the Cathedral, which is very grand and beautiful. I hoped we might meet the Bishop, but he is away on his visitations.

From Exeter I came in my Lord's wagon to Stanton Court. It was late when we arrived, and I could see little of the house, save that it was a grand one, with many lighted windows, and with large trees about it. We went up a long avenue, and round to a side door which opened into a square paved hall. Here I waited a good while, till I was ready to faint from weariness and hunger. At last an elderly woman appeared, and seeing me standing there alone, she asked me very kindly what I wanted, and whom I wanted to see. I made myself known to her, and gave her the note for my Lady which I had brought from Mr. Carey.

"Oh yes. You are the young lady from Chester, who is to live with my Lady Betty. But you should not be here among the servants. Come with me, and I will show you your room, and provide you some supper, for I am sure you must be tired and hungry."

I followed her through a door, across the great hall, up-stairs, and through passages, till I was thoroughly turned round and did not know where

I was at all. At last we entered a turret-room, where was a bright fire, which was all I could see at first, my eyes were so dazzled.

"I caused a fire to be kindled, lest the room might be damp, as it has not been used lately," said my companion. "You will find everything comfortable. 'Tis my Lady's pleasure that all under her roof should be so, each according to their degree. I will cause your mails to be sent up, as well as some refreshment, and you will do well to change your travelling dress, and be ready in case my Lady should wish to see you to-night."

"Is my Lady Betty's room near to this?" I ventured to ask.

"Yes, but I was not speaking of her, poor dear child, but of her mother, my Lady Stanton."

She lingered a moment, arranging the furniture, and then coming near me, she said, in a low tone:

"My dear, I do hope you will be kind and patient with poor Lady Betty. She is one by herself, and she hath so few pleasures, poor thing. You will, wont you?"

"Indeed I will," said I. "I love children dearly."

"That is well. But she is not like a healthy child, you see, and I sometimes think that her mind is as badly twisted as her body. Her late governess was very sharp with her, and I know she did her harm; and so my Lady thought, for she sent her away very soon. But I will say no more. I am the housekeeper, my dear. I am a far-away cousin of my Lord, but I never presume on my relationship, though they are all very kind to me. Do you ask for Mrs. Judith, if you wish to find me. Mr. Carey, with whom you travelled, is a nephew of mine. Now I must send your supper, and let my Lady know that you are come. She has asked for you to-day."

She went out, and presently came up a man with my mails, followed by a maid with a tray containing hot soup and other good things.

"Here is your supper, mistress," said she, pertly enough. "'Tis easy to see you have already got into Mrs. Judith's good graces."

"Set it on the table," said I, thinking her freedom very impertinent. She gave her head a toss, but said no more, and presently I heard her laughing with the man outside the door. "Pretty well for a poor parson's daughter," I heard them say. I opened my mails, and dressed myself neatly in one of my new gowns, and then sat down to enjoy the good supper provided for me. I had hardly finished, when Mistress Judith opened my door.

"You are to go to my Lady in her dressing-room at once," said she. "Dear me, how nice you look! But come, follow me, and mind the steps at the door of my Lady's room, and don't be over bashful when my Lady speaks to you."

Mrs. Judith was so evidently flurried, that I felt flurried myself, but I tried to compose myself. It came over me, that here was one of the occasions on which I needed the help of that great Master whom I was to serve, and I murmured the prayer for grace I was accustomed to use every morning and I don't know how it was, it seemed to quiet me directly.

"Mind the steps," said Mrs. Judith, as she opened the door; and it was well she did warn me, or I should have greeted my new mistress by falling on my nose before her. As it was, I made my courtesy, and followed my conductor into the room where sat my Lady Stanton. She almost dazzled my eyes, she was so beautiful and so richly dressed. She sat by her toilet-table, and seemed to be about undressing for the night, for her maid was getting out the things, and honored me with a stare behind her mistress' back.

"Come near to me, Mistress Merton," said my Lady, speaking with a clear, sweet voice, which struck me at once as having a ring of sadness in it. "You need not wait now, Brewster," she added, speaking to the dressing-maid. "I will call when I need you."

My Lady asked me kindly about my journey, and my mother, as if she meant to set me at my ease. Then she said:

"I suppose you have very little notion of what you are to do?"

"Very little, my Lady," I answered, which was the truth.

My Lady smiled. "You will find out by degrees. You are to spend most of your time with my little daughter—to amuse her and keep her contented, and to teach her what you can, and what she is able to learn without too much trouble. You will take your meals with Mrs. Judith, or else with the family, when we have no company. You will have certain hours to yourself, and are at liberty to walk out, so you go not too far from home; and I shall be glad if you can persuade Lady Betty to go out also. You will come to prayers with the rest of the family every morning. Mrs. Judith will show you where you are to sit. That is all I have to say to you at present, but I will see you again. I dare say you are wearied with your ride, and it is late."

She signed for me to go, and I followed Mrs. Judith back to my room, which was quite in another part of the house. When I was alone again, I thought over all I had heard, and I could not but feel that my position would probably be a hard one. It did not seem that I was to have any authority over the child, though I was expected to teach her. I was to have nothing to do with the servants, and yet I was not to be one of the family. I did not see my way at all, but I remembered what dear mother once said—that if we could see but one step before us, we were to take that step, and then the next would be made plain. So I consoled myself with thinking that at any rate I had nothing to do to-night but to make myself comfortable. I unpacked some of my chief treasures—my few books, my work-box, and especially my new Bible, and a pretty Prayer-book which Mr. Smith gave me. My room is a very neat and pretty one—a turret room, with a closet, and two deep, narrow windows. There is a small bed with green hangings, a chair, table, and chest of drawers, and what I prized most, a kind of desk, or cabinet, with a place on which to write, and a good many little drawers and shelves. I liked the aspect of my room, and after I had said my prayers, and read my Bible verses, I began to feel more at home, and to think that perhaps I might be happy here after all. I could not but shed a few tears when I thought how far away were mother and all my friends, and then the thought came across me, that we were all in the presence of the same Heavenly Father, and that His eye sees all at one glance, as it were. I never so strongly felt his presence as at that moment; and I did pray earnestly that He would make me to love Him more, that He would guide me, and make my way plain before me.

I did not sleep till late—there seemed to be so many strange noises, the wind did so roar in the chimney and among the great trees; and when it fell, there was another sound which I could not understand—a kind of long, low roar, which rose and fell, but never wholly ceased. At last my weariness overcame me, but it seemed as if I had not slept more than half an hour, when I was wakened by the loud, passionate crying of a child. I saw the sun was shining, and springing up,

I hastened to dress. I had hardly done so, the child crying all the time, when there came a knock at the door, and some one hastily opened it.

"I crave your pardon, mistress, but will you please come to my young Lady directly?" said a decent, kind-faced woman, who looked like a servant. "She has heard that you are come, and is determined to see you. Do make haste, before my Lord is waked by her noise."

"I will come at once," said I; and I laid down my Bible, having read only one verse—"Call upon me in the day of trouble, so will I hear thee."

"Is that Lady Betty crying?" I asked, as the screams struck more loudly on my ear, upon opening the door."

"Yes, she is in one of her takings, poor thing. Do pacify her if you can, for I can't, and that's the truth. You see her old nurse is lately dead, and she don't take to me yet."

She opened, as she spoke, first a door covered with green baize, and then one of wood, and ushered me into a large, airy room. It was the finest I had ever seen, except my Lady's, but I had no eyes for anything except the child who sat upright in the bed, her face red with passion, her poor little hands, as thin as bird's claws, clutching the bed hangings, as if she would pull them down, while she screamed at the top of her voice, like one distracted.

"See here, Lady Betty! Here's a pretty young

lady come to see you. Now be good, and speak prettily to her, wont you?"

But Lady Betty only screamed out some inarticulate words.

"There, see what you can do with her," said the maid, in a low voice. "I dare not go near her, that is the truth. She is like a wild cat."

I remembered how mother used to deal with me in my "tantrums," as Esther used to call them, and going up to the bed, I quietly sat myself down upon it, and looked at Lady Betty, without saying a word. At first she did not seem to notice me; but as I sat quite still and looked steadfastly at her, she presently ceased crying, and looked at me in a kind of wonder.

"Who are you?" she asked.

"I am Margaret Merton," I answered. "I have come to see you, but I can tell you no more till you stop crying."

"I want my mother," she said, pitifully.

"My Lady is not awake yet, I dare say," I answered. "I am sure you would not like to wake her with crying. That is not a pleasant way of being roused."

I saw I had gained her attention. "Did I wake you?" she asked.

"Yes, and I could not think at first where I was. I am not used to hear children cry."

"Haven't you any children at your house?" she asked.

"Yes, I have two twin sisters about as old

as you, and a little brother, but they do not cry."

She was interested directly, and began to ask me questions. I talked to her till she was quiet, and had forgotten her passion, and then I said, "I will tell you more when you are dressed."

"But I don't want to be dressed," said she, putting up her lip. "Mary hurts me so. I want my own old Mary!"

"But you can't have her, my Lady, because she is not here," argued the maid. "She is dead and gone, as you know very well." Then to me:

"Do persuade her. My Lady will be displeased."

"Will you let me dress you, Lady Betty?" I asked.

"Won't you take hold of my arms hard and hurt me?" she asked, looking doubtfully at me.

"Not if I can help it; but if I do, you must tell me, and I will be more careful."

She submitted with a good grace, and I took her in my lap and dressed her like a baby, Mary handing me the things. The tears were very near my eyes as I was doing it, for I remembered how I used to dress my poor little sister Phillis, the one next older than the twins, who died of a waste a year before my father. I did not wonder that Lady Betty dreaded to be touched, when I saw how thin she was—nothing but skin and bone. She is terribly hunchbacked, too. Her backbone is turned to one side, and curves out so that she has a great bunch on her shoulders. She cried out once or twice, but on the whole we got through pretty well. When I had done, she put up her poor face and kissed me, saying that I had hardly hurt her at all. I was glad to see that Mary looked relieved and pleased instead of seeming jealous.

"That is my good little Lady!" said she. "Now, I will bring your breakfast;" and she hastened away.

"Don't you say your prayers?" I asked the child, when we were alone together.

"Why, no!" she said, as if surprised. "I cannot go to the chapel."

"But you might say them here. Your Heavenly Father will know what you say as well here as in the chapel."

"Well, I will say them, if you will hear me, as Mary used. I like you, and I will do as you bid me."

I thought I had made a good beginning. I set her on the side of the bed, as she could not kneel, and kneeling by her, with her hands clasped in mine, I made her say after me the Lord's prayer, and another, which dear mother taught me as a child. Then I made her say, "God bless my father and mother, and all my friends, and make me a good girl."

She was very serious and reverent. After we had finished, she asked me to carry her to the window that she might look out.

"Cannot you walk?" I asked.

"Yes, but it hurts me. I like to be carried best."

She was nothing to lift, so I humored her by carrying her to the window. It was the first chance I had to look out, and I exclaimed at the beauty of the view which met my eyes. The green grass of the lawn—oh, so green—stretched away to the woods, of which the buds were at least two weeks in advance of those I had left at home, and in some places showed a faint tinge of their summer's hue. On one side I could just catch a glimpse of a fine formal garden, with statues, and a fountain, and high clipped hollys and yews. The church tower peeped from the trees at the end of the long avenue, and away at the horizon lay a broad belt of glittering blue. I was so taken by surprise, that I did not think what it was, and asked Lady Betty.

"Why, that is the sea!" said the child. "Did you never see the sea before? I love to sit and look at it, and at night I lie and listen to the sound of the waves, till I long to fly away over there, where the birds go. Would you not like to fly, Margaret Merton?"

"You are to say Mistress Merton," said Mary, who now came in with the breakfast.

"I shall say what I like!" retorted the peevish child. "Margaret is a pretty name, and I love to say it. I may call you Margaret, may I not?"

"Surely, my love, if your mother does not object."

"My mother wont care. Every one lets me do as I please, only my aunt Jemima, and you need not mind her."

"Come now and have your breakfast," said I.

"I don't want my breakfast. I am not hungry."

"But you will be hungry by and by," I urged; "and besides, your mother will not be pleased if you do not eat your good bread and milk. It is that which makes little girls fat and rosy."

"I shall never be fat and rosy, I know!" said Lady Betty, in so sad a tone for a child, that the tears came to my eyes. "But never mind, Margaret, I will eat it if you want me to. Only please sit by me and talk to me!"

I was quite ready to do that, and we grew very merry over the bread and milk, Mary putting the room to rights meantime. I was telling my Lady a long story about our old cat and her kittens, and how she carried them all back to the rectory in her mouth when we moved. I had just come to the most interesting part of the story, when the door opened, and a lady entered whom I had not seen before. She seemed to me about thirty-five, though I have since learned that she is not nearly so old. She was very plain, with hair, eyes and skin which seemed all of a color, and there was wonderful formal, precise air about her. I broke off my story and rose, of course, while Lady Betty greeted the new comer with:

"Now, Aunt Jemima, do go away! Margaret is

telling me such a pretty tale, and I want to hear the end of it."

"Margaret, forsooth! And pray who is this young person with whom you are so intimate already?" asked the lady, glancing at me, as if she suspected me of committing some great impropriety.

"Why, Margaret Merton, of course!" answered the child, pettishly.

"Oh, I understand. The young damsel who was expected a week ago. How did it happen, Mistress Margaret Merton, that you did not arrive at the time appointed?"

I explained to her that I had waited for Mr. Carey, who had changed his plans at the last moment. She seemed to consider my excuse as of little consequence, for she hardly heard me through before she turned to Lady Betty.

"Well, child, and how do you find yourself this morning?" Then, without waiting for an answer, she turned again to me:

"It appears to me, Mistress Merton, that it would be more seemly for you to *stand* in attendance upon your young mistress, than to be sitting thus familiarly by her side."

I felt my face grow scarlet at the reproof. The truth is, that I had never thought of Lady Betty as my mistress at all, but only as a poor suffering child who was to be made comfortable; and I had treated her just as I would have treated one of our own twins, or one of the village children in a fit of the earache. I knew not what to say, but Lady Betty answered for me:

"I choose to have her sit by me, Aunt Jemima, and that is enough. She is good to me, and I love her and she shall do as *I* choose, wont you, Margaret?"

I did not know what to say or do, for I had never heard a child speak to a grown person in that way. I thought the best way was to say nothing. Lady Jemima reproved the child sharply for her impertinence, and even went so far as to shake her. The child screamed loudly, at which I could not wonder, for the shaking must have hurt her very much, so thin and weak as she was. I thought, for my part, Lady Jemima deserved the shaking quite as much as Lady Betty; and I confess I should like to have given it her myself. At that moment my Lady Stanton appeared at the open door.

"What is all this?" she asked. Lady Betty at once began to tell her story, and Lady Jemima hers. My Lady said nothing till it came to the shaking. Then her great dark eyes flashed, and she turned upon her sister-in-law, and bade her never to touch the child again at her peril.

Lady Jemima at first began to justify herself, but stopped suddenly, burst into tears, and ran out of the room.

My Lady tried to quiet the child, who was still crying, and at last succeeded by telling her that her father would hear her, and be very angry. Then she bade me go and get my breakfast, and she would stay with Lady Betty. She followed me to the door and closed it after her.

"This is not a good beginning!" said she. "What did you do to displease my sister and make ll this trouble?"

"I told her, adding that I was very sorry, but I had no thought of doing anything wrong, but only of pleasing Lady Betty, who would have me sit down with her and tell her a story while she ate her bread and milk.

"Well, well!" said she. "'Twas no great matter to make such an ado about, but you must manage as quietly as you may. I am glad that Betty takes to you, and I hope you may be able to teach her something: but be very gentle with her, and above all, try to keep her quiet, for nothing vexes my Lord so much as her screams. There, go and get your breakfast, and look about you if you choose. I shall be with Betty for the next hour."

She went back to Lady Betty and shut the door. I did not know what to do, for I had been so confused the night before that I had not observed which way we had come, and had no notion in what part of the house to look for Mrs. Judith's room. As I stood hesitating, Lady Jemima appeared again, her eyes red with crying.

"What's the matter?" she asked, in a more gentle oice than I had yet heard her use: "why do you stand here?"

"Because I do not know which way to go, my Lady!" I answered. "I am to go to Mrs. Judith's room for my breakfast, and I don't know where to find it."

"I will show you," she said. "Follow me."

"But that is taking too much trouble for you, my Lady," said I.

"I choose to do it," she returned. "It is fit that I should humble myself as a penance for so forgetting myself before you this morning. Let it be a warning to you."

I did not understand what was to be the warning, and there was something very strange to my ears in the way Lady Jemima talked of doing penance. However I said no more, but followed her down-stairs, noting the turns this time, that I might not be at a loss again. We met several persons, who spoke to Lady Jemima and looked rather curiously at me, especially one tall, stately gentleman, who said to her, in a laughing way:

"Good morning, my Lady Abbess. Have you found a new penitent, or novice, or whatever you please to call her?"

"Certainly a novice, brother, but I fear not much of a penitent," replied Lady Jemima, primly. "'Tis Betty's new governess, or waiting-gentlewoman, which ever you please to call her."

"So!" said my Lord, as I now perceived him to be, looking at me with more attention. "You have undertaken a hard task, my young lady. I would as soon be nurse to a wild-cat. But 'tis no wonder the poor thing is cankered and crabbed, considering her misfortune. Be kind and faithful to her, and you shall lose nothing thereby, I promise you."

I courtesied, but did not speak. As mother says, "Mumchance is a safe game."

"Here is Mistress Judith's room," said Lady Jemima, opening the door.

"Many thanks, madam," I began, but she cut me short at once.

"You owe me no thanks: I did it to please myself." Then more graciously: "I will see you again, and perhaps I may be of use to you. I daresay you need instruction in your religious duties."

I courtesied again, and she left me. I could not but think that pleasing oneself was an odd way of doing penance. Mrs. Judith was very kind to me, and provided me a nice breakfast.

When I had eaten, I thought I would look about me a little, as my Lady had said. The trees of the park came up quite close on this side of the house, and I found myself directly in a little wood, where grew in profusion primroses and many other flowers which had not begun to think of coming out in the North. I gathered two pretty little nosegays, one for my own room, and one for Lady Betty; and finding some snail shells, I put them in my pocket, thinking that they might amuse the child. I could have spent my whole hour in the wood, but I remembered that my clothes were yet to be put in order, so I went back to my room, and unpacked all my things arranging them as I was used to do in my old room in the Rectory. Then, having still a few minutes, I read the one hundred and third Psalm, which came in my regular course, and said my morning prayers. The chaplain is gone away, so we have no prayers in the chapel at present. Then I went back to Lady Betty's room. My Lady was still there, and smiled as she saw my flowers, while Betty uttered a cry of delight, as she took them in her hands and smelled them.

"Do you then love flowers as well as myself?" said my Lady, gently.

"Yes, my Lady," I answered.

"Margaret used to have a garden when she lived at home," said Lady Betty. "She told me so this morning. I wish I could have one, but then I could not dig in it myself, as she used to."

"Perhaps you may, some day, when you are stronger," said my Lady. "You and Mistress Merton seem to have made friends very readily."

"She is so good to me," said Betty. "She dressed me without hurting me a bit. I love her better than anybody but my own old Mary."

"Mistress Merton was very kind to dress you," answered my Lady. "But, my daughter, she is not your nurse or waiting-woman—she is your governess, and you must be good and obey her, and strive to learn all that she can teach you."

I was not sorry to hear my Lady say this. It is much more comfortable to understand one's position, be that position what it may. But Lady Betty did not seem pleased at all.

"I don't want a governess!" she whimpered. 'Mrs. Burley was a governess, and she was cross to me: and I want Margaret to dress me and tell me tales, as she did this morning."

"Oh, very well! That is as you and she can agree;" said my Lady, smiling, as did I. "I dare say she will tell you tales if you are good; only, Mistress Merton, you must not let this imperious little girl make a slave of you."

"But you will dress me, won't you?" asked the child, turning to me.

"Surely, if your mother is willing," I said. "Why not?"

My Lady gave me a sweet smile, and a glance from her beautiful eyes, as she kissed Lady Betty, and sat her in her easy chair (for she had been all this while on her mother's lap). The child made up a crying face, but refrained, as her mother held up her finger, though her poor little mouth quivered piteously as my Lady left the room, and I feared we might have another scene. Luckily, I bethought myself of the shells in my pocket, and these and the rest of the story about the kittens diverted the impending storm.

But I am running on at too great length with my first day's experiences at Stanton Court. I will only add that I dined with Mrs. Judith at noon, the house being full of company; and being used to eat my dinner earlier, I was hungry enough.

Mrs. Judith says, 'tis the fashion now, not to dine till noon, and some very modish people put it off an hour later, which seems absurd enough. I had no more trouble this day with Lady Betty, who was good enough, only she has a pert, fretful way of speaking, which I do not at all like.

I have begun making her a great rag baby, such as Phillis and I used to play with. Lady Betty is much interested, and I mean the job shall be a good long one. I rise before six and thus have an hour to myself before I go to my child. I have dressed her every morning and undressed her at night, making the condition that she shall learn a Bible verse every time, from my repetition. Then we talk a little, and I sing a psalm to her, and she goes to sleep quietly enough.

Mary sleeps in the room with her, and is disposed to be very kind and faithful: but she does not know how to manage very well.

March 23.

I am getting settled to this way of life, and have began lessons with Lady Betty. She knew her letters, but that was all, so I begin at the beginning. We have half an hour's lesson, then an hour of talk and play.

I have had a long conversation with my Lady, whom I like more and more all the time. I told her how Phillis and John had died of wasting sickness, and how my mother had then taken a different way with the others, giving them little or no medicine, and plenty of fresh air and good plain food, and how they had improved under the regimen. She seemed pleased with the notion, and said, as it grew warmer, we might perhaps get Betty out of doors. She likes my plan of teaching and says I shall manage matters my own way Beside that, she hath caused my place to be fully settled in the family as Lady Betty's governess, and yesterday, hearing Anne give me a slighting answer about my room, which it is her business to take care of, she gave her a short but sharp setting down, and bade her beg my pardon, which she did, sulkily enough.

CHAPTER IV.

March 30.

EASTER is almost here. It has seemed strange not to go to church, as my dear father maintained daily prayers all through Lent; but the chaplain is come home now, so we shall have prayers in the chapel every morning.

I have quite shaken down into my place, and am beginning to feel at home, and even happy. Everybody is kind to me, even Anne. She came to me one day with her eyes red with weeping, and looking so sad that I asked her what the matter was; so she burst out crying and told me that her baby sister was dead. I comforted her as well as I could, and seeing her heart was full, I drew her on to talk about the child, and its winning ways, and finally read her what our Lord says about little children. She left me, quite consoled, and now thinks nothing too much to do for me.

As for Lady Betty, I have no great trouble with

her, except that I have now and then to fight a battle with her selfishness, and assert myself a little. The poor thing has taken to me wonderfully.

"I do love you!" she said to me, last night, as I was undressing her.

"And so do I love you!" I answered.

"Really?" said she, looking at me wistfully. "Really and truly?"

"Really and truly!" I answered. "Why not?"

"Mrs. Burley said I was so cross that nobody could love me," said she. "And I am cross, I know. I was cross to you this morning!"

"Rather!" I answered, smiling.

"Well, I am sorry!" she said, impulsively. "Will you love me if I am cross?"

"Yes, my dear," said I: "only, Lady Betty, why should you be cross?"

"I don't know—because I am so sick and so—you know, Margaret. I am not like other people, and I can't help being cross!"

"Are you sure?" I asked. "Did you ever try?"

She opened her great eyes as if such a notion had never occurred to her mind; but she answered frankly: "No, I don't know that I ever did."

"Then you can't tell whether you can help it or not," said I. "All sick people are not cross. Phillis was not, neither was my little playmate and friend, Grace Forrester."

"Tell me about them," said she.

I am glad every time I find something new

to talk about, and Lady Betty is never weary of asking questions about Phillis and Grace.

"Well, I wish I *could* help being cross," said she, finally. "How can I?"

"You must ask the Lord to help you," said I

"And will He?"

"Yes, if you ask Him earnestly. But then you must try hard not to let the cross words come out, even if you feel cross inside. If you don't say a word, you will get over it all the quicker."

I noticed the next morning that she was not nearly so sharp with Mary, even when Mary hurt her by shaking her chair. I felt myself reproved at seeing the effort she made, thinking how ready I have all my life been to resent and retort.

I have quite settled down, as I said, and everything goes on regularly. There are a good many ladies staying in the house, but I see none of them except by accident, as my room and Lady Betty's are quite by themselves, away from the company part of the house. If only I were not so homesick.

April 6.

Something has really happened since I wrote last. I have had a visit from Mr. Carey, and have written a long letter to send home by him, since he was so kind as to offer to take charge of one. Mr. Carey stopped at the parsonage in the village with old Doctor Parnell, and walked up to Stanton

Court to see his aunt Mrs. Judith and myself. I was overjoyed at seeing him, and was so silly as to let my joy overflow at my eyes. It did seem so like meeting some one from home. He told me he was going back to the Rectory next week, and would gladly take charge of a letter for me. So I wrote my letter, saying everything I could to make dear mother think me happy (as indeed I am, were I not so homesick).

Hearing that I was writing home, Lady Stanton gave me a kind message for my mother, and a new silver groat apiece for each of the children. Lady Betty too would send her gifts to the twins, in the shape of a piece of gay ribbon, which she begged of her mother for the purpose. When my package was ready my Lady kindly gave me leave to carry it down to the Rectory myself. I was glad to go, both for the sake of the walk, and that I might see something of the village, where I had not been except once to church. Mrs. Judith bade the gardener show me a shorter path to the village, through the wood, and down a ravine or coombe, as they call it here, in which runs a beautiful brook. About half way down a beautiful spring comes boiling up from under a large rock, in quite a large stream, and the water is deliciously clear and cold. I could easily have wasted half the afternoon in this charming place, which, though very different, made me think of our old haunt, the Holy Well in the deer-park, where dear Dick and I used to have so many long talks; but I knew that I must not be out too long, so I tore myself away and hastened onward. It seemed pleasant to be within the very walls of a rectory once more, though that at Stanton Corbet —as the village is called—is by no means so fine a house as ours at Saintswell. A part of it is very old, however, and it is all overgrown with climbing plants, (there is such a passion flower as never would flourish with us); and somehow the very air did smell like home. Mistress Parnell made me very welcome. She is not the rector's wife, but his sister, neither of them having married. They are both old people, with a wonderful likeness to each other, both in features and expression. Mistress Parnell would have me sit down to eat a cake and drink a glass of mead.

"And so you have a new chaplain up at the Court?" remarked Doctor Parnell to me.

"Yes sir," I answered. "He came only yesterday."

"Did you ever know him?" asked the Doctor, turning to Mr. Carey. "His name is"—

"Penrose," said I, seeing that he turned to me to supply the name which he had forgotten. "Mr. Robert Penrose."

"Oh! aye!" said he, smiling, "a Cornish name, belike.

"'By Pol, Tre, and Pen,
You shall know the Cornish men.'"

"He is a Cornish man, I know," said I; "I heard Mrs. Carey say as much."

"I rather think I know him," said Mr. Carey. "He is an Oxford man, and one of the new lights. He was at Exeter awhile, and was to have been my Lord's chaplain, but the arrangement fell through. I fancy my Lord thought him too much of the Archbishop's way of thinking."

"Oh, well," said Doctor Parnell, "I hope he may prove a trusty shepherd, and preach the root of the matter, after all. For myself," he added, smiling, "I must even go on in my own way. I am too old to change my old Mumpsimus, for the Archbishop's new Sumpsimus."

Whereat both the gentlemen laughed, but 'twas all Greek to me. However, I fancied I understood something, when I came to hear Mr. Penrose read prayers—for he used so much ceremony, and read in such an artificial tone, that I could hardly understand him.

Mistress Parnell would have me carry a basket of Guinea fowls' eggs to my Lady, so I waited a little for them, and had a pleasant talk with Mr. Carey. Oh, how I did wish I were going back with him; but there is no use in that. Here I am, and here must I stay; and, in truth, 'twould cost me no small pang to part with my poor child. I begged him, if he saw Dick, to put him in mind to write to me, if ever he had a chance.

"I think the opportunity is more like to be wanting than the wish, Mistress Margaret," said he, smiling. Nevertheless I will give your brother your message, and also when I write to my mother, I will try to send you news from home. I could wish there were a regular post for letters from one part of the kingdom to the other, as it is said there is in Holland."

"It may come to pass, though belike not in our day," said Doctor Parnell. "This maiden may live to see such a post passing regularly as often as once a week between London and Exeter."

That does not seem very likely—however, there is no telling.

When I parted from Mr. Carey, it was almost like leaving home once more, and I wept so much after I got into the woods, that I was fain to stop at the spring, and bathe my eyes a long time, before I went up to the house. As I was bending over the little basin, I was startled by a step, and looking up hastily, I met the eye of a fine-looking gentleman, whom I had never seen before. He had a look of my Lord, but much younger, and with a difference, as the heralds say. He was much bronzed, and I took him for a sailor. He raised his hat, and bowed in courteous fashion, as our eyes encountered, but passed without speaking. I wondered who he could be, but was soon enlightened by Mrs. Judith, who told me that young Mr. Corbet had come down to see my Lord. He is my Lord's cousin, and the master, now his father is dead, of the fine old house in the woods, about a mile from here; and unless my Lady's child prove a boy, he is like to be heir of all."

Lady Betty was full of news about Cousin Walter, as she called him. "Cousin Walter," had been to see her already, and had brought her a little dog from foreign parts, which she was to have to-morrow, and a fine picture-book from London. I am not likely to see much of this fine gentleman, but I cannot help fancying him for his kindness to my poor little nursling. And I could see that my Lady was pleased, also. It seemed that his mother, Mrs. Corbet, wishes to return to end her days in the old house, and he has come down, like a dutiful son, to see it put in order for her.

April 9.

Our company have all gone now, and we are not to have any more for some time—only Madam Corbet is to be here for some two or three weeks, before she goes to her own house. Mary shook her head and looked grave upon this, but would not tell me why. I am glad, for my part, that we are likely to have a quieter house. I am sure so much of care and company cannot be good for my Lady. I now take my dinner and supper with the rest, an arrangement which makes me more one of the family than I have been before. My seat is next the chaplain's, so we are becoming well acquainted.

April 10.

Last night Lady Jemima came to my room before I had finished writing, so that I was forced to put my book away in a hurry. I thought

at first that something must have happened, and
stood waiting to hear what it was, but she bade
me be seated, and taking a chair herself she began
turning over my books. They were but few—
my Bible and Prayer-book, the book of "Contemplations" my Lord gave me, and Spencer's Fairy
Queen, a present from Dick, besides my old Latin
grammar and Virgilius, which I had brought
partly for association's sake, and a volume of
father's sermons.

"Do you read your Bible every day?" she
asked, presently.

"Yes, my Lady," I replied.

"And do you understand all that you read?"

"No, my Lady," said I, adding: "I suppose
nobody does."

"Of course not, child. And what other books of
devotion have you?"

"None, my Lady, only this;" and I showed her
the Bishop's "Contemplations," which I am reading by course. She looked at it rather slightingly,
I thought, and laid it down. Then she began to
catechize me. Had I been confirmed? Had I
received the Communion, and how many times?
Did I say my prayers, and how often?" and
finally—"Did I fast?" I did not quite know what
to answer, so she asked me again if I ate meat at
this holy season. I told her I did.

"And why do you so?" she asked, sharply;
"there is always fish on my brother's table."

I told her that fish did not suit me; that it

made me ill, and that if I went without meat I had the headache, and was not fit for my work : but that I had always been used to deny myself in the matter of dainties in time of Lent. She looked but half satisfied.

"'Where there is a will there is a way,'" said she. "If your heart were right, you would not mind a little inconvenience. I will give you a book of devotions, which you will do well to use, and which will do you more good than all this Puritan stuff!" giving my Lord's volume, a contemptuous push from her. I was nettled to see her treat the volume so, and said, I fear rather sharply:

"'Tis no Puritan stuff, my Lady. It was writ by the Bishop of Exeter, and I am sure he is a good man, besides being a Bishop."

"It is not the rochet that makes the Bishop, or the title either," said Lady Jemima. "An open enemy is better than a half-hearted or treacherous friend. Your Bishop Hall is no better than a traitor, I fear. How do you like Mr. Penrose?"

"Well enough," I said.

"But his preaching and services—how do you like them?" persisted Lady Jemima.

I was rather confused. I said I was not used to that way of reading or speaking, and that Mr. Penrose's sermons seemed to me not very clear. I could not make out what he would be at, and it seemed to me as if he did not quite know himself.

"That is a very improper way of speaking," said Lady Jemima, with great sharpness. "You should know that it is not your place to sit in judgment on a priest. You would do much better to learn in silence and humility, than to carp and criticise."

I felt my face flush at her tone and manner, which were very severe, and even contemptuous, and I answered, quickly:

"You asked me, my Lady, and if I speak at all, I must needs say what I think. I have no desire to criticise bishop, priest, or deacon, unless I am asked."

It was now Lady Jemima's turn to color, and she bit her lip, as if she did not quite know what to say.

"You are malipert, mistress!" she said, at last. "I came to do you a kindness, but this is not encouraging. I will leave you this book, however, and I hope before I see you again you will have come to a better mind."

And with that she rose, and laid a book on the table.

"I beg your pardon, my Lady, if I have displeased you," said I, seeing that she was about to go. "I meant no offence."

She seemed mollified, sat down again, and began giving me a lecture on my religious duties, as that I ought to spend so many hours a day in reading and devotion; that I should learn by heart the seven penitential psalms, and say them every day, and so on.

"But, my Lady," said I, "if I were to do all that

you have laid down for me, I should have no time for my duty to Lady Betty, which is my chief business, and for which my Lady keeps and pays me."

"You should serve God first of all," said she, solemnly: "no matter what other interests may suffer. How do you expect to go to heaven unless you give up your whole life to God's service? The work of the longest life may not be sufficient to secure your salvation, and yours may, for aught you know, be very short. You may die this very night!" And then, the clock striking ten, she went away, much to my relief. The book she left was one of devotions and prayers for the seven canonical hours, which seem very good, though to use them all, methinks, would occupy the most of the day.

April 11.

Lady Betty has begun to spell words of two syllables. She learns very fast, and since she has really found out that reading means getting stories out of books, she is so eager to get on that I have to check her. She is usually very good, I must say, but now and then I have a little scene with her. She had a great crying time this morning because the little dog Mr. Corbet promised her has not yet come. I tried to soothe and quiet her, but she only screamed the louder, and struck right and left. As I came near her, she struck me a severe blow, and really hurt me. At last I said to her, "Lady Betty unless you try to stop crying and be good, I cannot tell you any story to-night." (I have lately told her a story every night.) But she would not be still, till at last the door opened suddenly, and there was my Lord.

"What's all this?" he said, angrily. "What is this noise—enough to deafen one?"

He spoke very harshly, I thought, and Lady Betty stopped crying and seemed to shrink into herself.

"What are you about, Mistress Merton, to suffer this uproar?" continued my Lord, turning to me.

I said that Lady Betty had been disappointed about her dog, which Mr. Corbet had promised her.

"Then, if she does not be quiet, I will have the dog's neck broken when it does come. Mr. Corbet had better mind his own business. He is not master quite yet, I trow. And for you, Betty, I will try what virtue lies in a birch rod, if I hear any more noise. You are cosseted and cockered out of all reason." So saying, he shut the door violently and went away.

Poor Betty had sunk down into a shapeless heap in her chair, and was quite silent. I went to her, and found her shivering and trembling, as if in an ague fit. I took her in my arms, and she burst out into a fit of crying—not frantic screaming, as before, but deep drawn sobs, which seemed to rend her bosom.

"Oh, if I had only never been born! if I had only never been born!" I heard her say over and over to herself, as her head lay on my shoulder.

"You should not wish yourself dead, my love!" I began, but she interrupted me.

"I didn't say I wished to die. That would make my mother sorry. I wished I had never been born at all, and then nobody would have cared. I wish God had not made me!" she added, with a fresh burst of sobs. "I don't see why He did. I am of no use to anybody, and now I have angered my father, and you, and"— The poor little head went down again.

"I am not angry, my dear!" said I, which was true, as far as she was concerned, though I confess I was angry enough with my Lord. "I am sorry that you have been naughty, but I am not angry. I think you will try to be good now, and stop sobbing, for that will make you sick and vex your mother, and I am sure you would not wish to do that."

She did really try to be quiet, but it was of no use. The sobs would come, in spite of her. At last, however, she grew more composed, and lay still, with her head on my breast. I held her in silence for a little while, my heart aching for the poor thing. Presently she raised her face, all stained with tears, and said, in a quivering voice: "Oh, I am *so* tired!"

"Poor dear!" said I, kissing her: "I will sing to you, and you shall go to sleep, and feel better."

"I shall *never* feel better," said she, pitifully. "I am tired all the time—tired of everything. I shall never be rested, I know. Is it wicked to wish I had never been born—for indeed I cannot help it?"

I did not quite know what to say. It seemed to me, that in her case, I should wish the same.

"And now I have angered my father again," she continued: "and I have hurt you, and all—and oh, Margaret"—and her poor frame quivered with new excitement—"do you think papa will have my dog's neck broken when it comes?"

"No, my dear love," I answered her: "not if you are good. Don't disturb yourself about that. I do not think my Lord will let the dog be hurt, unless you are very naughty about it."

"But he—he said he would, and he is angry with me, and wont forgive me, nor come and see me. Oh, Margaret, do ask him to forgive me, and not let my poor dog be killed!"

"I will, by and by," said I, "but not now." For the truth was I did not believe my Lord would think of the matter again after he had gotten over his fit of temper, which seemed to me quite as bad as Betty's, if not worse. "I will ask him at supper time. I do not think he would like it if I were to go to him at present. Now let me wash your face and make you neat before my Lady comes in."

She was very docile now, and I dressed her without any trouble. She was very tired, so I laid her on the bed and sat down by her.

6

"Margaret," said she, presently, "how can I help being angry?"

"I don't know that you can help feeling angry," said I; "but I will tell you how I help it sometimes. I just shut my mouth and don't say one word, only I repeat to myself the prayer for charity, and the Lord's prayer: and if I am firm, and don't let myself speak one word, I can generally put down the feeling pretty soon: but if I begin to talk, all is over!"

"I didn't suppose you were ever angry," said Lady Betty.

"I have naturally a very hasty temper," I answered. "I don't believe yours is any more so."

"But you had such a nice home, I should not think that you would ever have had anything to vex you."

I could not help smiling as I thought of Felicia. I told Betty I did not believe there was any place in the world where there was not plenty of provocation of one sort or another.

"There wont be any in heaven, I suppose," said she, wistfully.

"No," I told her. "Everything will be good and peaceful there."

"But I am afraid I shall never go to heaven!" she continued, sadly. "Only good girls go to heaven, and I am not good, though I do try to be!" she added, earnestly. "Nobody knows how hard I try to be good, sometimes!"

"Your Father in heaven knows," said I. "He

knows all your hindrances, too, and will help you. Now lie still and try to sleep, and I will sing for you."

She dropped asleep presently, for she was very tired, and I sat still by her side, holding her hands. My head was very full of thoughts. "Only good girls go to heaven!" Then what am I to do? I am not good, I know very well. Surely I must be better than I am, if I am to escape at last.

Lady Betty waked when the bell rung for chapel, and Mary came with her supper. She said she did not want any, rather fretfully at first, and then, as if recollecting herself, she added:

"But I will try to eat something, Mary."

"That is a good little lady!" returned Mary, who is always kind and patient. "Eat your supper, and let Mrs. Margaret go to chapel."

"But you will do what I asked you, wont you, Margaret?" asked Lady Betty. "I can't go to sleep to-night unless you do."

I promised her that I would do my best, and having arranged my dress, I went down to chapel.

It being Friday, Mr. Penrose preached a short sermon. I don't recollect the verse of Scripture, but the real text was poor Betty's, "You can't go to heaven unless you are good." He spoke much of the duties of fasting and mortification, and of our making satisfaction for our sins by repentance and good works. I am sure I never heard such a sermon from my father, but papa's discourses were generally very simple and plain. Mr. Penrose is a good speaker, when one is used to his voice, and certainly he seems very much in earnest, especially when he spoke of the horrors of perdition and the anger of God against sinners. His sermon made me miserable—if that does one any good. I did not forget my promise to poor Betty, and waited for my Lord as he came in to supper. He had slept, by the way, all through the sermon. He looked pleasant enough, and seeing me standing there, he stopped and said, in his usual cheerful, jovial voice:

"Well, Mistress Merton, what can I do for you?"

I told him my errand, adding that Lady Betty was very unhappy, thinking that he was angry with her. He stared as if he had forgotten all about the matter, then said, as if he were a little ashamed, as well as sorry, I thought:

"Oh, poor thing, does she think so much of my words as that? Tell her I am not angry with her, only she must be a good girl, and not do so any more."

"And about the dog?" I ventured to say. "Lady Betty has so set her heart upon it, I hardly know what she would do if it were killed. May I tell her that you do not mean to "—

"Of course," said he, interrupting me with some indignation in his voice. "Whoever thought of killing the poor thing? I wonder you should think of such a thing. What do you take me for, Mistress Merton?"

"For a man who throws stones, and then wonders that any one should be so foolish as to be hit," I thought, but I only said, "I thank your Lordship. I will set poor Lady Betty's mind at rest, then."

"Of course. And here, give her this," said he, giving me a gold piece from his pocket.

"Much use she has for money, poor thing; a few kind words would be worth far more," I thought, but I said no more. I sat next Mr. Penrose at supper, and noticed that he ate almost nothing —only brown bread and cheese. Methought he looked reprovingly at my dish of cream and slice of white bread. He has been in Chester, and we had a pleasant little talk about that part of the country. I think I could like him well enough if he were not so solemn.

I set poor Betty's mind at rest by giving her my Lord's message and present, at which she was wondrously delighted, and said again and again how good he was. I did not see the great goodness, but I was content that she should think so.

CHAPTER V.

April 15.

THIS is Holy-week, and I have very little time to write in my journal. I am trying to pursue the course of devotions Lady Jemima gave me, and of which Mr. Penrose highly approves; and that, with my attendance on Lady Betty, takes all my time. Lady Betty has not been so well, and is rather fretful and exacting. I try to have patience with her, but it is hard work, sometimes.

I don't know what to do about receiving the Sacrament at Easter. I don't like to miss it, but Mr. Penrose and Lady Jemima say so much of the peril of unworthily receiving. Lady Jemima is very kind to me, and gives me much good advice. I told her that I felt very unhappy because I was no better, and she said that was right—that we ought constantly to contemplate our sins and short comings in order to make us humble and contrite, and that it became sinners, in a state of probation, and likely to be called to judgment at any time, to be grave and sad.

I have no time now to read the "Contemplations," and not much for the Scripture. To be sure, we hear it in chapel every day.

April 17.

Betty said to me, this morning : "You are not my sunshiny Margaret, any more. You look so solemn all the time, just like Aunt Jemima!"

And with that she pulled a long face, and put on a look so exactly like her aunt that I could not forbear laughing; at which she laughed too. I don't look any more sober than I feel, however. Mr. Penrose's sermons have made me realize the things of eternity more than ever I did before, and they are dreadful to me. To be sure, there is heaven, but how am I to know it is to be my portion? How can I know that my repentance is sufficient—that my sorrow for sin is real and sincere? And I have been such a sinner! In looking back over my life I can see nought but sin. Sin where I never suspected it before—and nothing good anywhere: and the harder I try to conquer myself the worse I am.

Lady Betty's doll is finished. She is very much pleased with it, and we have had many games of play at "making believe:" she being the mother, and I by turns doctor, nurse, and aunt.

"But if you are an aunt you must be cross," said Betty, this morning: "aunts are always cross."

"O no!" I answered. "By no means. My

dear Aunt Magdalen was not cross, nor aunt Willson."

"Aunt Jemima is—almost always, I mean," persisted Betty.

"Aunt Jemima is always what?" asked the lady, who had come in softly, in time to hear Betty's words—for the door being set open for the sake of air, and Lady Jemima always walking like a cat, we had not heard her approach.

"Aunt Jemima is always what?"

"Cross!" answered Lady Betty, simply. "But I suppose you can't help it, can you, Aunt Jemima?"

Lady Jemima colored, but she did not answer Betty directly. Presently she said, "Who made you that great doll?"

"Margaret," answered Betty. "She has just finished it." And she began to display all the perfections of the rag baby. Lady Jemima looked at the clothes, and said that they were neatly made.

"But, Margaret," said she, "I have come to sit with Betty while you go down to the chapel."

"It is not chapel time," objected Betty; "and I don't want Margaret to go away."

"But Margaret wants to say her prayers, if it is not chapel time," returned Lady Jemima. "You would not be so selfish as to keep her from them, would you? It would be much better for you to be saying your own, than to be playing with your doll, at such a time."

"Well, she may go, if she wants to," said Betty, rather sadly.

So I went down and said my prayers in the empty chapel, out of the book Lady Jemima gave me; but I cannot say I found any great comfort therein. Lady Betty's sad, grieved face haunted me all the time, and I could think of nothing but getting back to her. When I finally returned, I found Lady Betty sitting looking out of the window, with her elbow on the sill, and her chin on her hand. Lady Jemima was reading to her out of the Bible, but I don't think she paid any attention.

When Lady Jemima saw I had come back, she ceased her reading, and rose, but Lady Betty did not look round nor move.

"Good-by, Betty," said Lady Jemima.

"Good-by," said Betty.

When her aunt left the room, she said, sorrowfully enough, "Don't you love me any more, Margaret?"

"Of course I do!" said I, sitting down by her. "Why should you ask me such a question?"

"Aunt Jemima says you don't," replied the child. "She says I am so selfish."

"Selfish about what?" I asked.

"She said it was selfish in me to let you work so hard at the doll just to please me, when there are so many poor people that need clothes, and that—that"—

"Nonsense!" said I. I could not help it, so vexed was I at Lady Jemima. "I was very glad to make the doll, and shall be always glad to do anything for you."

She brightened a little on this, but I could see all the afternoon that she was cast down, and I was sorry enough that I had left her to her aunt, who, good as she is, never seems to come near Betty without hurting her in some way. After all, my work here is to take care of Betty, and I don't believe God means I should let her suffer for the sake of saying my prayers, more than anything else.

April 18.

I have had a sharp dispute with Mr. Penrose. I had been walking as far as the Abbey ruin in the park, when he joined me: and after some discourse, began to ask me what I was reading. I told him that I was reading the Bishop's "Contemplations;" whereat he spoke slightingly of the book, and said he would give me something better. Now, when I have learned to love a book as I have this one, 'tis all the same to me as a friend, and I cannot bear to hear it spoken against; so I answered something quickly, that I wanted nothing better, and beside that, I had promised to read it.

"But, Mistress Merton," said Mr. Penrose, "are you sure that you are the best judge? Am not I, your pastor, best fitted to direct your reading? And if I tell you that any book is unfit for you, are you to sit in judgment on what I say?"

"Why not?" I answered, hotly enough: "since you yourself, as it seems, presume to sit in judgment on your Bishop?"

He was silent a moment, and did seem somewhat taken aback. Then he said, "You are something sharp. What is the Bishop to you, that you defend him so earnestly?"

"He has been a good friend to me and mine," I answered; "and he is a good man, and a good preacher. He preached the best sermon in our parish church that ever I heard in all my life."

I saw he was touched at this, and I was wicked enough to be glad I had given him a pinch, though no such thing was in my thought when I spoke.

"Then," said he, "I am to conclude that my preaching does not please you?"

"I don't sit in judgment on it," I said, demurely. Then willing to turn the conversation, I said, looking up to the great window which is still almost entire: "What a splendid pile this must have been in its day!"

"Ah, yes!" he answered. "There was piety and zeal in England in those days."

"And is there none now?" I asked.

"Nay!" said he; "where do we hear now of bodies of men and women retiring to devote themselves to God and His service, as in those days? Now every priest must have his house and his wife and children. The service of His Maker is not enough for him."

"You can hardly expect me to quarrel with that, since I am a priest's daughter," said I, laughing. "And does not St. Paul himself say both of bishops and deacons that they should be the husband of one wife? Besides," I added, more soberly, "I see no need of people retiring into convents and abbeys to serve God. Why should we not serve him in the daily work He has given us to do?"

"'Tis a good thought, at least," he said, and so we parted good friends at last.

April 20.

Well, Easter is passed and gone. I know not whether I spent it well or ill. I did not go to the service in the chapel, but, with my Lady's permission, walked down to the church in the village. The old rector preached on the Resurrection—a mild and gentle sermon enough, not very deep or brilliant, as are Mr. Carey's, nor so solemn and awful as those of Mr. Penrose; but somehow I felt it comforting and soothing; and though I shed many tears, they were not all sad. I went to the Sacrament with fear and trembling, but the words, "Come unto me!"—and the others, did seem a voice bidding me draw near—so I went. There were a good many communicants, and all were serious and devout. I specially noticed a large and majestic old man, supported by his son, as I suppose, who approached the table. He stumbled a little at the step, whereat Mr. Corbet, whom I had not seen before, came forward and took his other arm. After the service, as I waited a little in the church-yard to speak to Mistress Parnell, this same old man came out of the church door, leaning on Mr. Corbet's arm.

"And so, Master Watty, your lady mother is coming among us again?" I heard the old man say. "I hope I shall be able to pay my duty to her; but the path grows steep to my old feet now-a-days."

Mr. Corbet made him some pleasant answer, and then fell into conversation with the son—a man of about his own age. Meantime Doctor and Mistress Parnell came along and spoke to me.

"Did you not have service in the chapel at the Court to-day?" asked the Doctor, after he had saluted me politely. "I understood it was to be so?"

I told him that it was so, but that my Lady had given me leave to walk down to the village. "The parish church seems to me so much more pleasant and homelike than the chapel!" I ventured to add. "It does not seem like the church, where there are no poor people, and no school-children."

The train of school-girls passed us at this moment, with their mistress walking behind them, and leaning on the arm of the oldest girl. She was quite elderly, and looked feeble, but had one of the finest and sweetest faces I ever saw.

"You must find time to visit our school and almshouses, and that will make you feel still more at home!" said Doctor Parnell, kindly. "We have plenty of poor people here, as everywhere else. There is a poor woman down at the Cove, who was brought to bed last night, and is but poorly off for clothes. If you will mention the case to my Lady, perhaps she can do something for them."

"I will," said I: and just at that moment a plan popped into my mind, which I hope to bring to good effect. Mistress Parnell would have had me stop at the Rectory and take some refreshment, but I excused myself, knowing that Betty would count the hours and minutes till my return, and hastened toward home by the shortest path. I stopped a moment at the entrance of the glen walk, to gather some wild flowers for my child, when Mr. Corbet overtook me and walked the rest of the way by my side. He asked after Betty, and sent her a kindly message, and told me his mother was coming to Exeter in the Bishop's company to-morrow, and that he should meet her there, and bring her home.

"That will be pleasant to you," I said.

"I want you to know my mother," said Mr. Corbet. "She is one of a thousand. Nobody ever knew her without being the better for it."

"I think nobody can be like one's mother!" I said, and then I stopped and choked, and had much ado not to burst out crying, as I thought of my own dear mother, and how last Easter we were all together—father, and Dick, and all!

Mr. Corbet took no notice of my emotion, and presently began talking of other things. He asked me if I had noticed that tall old man in church? I said I had, and asked who he was.

"That is old Uncle Jan Lee!" replied Mr. Corbet, smiling; "uncle to half the village and all the Cove. He sailed with my father around the world, in Franky Drake's expedition, and can tell you tales by the hour about those times. He and his nephew, Will Atkins, have been my sworn friends ever since I could run alone, and I owe them far more than my own life. I will tell you the story some day—though perhaps I had better not," he added, with his sudden smile, which lights up his grave face at times like a flash of sunshine. "It would not be wise in me to do so, for the tale does not tell very well for me, and I should be loth to lose your good opinion, Mistress Merton."

I don't see what my good opinion has to do with him. I am only a poor parson's daughter, and a governess, to make the very best of my position. However, we had a very pleasant walk, and I must say I have felt better and happier since than I have done for a long time. I suppose the long walk in the fresh air may have something to do with the matter, for I do miss the exercise I was used to take at home.

I went up to my child, and was glad to hear Mary say that she had been very good; but the tears came to the poor thing's eyes as she kissed me.

"I wish I could go to church!" said she. "I do get so tired of this room all the time!"

It is no wonder, poor dear! I mean she shall have a change of scene, now that there are no strangers in the house to stare at her.

When I sat down to dinner with the rest, I thought Mr. Penrose looked mighty stiff and dissatisfied, and I wondered what the matter was. Presently, however, it all came out:

"I did not see you in chapel, Mistress Merton!" said he to me, when the dinner was fairly in progress. "Why was that?"

I felt in very good spirits, and not, I am afraid, in any mood to be catechised; so I answered merrily enough: "I am not sure, Mr. Penrose, but I think it must have been because I was not there;" and then seeing that he looked a little displeased, I added that I had been to church at the village.

"Yes, I saw you walking home!"

"Oh, you did!" thought I. "Then why need you ask me anything about the matter?"

"I hope you enjoyed the services!" he said, in a tone which contradicted his words.

"I did," I answered. "It seemed like being at home again."

"I had hoped, however, to see all the family present at the chapel," said Mr. Penrose; "and said so to my Lady. I presume, however, you had her permission for absenting yourself?"

"I should not be very likely to go without it!" I replied with some heat, for I was vexed at his tone and manner. "If you doubt my word, you had better ask my Lady herself."

By ill-luck occurred at this moment one of those unaccountable silences which will fall at such times, and my words were heard the length of the table. My Lady looked up, and said, smiling, while all eyes were turned on us:

"What is that which is to be referred to me, Mistress Merton?"

I don't know whether I felt more like sinking into the earth, or boxing his ears who had brought me into this scrape: however, I answered, smiling in my turn, though my cheeks were as hot as fire:

"Mr. Penrose seems to think I have been playing truant, my Lady, in going to the village church this morning; but I tell him that you gave me leave to do so."

"I did so, certainly!" answered my Lady. "I thought you would feel yourself more at home, being a clergyman's daughter, and used to a parish church. I trust you had a pleasant time!"

"I did indeed, my Lady," said I. "I enjoyed it very much."

"Especially the walk home," said Mr. Penrose, in an undertone, intended only for my ear. I was so vexed I would not speak to him again all dinner-time. I am afraid, after all, that I am not much the better for my church-going—but Mr. Penrose was certainly very provoking.

After dinner I gave my Lady Doctor Parnell's

message, and then opened my plan to her, which was to set Lady Betty to work on some clothes for the poor babes. I told her I thought it would make an interest for Lady Betty outside of herself —that it would divert her, and be good for her in many ways. She seemed much pleased, I thought, and gave me leave to do as I saw fit, only cautioning me against letting the child overtire herself, as she is apt to do with any new fancy.

"You look brighter and better than you have done lately!" observed my Lady. "I have feared that you were finding your work too hard for you."

"It is not hard at all, but too easy, if anything!" I answered. "Lady Betty makes me no trouble. I only wish I could do more for her." And then I told my Lady what I had thought of—that Lady Betty would be better for a change, and for more exercise, and I asked her if I might not have her chair carried into the long gallery on the other side of the house, and encourage Lady Betty to walk there a little.

She seemed pleased at first; then, to my surprise, hesitated, and said she would speak to my Lord. I did not see why he should object, but afterward, talking with Mrs. Judith, when Betty was asleep, the murder came out. My Lord is ashamed of his oor little humpbacked girl, and does not like to nave people see her, forsooth! It is a fine thing to be a man and a nobleman, to be sure. If one is to look up to them so much, 'tis a pity that they are not a little higher, so that one need not have to go down on one's knees in the dirt!

Easter Monday.

My Lord has given his gracious consent, and so his morning Mary and I pushed Lady Betty in her chair across into the long gallery, and placed her at a sunny window. It was touching to see her delight. The gallery is a fine one, with a noble vaulted ceiling, and is hung with many family pieces, besides old armor and weapons.

After Betty had rested a while, I proposed that she should try to walk as far as the next window.

"But it hurts me to walk!" she said.

"I dare say it does, my love!" said I, "but I want to see whether you cannot, by degrees, get to walk without its hurting you. Just think, if you can once learn to use your limbs, how many nice things you could do."

"Well, I will try!" said she: "I will do anything for you, Margaret, because I love you so."

"You are my dear good little girl," said I, kissing her, while the thought passed through my mind, "Love makes easy service!"

Betty walked to the next window easily enough, and was so pleased with her progress that she would have gone still farther, but that I would not allow.

"No, you have done enough for once," said I. "If this does not hurt you, you shall walk into my pretty room, and I will show you the pictures of my little brother and sisters." For having a knack at drawing, I had sketched a little portrait of each of the children before leaving home, and the likeness was not contemptible. "See, here comes good Mrs. Carey. How surprised she will be!"

Mrs. Carey was surprised enough to satisfy all our expectations. She said she was sure Lady Betty needed some refreshment; and going back to her room she brought us some gingerbread and dried pears, and some milk. So we had quite a feast.

"I wish, Cousin Judith, you would tell us something about the picture," said Betty. The ladies all call Mrs. Carey, Cousin Judith. "Tell me who is that beautiful dame with the pearls in her black hair?"

"That is your great aunt, Lady Rosamond, who set up the almshouses," said Mrs. Carey.

"And who is that old lady in the close coif and black veil?" I asked. "She looks like a nun."

"And so she was a nun. That is Mrs. Margaret Vernon, my dears. She was a Lady Abbess of Hartland, and brought up your grandmother, my old Lady. So after King Henry put down the convents she came and ended her days with great content at Stanton Court. Mistress Corbet says she can just remember her, a very aged lady."

"And who is that beautiful fair woman in black?" I asked. "I never saw a lovelier face, if she were not so pale. But she looks very sad."

"That is called the fair Dame of Stanton!" said Mrs. Judith; and then followed a long tale, too long to write here.

"Anne says my Cousin Corbet is the fair dame come back again!" said Betty, "and that it was she who made me crooked by her arts; but Mary says it is not true."

"Of course it is not true!" returned Mrs. Judith, indignantly. "I wonder at you, Lady Betty, for listening to such stuff about your dear cousin, who has always been so kind to you; and I will give Anne a good rating, that I will! There has been mischief enough done by such talk, before now. Everybody knows how your misfortune happened, my dear, and that was by being shrew-struck—beshrew the careless wench by whom it came about."

"How was that?" I asked; "and what do you mean by being shrew-struck?"

"Bless you, my dear, don't you know? It was Judith Hawtree did the mischief, not that she meant it, 'but evil is wrought by want of thought,' my dears. Old Mary left my Lady Betty in her charge, awhile; and what does Judith do, but lay the child down under the tree on the grass to sleep, while she gossipped with her sweetheart. There were always shrew-mice in the park, and one of them no doubt ran over my poor dear lady as he lay asleep on the ground, for there were the marks of its feet on her dress, and from that time the troubles begun."

"Perhaps it was not the shrew-mouse, after all," I ventured to say. "Perhaps Lady Betty took cold from lying on the damp ground. It seems more reasonable, than that a mouse should cripple a child by just running over its dress once."

"Ah, well! That may be your notion, Mrs. Merton. For my part, I don't pretend to be so much wiser than my father and mother before me," said the old lady, rather offended. "I don't profess to understand how a sting-nettle, that looks much like any other plant, should poison one's hand for hours; but I know it does. Anyhow the poor child pined from that day; but it is absurd and wicked too, to bring up that old story, which once nearly cost the dear lady her life."

And then she told me that Mrs. Corbet had once been taken for a witch, and assaulted by the village rabble, so that she would have lost her life, but for the valor of the old schoolmaster, Master Holliday, and Will Atkins, "for Master Walty, he was away on some wild goose chase or other. He was but a wild lad then, though he is sober enough now, with his Puritan notions and ways."

"What Puritan ways?" I ventured to ask, but got no answer, for just then Lady Betty said she was tired, and we took her back to her room again. If she seems no worse to-morrow, I shall try again. I do not despair of getting her out of doors.

Wednesday.

Lady Betty was no worse for her journey, and

yesterday we tried it again. I let her walk the length of two windows, and then she sat a long time looking out and watching the deer, which were feeding out in the open spaces of the wood, listening to the birds, and seeing the rooks, which are now busy with their nests. We were much amused to see them stealing twigs from each other. While we were looking at them, Mr. Penrose came along, and stopped to talk, but he was, methought, awkward and restrained, and I did not give him much encouragement, for I felt vexed at him; so he soon went away. At supper there arose, I know not how, a debate on the celibacy of the clergy. My Lord and Lady were for having them marry, and my Lord made some not very delicate jokes on the subject, I thought. Lady Jemima was vehemently against them, and, as her fashion is, grew very warm, and said some sharp things. Mr. Penrose appealed to me—small thanks to him for drawing the notice of the whole table upon me. I said, what was true enough, that I had never thought about the matter, but presumed it could not be wrong, as St. Peter and St. James at least had wives, as did some other of the apostles: and St. Paul expressly said that a Bishop was to be the husband of one wife; but, I added, that it did not seem to me desirable that clergymen should think of marrying till they were settled and knew what they were likely to have to live on. Whereat my Lady smiled, and Mr. Penrose looked wondrously dashed. I am sure I can't guess why. I don't see why it should be anything to him.

Friday, April 25.

Well, Betty has her dog at last, and a pretty, gentle little creature it is, just fit for her to play with. And I have something better brought by the same kind hand. Mr. Corbet himself brought the dog to Betty, as we were sitting in the gallery, whither we now go every morning when the sun shines; and after she had become a little quieted with her ecstasy, he turned to me.

"I have a token for you also, Mistress Merton, if you will take it. My mother sends you this box, as an Easter gift."

I took it, of course, with due thanks.

"Nay, open it," said he: "the best part is within."

So I opened it, and there lay two letters—real goodly-sized letters—one in Dick's hand, the other I did not know. Mr. Corbet explained to me that his mother had brought the one from London, and the other had been sent in a packet of Mr. Carey's to his friend in Exeter. I could hardly believe my eyes, and I am afraid my thanks were clumsily expressed. However, Mr. Corbet appeared satisfied, and, saying he knew I wished to read them, he withdrew. I had hardly time for more than a glance at them through the day, but I have feasted on them this night to my heart's content. One is from Dick, as I said; the other from my Aunt Willson, enclosing two gold pieces, and telling me that she had made the acquaintance of Mistress Corbet in London, who had kindly offered to carry a parcel for her: so she sent me a piece of fine lawn for kerchiefs and aprons, with some laces and other small matters. 'Tis a kindly letter, full of good counsel and sympathy, somewhat roughly expressed, as is Aunt Willson's fashion. She says, in conclusion: "Remember, child, to keep your place. Every man, woman and child is respectable in his own place, whatever that may be, for the time."

Felicia also sends a note, written in rather a mournful strain. I can see that she has found trouble already, and I dare say she and aunt have had more than one battle. She warns me against expecting happiness in this world, as that is the lot of but few—certainly never of the dependent and the poor. But I don't know that. I am both poor and dependent, and I am reasonably happy— or should be, only for some things which have naught to do with my condition in life. As for poor Felicia, I don't believe her condition makes so much difference with her. She always makes me think of a speech of one of the old almswomen at Saintswell, about her daughter-in-law. The old woman had been saying somewhat about her laughter's fretting, when my mother remarked, "Ah, well, Goody, I would not disturb myself about the matter. You know poor Molly's way—if she had no trouble in the world, she would make it."

"Mek it!" cried the old dame, in her shrill voice. "Mek it, madam—she'd buy it!"

Dick's letter is like himself—grave beyond his years, full of kindness and of a certain kind of humor too. He tells me a great deal of new about home matters, as that mother is well and seems much more cheerful than she did in the Rectory, and that she has taken to working in the garden. The twins and Jacky are doing well in school, and Jacky is much less forward and pert. I can guess why. He says Mr. Carey is much liked already in the parish, and is especially kind to the poor women at the almshouses, though he had a great argument with Dame Higgins on the claims of the Romish church. My father would never argue with her. He used to say 'twas a case of "invincible ignorance," and there was no use in fretting the poor old body, who, I verily believe, never remembers that she is a papist unless somebody puts her in mind of it. However, this dispute did not end in a quarrel, so it does not matter.

Dick is getting on with his studies, and says his master is very kind in giving him time to read; so that he feels doubly bound to serve him faithfully. He says Master Smith's shop is a kind of rendezvous for all the learned men in Chester, and that the Bishop himself sometimes drops in to hear the news. He says, too, what I am very sorry to hear, that public affairs grow more and more disturbed, and that this attempt of the Archbishop's to revive the book of Sunday sports, put forth by King James, will cause great divisions among the clergy. Dick's letter closes with a gentle admonition to remember Goody Crump's motto: "'Tis all in the day's work." Ah, bu then, if one cannot do one's day's work—if the more one tries the more hopeless it seems—what then?

April 27.

Lady Jemima is going up to London to visit her cousin, who is to be married soon. She leaves next week. I should like to send a letter by her to Aunt Willson, but I don't like to take the liberty of asking her.

My Lady again gave me leave to walk to the village to church, saying that she would herself remain with Lady Betty. She is wondrously kind to me, and seems altogether satisfied with the way that I manage the child. Well, I was very glad to go, and enjoyed my walk, as usual, pleasing myself with the thought that I should hear good Doctor Parnell; when, lo and behold, I found, as I entered the church, that the Doctor was gone away, and Mr. Penrose was to preach. I could not help feeling vexed and disappointed. His sermon was on the text about the strait gate and narrow way, and he drew a wonderful picture of the difficulties of the way and the gate, assuring us that even a life-long devotion, and that of the most austere, would hardly be enough to win an entrance. Dick used to say that his religion made him happy; but I can't see how any one is to be happy, according to Mr. Penrose—working so hard, with all our failings noted and set down against us, and, hanging over all, the fear of final failure and its dreadful consequences. Yet, if it is true, of course one ought to know it. I must say it makes me very wretched, and I don't know what to do. My temper is so warm and my feelings so quick, that I am always saying and doing what I wish unsaid and undone; and sometimes, the more I try the worse it seems to be with me. The very effort makes me feel fretful and impatient.

I don't believe Mr. Corbet agrees with Mr. Penrose in his notions. I saw him several times glance at his mother, and slightly shake his head. Mrs. Corbet is a beautiful old lady—I think the most beautiful I ever saw. She must be past sixty a good deal, yet her eyes are bright and clear, and her hair unchanged. To be sure, it is so nearly silver in its natural color that a few gray threads would not show. She seems quite feeble, and, indeed, Mrs. Judith told me she had never been really well since the time of the riot, when she was struck down by a stone and otherwise maltreated. She spoke to me kindly, and said she would send me the parcel she had brought from my aunt, or perhaps bring it to me, as she meant to come to the Great House before long.

Mr. Penrose came up with me as I was hurrying

home, and asked me why I walked so fast? I told him I was in haste to return to Lady Betty.

"The child seems to love you very much," said he.

"And I love her;" I returned. "Nobody could help it."

"Yet you must find your life somewhat irksome," he went on to say.

"Not at all!" I answered. "Why should I? 'Love makes easy service,' and besides she really gives me very little trouble, considering all her misfortunes. I knew what I was undertaking when I came, and it has not been so hard as I expected. Every one is kind to me, my Lady especially, and as for the rest, why it does not signify. ''Tis all in the day's work.'"

"My lady is kind to every one, I think," said Mr. Penrose, to which I agreed. "'Tis a pity she has been so unfortunate with her children. If the next child should prove a girl, or should not live, Mr. Corbet will come to be lord of all."

"So I suppose," said I; "but we will hope for better things."

"Then you would not wish it?" he said, looking at me.

"Wish what?" I asked.

"That Mr. Corbet should be lord of all!"

"Of course not!" I answered: "why should I? Mr. Corbet is well enough off; beside that he is nothing to me, and my Lord and Lady have been my very good friends. I don't understand you at all—and it seems to me that you do not understand yourself, very well!"

"I beg your pardon, Mrs. Merton, if I have offended you," was all his answer. Then, after a pause, "I suppose you were very much disappointed at seeing me in Doctor Parnell's pulpit?"

What could I say? I *was* disappointed, but I would not tell him so. I said I was surprised, as I did not know that the Doctor was away. So then we walked the rest of the way in silence. It seems we never can meet peaceably. I wanted to talk to him about his sermon, but of course I could not, after that. I do think he is very odd.

Monday, 28.

Lady Jemima has herself offered to carry a letter to my aunt, so I have written one to her, and one to Felicia—the latter as kind as I could make it. I am certainly glad that she has gone away, but yet I can see, now that we are separated, that I was often to blame in our quarrels.

After I had finished my letters, I went to carry them to Lady Jemima's room, where I had never been before. It is very bare and plain—more so than mine—and looks, I fancy, like a nun's cell. She has several religious pictures, and many books of devotion, but none other, that I saw. Her bed looked hard, and as if it had very little covering upon it, and there was not even a rug by the bedside. Lady Jemima was looking over a great basket of work, not tapestry work, or any such thing, but coarse garments of various kinds. She made me welcome, and bade me sit down.

".What are you busy about with your needle?" said she.

I told her (what I forgot to mention in the righ place), that I was making some clothes for the twins of the poor fisherman's widow down at the Cove, and that Lady Betty was helping me about them—adding that I was at work on a christening frock, for which my Lady had given me the material. She seemed pleased, but when I added that I liked the work because it made me think of home, she said, decidedly:

"That is not a proper motive, child! You should do it because it is right, and because our Lord has commanded it—not because it gives you pleasure!"

"But suppose it gives me pleasure to do what is right, my Lady?" said I. "Am I therefore to leave it off?"

"That is a quibble!" said she, though I am sure I did not mean it so. "One must be arrived at a great degree of saintship to take pleasure in doing right because it is right; and if we only delight in it because of some pleasant remembrance, or pride in our own skill, there is no merit in it, whatever."

Now I had never once thought of any merit in connection with my work for Mary Hawtree's twins. I knew the babes needed the garments, and I thought, beside, that it would make a good healthy interest for poor Betty. However, the more I say, the less Lady Jemima understands me, so I held my peace.

"I had hoped to leave you this work of mine to finish," continued Lady Jemima; "but you seem to have your hands full already. Do you think you could find time?"

"I fear not, my Lady," I answered, after a little consideration. "You see the most of my time must be given to Lady Betty, either in teaching or amusing her."

"Of course, but have you no time given you for recreation or devotion?" I told her that I had an hour in the morning and another in the evening, beside what I could gain by rising early.

"And cannot you devote some of this time to the service of the poor? How can you hope for heaven, if you cannot make such a little sacrifice as this—or what would you do if you were called upon to give up everything for His sake?"

Well, it ended with my promising to see what I could do, and taking the great basket to my room, where it stands now, and as I look at it, seems to reproach me for wasting so much time over my journal.

May 1.

We have done great things to-day. Lady Betty as really been out of doors.

The way of it was this. My Lord and Lady, Mr. Penrose, and about all the household except Lady Betty and myself, had gone down to the village to see the May games on the Green. Mary would have had me go and let her stay, and Anne afterwards made the same offer, but I would not hear of it. I knew that Mary and her sweetheart would both be disappointed, and I don't like to leave Anne with Lady Betty; she is such a gossip, and fills the child's head with all sorts of unwholesome stuff. So I stayed at home, right willingly, for I don't feel in spirits for any such follies.

Lady Betty was sitting at the window in the long gallery, and I by her, both of us feeling rather silent and doleful, when the door opened and the little dog jumped from Lady Betty's lap and ran barking and frisking to meet Mr. Corbet.

"Why, Cousin Walter!" said Betty, "I thought you would be at the May games?"

"And I thought I would come to see my little lady!" he returned, kissing her. "Mistress Merton, the air is very warm, and the sun is like June. Could we not, think you, carry Lady Betty down to the garden and let her see a little what the world is like on a May-day?"

It was just what I had been wishing to do, but I hesitated, because my Lady was away. However, I could not withstand my child's pleading, so I wrapped her in a shawl and hood of my own, and took down some cushions and cloaks, while Mr. Corbet brought Betty in his strong arms, and set her on the garden seat. I never saw any poor child so delighted as she was. She had not been out of doors in so long that 'twas like fairy land to her. After sitting in the garden a while, Mr. Corbet proposed to carry her in the woods, and that was still more wonderful. We found a safe seat on the dry grassy root of an old tree, and I sat down by her, while the little dog ran hither and hither, as well pleased as his mistress. Mr. Corbet exerted himself to entertain Betty, telling her stories, bringing her flowers, and pointing out various things to her notice. I dared not leave her stay too long this first time; and though she was unwilling at first to go in, she gave up very pleasantly at the last.

"Why, that's my brave, good little maid!" said Mr. Corbet, as she consented to go in. "You have worked wonders, Mrs. Merton. I was afraid of a scene."

"I don't cry any more, now!" said Betty; "I am trying to be good, like my mother and Margaret."

When I reported the matter to Lady Stanton, I thought she looked rather grave upon it: so I hastened to say, that I did not think Lady Betty had taken cold, and I was sorry if I had done wrong; but that the child had been so overjoyed at her cousin's offer, that I could not bear to disappoint her.

"You have done no wrong, sweetheart!" said my Lady, "and I dare say nobody will be the worse; but we must not trouble Mr. Corbet. The next time, we will have John Footman carry her down."

May 9.

Lady Jemima is really gone, and Mr. Penrose with her. They travel in company with some friends from Exeter. She left on the fifth of the month; and is to be away four weeks, she says, at the very most. I am rather sorry I gave her th letter for Felicia. I somehow feel as if trouble would grow out of it. I don't know why, only that Felicia has been my great cause of trouble hitherto, and I doubt if she will be able to let slip a chance of saying something to my disadvantage. Aunt Willson will speak for me, that is one thing.

Betty has been out every pleasant day, and I think the fresh air, the change, and exercise, really do her good. She has gained strength, appetite, and a little color, and Mary says she sleeps more quietly at night. She gets on finely with her reading, and wants to begin writing; but I put her off as yet. My Lady demurred a little at this, because Lady Betty is so very backward for a child of her age; but I told her I was sure it was best not to overcrowd her, but to better her health, if possible, first of all; and to this she agreed. Betty herself is growing ambitious, and I now have to check her instead of urging her on, as at first. She is very much pleased at being god-mother (by proxy, of course,) to one of the twins for whom we have been working, and I have promised that the babes shall come up to see her when the mother is able to bring them. I have sometimes debated in my own mind, whether she ought not to be told of what is coming, but on the whole I do not think it best.

Mrs. Corbet has been up at the Court, and made us quite a visit in the nursery. How any one could for one moment impute evil to her, I cannot guess. I should think the very sight of her face would be enough to banish suspicion, if one had entertained it. There is somewhat in her very presence so *restful*—I know not how else to express my meaning. I think if I were ill, or in trouble, I should feel it a comfort only to have her in the room, if she did not say a word. She looked with a real interest at Lady Betty's sewing, commended its neatness, and said she was glad to see her busy about such work.

"It was all Margaret's doing," said Lady Betty, frankly. (She will always call me Margaret, even before strangers, and I have begged my Lady to let her have her own way.) "I should never have thought of it only for Margaret; and oh, cousin, it is so nice! so much nicer to be thinking about my little god-daughter, and what I can do for her, than to think only of what I want myself."

"Dear heart!" said Mrs. Corbet. "It is always much pleasanter and happier, even for oneself, to think of the wants and pleasures of others, than to dwell forever on one's own. That would be the worst punishment that could befall any one in this world or the next. Do you not think so, Mistress Margaret?"

"I do, indeed!" said I; "and yet"—And here I

stopped, fearing lest I should be thought forward.

"And yet"—she repeated, with that sweet, sudden smile of hers.

"And yet we are told to think about ourselves in some things!" I went on to say. "Mr. Penrose says we are to watch ourselves constantly, lest we fall into sin, and we must think about ourselves, to do that—or, so it seems to me. You heard him last Sunday, madam?"

"I did," replied Mrs. Corbet.

"Well," I said, marvelling at my own boldness, but something seemed to draw me on—"if life is what he said—just one constant struggle with the power of evil within and without—if we are in every way to keep under and bring into subjection our bodies by fasting and penance, and our souls by mourning and mortification, with but a doubtful hope of succeeding after all—what can we do but think about ourselves?"

"Dear heart!" said Mrs. Corbet, again. (She uses these Devonshire phrases so sweetly and tenderly.) "Dear heart, do not you go to making bricks in Egypt with Mr. Penrose—albeit I think him an earnest, painstaking young man, and I believe he will yet work himself right. But, my child, remember who it was that bade us take no thought for the morrow, and commit thy soul to His keeping. Believe me, when I tell thee, that one good earnest look at thy Lord, will do more to keep thee in the right way than gazing on thyself forever."

How I did want to go on with the conversation! but at that moment my Lady came in, and carried away her cousin to see something in her own room—baby things, I suppose.

I know how to work satin stitch wondrous nicely, and I have a great desire to work something pretty for my Lady; but here is this great basket of Lady Jemima's staring me in the face all the time. I wish I had refused to have anything to do with it at first; and yet, according to her, there would be no merit in doing the robe for my Lady, because it would be a pleasure from beginning to end. I am sure it is no pleasure to work on these garments. They are so coarse that I think it will be no mean penance to wear them, and I must say, marvellous ill-contrived. I have neglected my journal and my recreation to work at them, but I am sure I am no better for the sacrifice, as yet. I wish I could talk the matter over with Mrs. Corbet. I feel as if she might shed some light on my difficulties.

Mrs. Corbet brought me my parcel from Aunt Willson. The lawn she sent—a whole piece—is beautifully fine and sheen, and would be just the thing for my embroidery. There are besides some dressing things, cords and laces, pins, needles, bodkins, and a nice housewife, stored with abundance of thread of different kinds, and a new book for my journal, with some other papers. I wonder, by the by, how Aunt Willson knew I kept a journal? I suppose Felicia must have told her

Felicia herself sends me a kerchief and apron, of fine stuff, indeed, and well made, but *green*—just the color she knows I never can wear, even if I were not in mourning.

May 12

Mrs. Judith says Mr. Corbet is going southward on a journey, and is expecting to be gone some time. His mother, methinks, will be lonely without him. Of course I shall not see him before he goes, unless he comes to say good-by to Betty. I have not told her that he is going.

I don't know how it is, but I do not feel like myself for a few days past. I feel fretful, and the least thing troubles me, and I do not sleep well, for the first time in my life. My head aches and feels heavy, so that I find it hard to exert myself to amuse Lady Betty, and I am glad that she has her dog to play with. I think I miss my afternoon walks, which I have given up to sew on the work which Lady Jemima left me.

May 13.

Mr. Corbet did come to bid Betty good-by, after all. More than that he told me that he meant to go and see Mr. Carey, and most kindly offered to take charge of a packet for me; so I have written two long letters to mother and Dick. How pleasant it seems to think that he will see them all, and can tell me how dear mother is looking.

May 16.

I have finished all the work that Lady Jemima left me, and oh, how glad I am that it is done! I am afraid it has done me no good, however, because I have disliked it so much; and more than that, I am afraid that the poor women at the almshouses, for whom it is intended, will not be so very much the better either, for the garments are not well-fashioned, and though I did my best to reform their shapes, I did not succeed very well. I asked my Lady if I might go and carry the basket to the almshouses.

"What is it?" she asked.

I told her about it.

"And when have you found time to do so much?" she asked, looking not very well pleased.

I hastened to tell her that I had sewed during my hours of recreation, instead of going out to walk; but she was no better satisfied than before.

"I thought you were not looking well," said she. "Lady Jemima should have had more consideration than to lay such a task upon you. Henceforth, Margaret, remember that I wish you to walk every day when the weather is pleasant. You will fulfil no duty to anybody by making yourself sick."

"I did miss my walks very much, my Lady," I said; "but my Lady Jemima wished the work finished, and she said I ought to deny myself daily."

I stopped, for I did not wish to repeat all that Lady Jemima had said. My Lady smiled.

"Well, well!" said she. "My sister meant well,

no doubt, and so did you; but remember, sweetheart, that your time and your health are not altogether your own, and that you must first do your duty in the state of life to which you have been called. I am not angry with you, child, so you need not look so downcast."

"But, mamma!" said Betty, anxiously, "Margaret and I want to make some more clothes for the twins, and for their mother. You don't mind that, do you? I do love it so much, and I am learning to work nicely. Margaret says so."

"O no. That is quite another matter. Let me see this same work."

So I brought out our basket, and Lady Betty displayed all we had accomplished between us, scrupulously avoiding the taking any more than her due share of credit. She is a wonderful truthful child. My Lady examined the work, and seemed much pleased.

"You have done wonders," said she. "But whose work is this pretty christening dress, for so I presume it is?"

"That is Margaret's!" said Lady Betty, as proud of the modest little row of satin stitch, as if she had done it herself. Is it not pretty, mamma?"

"Very pretty, indeed!" replied my Lady.

"Margaret knows how to do all kinds of pretty work," continued Betty. "She can work tapestry, and make knotting, and knit!"

"Margaret is a wonderful person, no doubt. I think we are much obliged to good Mr. Carey for bringing her to us. You must ask her to teach you some of these feats of hers," said my Lady. "Have you any of your work by you, Margaret? I should like to see it."

I had some few little pieces, so I brought them and my Lady looked them over, and was pleased so to commend them, that I found courage to make my request, which was that she would let me work something for the baby that is coming, on the fine linen that my aunt sent me. She consented, on condition that I should not abridge my hours of recreation.

"But how shall you manage about Betty?" she asked. "I suppose she knows naught of the matter, and she will be all curiosity about your work."

"If I might venture to speak my thoughts about that, my Lady," said I, and then stopped, fearing I was too bold.

"Well!" said my Lady. "Speak out. Your thoughts are usually to the purpose, I find."

Thus encouraged, I did venture to tell her what I was thinking of—namely, that she should tell Lady Betty herself.

"You see, my Lady, she is sure to find out in some way. Lady Jemima is very outspoken, and the maids will talk: and if she learns the story from you, she will be less likely to take up any wrong impression, or to ask inconvenient questions. My mother did so by me when Jacky and Phillis were born, and she said she thought it the best way.

"Your mother has made a wondrous wise maid of you!" said my Lady. "I wonder she could make up her mind to part with so notable a daughter.'

I told her that Dick and myself, being the eldest children, were obliged to do what we could to help the others, dear father's death having left us poor, and besides, I said, people at home did not give me credit for so much wisdom. She laughed and said something about a prophet being without honor in his own country; and then bidding me take a good long walk, and enjoy myself in the fresh air, she went back to Lady Betty, and I took my bundle of work and went down to the almshouses.

They are pretty cottages enough, five in number, and stand on the village green, near the church-yard. I thought the thatch would be the better of mending in some places, but, on the whole, they looked comfortable, though not so nice as ours at Saintswell. I wonder, by the way, whether Mr. Carey will hold Sir Peter Beaumont up to the point of keeping them in repair, as my father used to do.

Well, I knocked at the door of the first one, and a voice said, "Come in!" so I entered. There, in her bee-hive chair, sat an old woman, looks so like dear Dame Crump, that I could have kissed her. She made me most civilly welcome, and asked me to sit down. I told her that I had brought her a cap and petticoat, which Lady Jemima had left for her. She smiled, and said my

Lady was very kind, but I can't say she showed any great enthusiasm about the matter.

"You will be the young lady now to take care of my Lady Betty," she said, presently. I told her I was.

"And how is she, poor dear maid? No better, I suppose?"

I told her I thought Lady Betty was stronger than when I came, adding that I believed the fresh air did her good.

"No doubt, no doubt!" said Dame Yeo, for such I found was her name. "Fresh air and good food are better than doctor stuff. You are not from this part of the country, Madam, or so I judge, from your speech?"

I told her I was from a little village not far from Chester.

"Chester!" said she, musingly. "I had a sister that married and went to live somewhere near Chester. Her husband was a sailor, and when he went away on his long voyage to the Indies, Madge went to live with his old mother. She was much older than I. I doubt she is not alive. A fine stout lad was Thomas Crump, and Madge was a handsome maid as ever I saw. But she would be near a hundred an she were living. I am past eighty, myself."

The resemblance to my old friend was explained.

"I can give you news of your sister, I believe," said I. "She is still living in one of the almshouses in Saintswell, and though old, as you say, is well and cheerful. I saw her the day before I left home."

Never was any poor old creature so pleased. The tears ran down her withered cheeks, as she thanked God again and again for sending her news of her sister. I told her all I could think of about Dame Crump, and when I had stayed as long as I could, I rose to go.

"Come again, my dear, tender soul! My dear young lady, now do, wont-e?" she said, detaining me with a trembling hand. "It does seem to do me good to see you!"

"And I am sure you have done me good," I answered. "It is so pleasant to talk of home."

"Aye, that it is—that it is!" replied Goody Yeo. "There is no place like home, my maid; now is there? There, bless thy heart! I didn't mean to make thee cry. Don't-e cry, now, but keep up a good heart, dear soul, and when you are downcast, think about the home above. We shall all meet there, you know!"

"Can I do aught for you, Goody, before I go?" I asked, brushing the drops from my eyes.

"If it wouldn't be asking too much, if you would ust take the Bible and read me a psalm and chapter. My eyes are not worth much now-a-days, though I do spell out a verse now and then."

"What shall I read?" I asked.

"Oh, the psalms for the day, first of all."

So I read the psalms for the day, the old woman

listening devoutly, her wrinkled face full of peace. Then, at her request, I read the last chapter of Revelations.

"And to think that is all ours—our purchased inheritance!" said Goody, when I had done. "Truly we need not murmur over the hardships of the way when it leads to such a home at last."

The old woman does not seem to have any of those doubts which Mr. Penrose thinks we ought to have, to keep us humble. I would have liked to talk farther with her, but I had stayed too long already. I see the cushion of her chair is worn out. I will beg some pretty piece of my Lady, and when Betty has finished her present work, she shall make a patchwork cushion for Goody Yeo.

Goody Hollins was in a very different mood. The world was out of joint, according to her. Nobody cared for her. Parson never came to see her, and Mistress Parnell was always corsetting up Goody Yeo and old Master Dean with good things, while she had nothing to eat, and nobody would care if she starved. "Nobody don't take no care of we!" were her last words. "We is naught but poor old folk that they just want to get rid of!"

She was deaf as a post, so there was no use in talking to her. I found Gaffer Dean, a cheerful old man, sitting out in the sun, and as chirruping as an old cricket. I would have liked to stay longer and chat with him, but the afternoon was wearing away, and I wanted to call at the Rectory.

Mistress Parnell made me welcome, as usual. I told her I had been at the almshouses, and she laughed at my account of Goody Hollins.

"I carried her a jug of broth this very day!" said she: "but the poor old soul is sadly crabbed and cankered."

"She seems to think that every one neglects her," I said: "even her own daughter."

"Her daughter has as much as she can do and more to take care of her own," said Mistress Parnell. "Besides that, she is and always was a sad slattern. Even Mistress Ellenwood could make naught of Peggy Hollins. And then she told me a great deal which I have not time to set down here, about Mistress Ellenwood the schoolmistress, and all the good she had done.

May 18.

I have begun my work for my Lady, which I think will be very pretty. The lawn is so fine it shows the embroidery to great advantage, and the thread Aunt Willson sent with it is just the thing.

Betty has heard the secret, and seems to take it kindly. She says little, but I see that she is turning the matter over in her own mind, in her silent fashion. Last night, after I had put her to bed, she asked me:

"Margaret, do you think the baby will love me, when it comes?"

"Yes, if you are a good kind sister!" I answered.

"You don't think mamma will leave off loving me then, do you, Margaret?" she asked again, with a quivering lip.

"No, of course not," said I. "She will love you all the more, and if you are a good girl, and try to learn, you can be a great help to her by and by."

This notion seemed to comfort her, and she lay down contented.

May 30.

This morning Lady Betty walked farther than she had ever done before. She is delighted with being out of doors, and it certainly does her good. The wild flowers, of which the wood is full, are an endless delight to her, and she is never weary of gathering them and observing them. This morning she saw a squirrel. The dog ran after it, and Betty was in a terrible taking lest he should hurt it, but it escaped easily enough, and sat on a branch, scolding us, at which the child was delighted. She is certainly stronger, and complains much less than she did, either because she really suffers less, or because she has more to think about, and so dwells the less on her own discomforts. She has not had a crying fit in a long time. I talk to her about all sorts of things—about the village and the poor people here and at home, and everything else I can think of to interest her. She was much delighted with my story of finding Dame Crump's sister in Goody Yeo, and in hearing of Gaffer Dean's jackdaw, which I forgot to mention in its place. She wished she could go down to see it. I wish she could. I wonder much whether she could learn to ride a donkey?

June 1.

Mr. Penrose is come back, but not Lady Jemima. He brought letters for my Lord and Lady from her, and one from Felicia to me—the most cordial I have ever had from her. Perhaps if we do not see each other for a year or two longer we shall become quite intimate and friendly. Felicia seems to have seen a good deal of Lady Jemima, and has much to say in her praise.

Mr. Penrose has brought down some beautiful furniture for the chapel—candlesticks, vestments, and what not, and he is busy arranging them in order. He would have had me help him, but I could not leave Lady Betty, who has been ailing for two or three days, and is so restless at night that I have taken turn about with Mary to stay with her. She seems to get no sleep unless some one is sitting by her. I almost fancy she is afraid.

June 2.

I have found out what ails Lady Betty. Anne has been telling her ghost stories. I hardly ever let Anne stay with her, but Mary's mother-in-law that is to be is sick, and she, like the good girl that she is, wants to take her share in nursing the old woman. Then old Brewster has also been ill, and my dear Lady has asked me to see that she had her medicine properly, and to attend to various little matters for her: so I have been much more away from my child than usual. Last night she was very restless, and started so at some strange sound, of which there are always plenty, that I asked her what was the matter.

"I am afraid!" she replied.

"Afraid of what?" I asked.

She would not tell me at first, but at last I coaxed her. Anne has told her I know not what tale of the ghost of a knight who walks in the long gallery. He is called the Halting Knight, because he had one leg shorter than the other, and Anne says that when any misfortune is about to happen to the family, he walks up and down all night, wringing his mailed hands, and tossing his arms over his head.

"There!" exclaimed the child, clinging to me. "Don't you hear it? Oh, what if he be come to presage the death of my mother!"

I certainly did hear something like a halting step: and at another time I might have been afraid myself: but I saw how necessary it was to soothe Betty, who was trembling all over.

"Dear heart! That noise you hear is not the Halting Knight," said I. "I cannot tell you just what makes it, but very likely it is the wind knocking a branch of ivy against the wall. Do not think about such frightful things, but remember how you have asked God to take care of you, and think about the holy angels that he sends to have charge of us."

Then I repeated the ninety-first psalm to her, and by degrees she grew more composed.

"So you don't think it is the Halting Knight?" said she, presently.

"No, I don't," I answered: "and I will tell you why. If the knight was a good man when he was alive, and served God, I am sure he is in heaven, and that he would never care to come from that holy and happy place to walk up and down all night in the dark windy gallery. And if he is with wicked spirits, I am quite sure that God will not let him come out of prison to hurt them who put their trust in Him. So I soothed her to sleep, and the rest of the night she rested tranquilly. She has been better to-day, though not well enough to go out of doors, and I have tried in every way to keep her mind diverted. Poor thing, she has trouble enough, without any fanciful fears.

June 4.

My Lady asked me to-day some questions about my friends in London. I told her I had none except my aunt Willson and Felicia, who was also my aunt, though I had never called her so, we being brought up together, and so near of an age. I spoke warmly, as I felt, in praise of Aunt

Willson, and told how nobly she had come forward to help us in our troubles. Then she asked me about Felicia. I hesitated, and then said, frankly:

"To tell you the truth, my Lady, I would rather not talk of her. We were never good friends, and I am afraid I might say more than I ought."

"Well, well!" said my Lady. "I will not ask you any more questions. My sister seems to think highly of her, but she is apt to take sudden fancies, especially when people are of her own way of thinking."

"Felicia must have changed a good deal if she is of Lady Jemima's way of thinking," said I. "But she can be very pleasant when she pleases, and she is very pretty. I hope she gets on well with my Aunt Willson. I hope she will not be discontented, and go back to mother again. I was so glad she went away before I did."

"Now you have told me all I wished to know," said my Lady. Then laughing merrily at my discomfiture, she bade me not be disturbed—she should think none the less of me.

June 8.

Mr. Penrose has finished all his decorations, and called me in to see them. There is a deal of gold lace and purple cloth, with silver-gilt candlesticks, and other trinkets, of which I do not even know the names. He would have me say how I liked it all.

"Honestly?" said I.

"Honestly, of course!" said he.

"Well then, to be plain with you, I like it not so well as before!" said I. "I think the old carven wood you have covered up much more beautiful than the embroidered cloth on it; and for the rest, I must say it puts me in mind of my little sister's baby-houses, or the Papish chapel my father once took me to see at my Lord Mountford's."

"You are something of a Puritan, I see, as your cousin says," said Mr. Penrose.

"I don't even know what a Puritan is," I answered, I am afraid rather too warmly for the place. "Felicia—I suppose it is she you mean by my cousin—used to call me a Puritan, because I did not like the East window in our church."

"And why did you not like it?" he asked.

"Because there was painted thereon the image of Him of whom no image should be made:" I answered. "I could not think it right. It seemed to me like blasphemy. I don't see anything wrong about these decorations of yours, but they seem to me not at all suitable for a church."

"I am unfortunate in incurring your disapprobation," said he, stiffly.

"You asked me, you know," said I. "I could but say what I think. I am sorry if I have hurt you!"

"You have not hurt me—only as you always do hurt me," he answered, with such a strange quiver in his voice, that I looked at him in surprise. He turned away, however, and began arranging some of the drapery about the altar. In doing so the fringe caught on one of the tall, heavy candlesticks. I saw that a fall was imminent, and sprang to save it: but I was too late. The candlestick fell, and as ill-luck would have it, struck me on the forehead, and the edge being sharp, made a pretty deep cut, from which the blood flowed freely. I felt stunned and sick for a minute, but recovered myself, to see Mr. Penrose gazing at me with a face whiter than his band.

"It is naught!" said I, pulling my kerchief to my forehead. Don't look so frightened, but help me to find Mrs. Judith."

For I was vexed at him, standing there as if rooted to the earth, never offering to help. It was rather unreasonable in me, too, but I do love folk to have their wits about them. He started, and recovered himself, and came forward to give me his arm.

Well, at last I got to Mrs. Judith's room, narrowly missing meeting my Lady, which was what I dreaded above all things. Mrs. Judith knew what she was about, at any rate, plastered up my head and bathed my face, and then helped me to my room. She would have had me lie still the rest of the day, but I did not like to leave my child, and I have felt no inconvenience since, save a headache, and now and then a strange sickness.

June 28.

I did not think, when I laid down my pen, that

three weeks would pass before I took it up again.

I felt the sickness coming over me again, and I suppose went to the window for air, for I was found senseless on the floor under the open casement, by Mrs Judith, who, in her kindness, had come up before going to bed to see how I was. She called Mary and got me to bed, and for three or four days I was in considerable danger, it seems, but my good constitution and Mrs. Judith's nursing brought me through. I had no surgeon, for the nearest, who lives at Biddeford, had been called away. I was not sorry, for I did as well without him, and perhaps better.

I have been sitting up now for a week, and to day ventured out of my room into the long gallery, greatly to the delight of Lady Betty, who thinks I must be almost well. The dear child was as good as possible all the time I was at the worst, so Mary tells me, even stifling her sobs when she was told that she would make herself sick, and that would grieve Mistress Merton. Since I have been getting better, Mary has brought her in to see me every day, and she has spent hours, sitting in her chair, or lying on the bed beside me. At first I had hard work to persuade her to go out of doors without me, but at last she let old John carry her down, and Mary go with her. She brings me great nosegays of flowers every day, as well as long stories about the squirrels and the young birds, for now, as ever, she prefers the wood to the garden.

Every one has been very kind to me since I was sick. Only I fancied Lady Jemima (who has been at home more than a week,) treated me rather coldly. She brought me letters from aunt and Felicia, the latter sweet as honey—rather too sweet, in fact. Felicia is not apt to be so loving, unless she meditates a bite, or a scratch at the least.

Mr. Corbet has not yet returned, but his mother, who has been once to see me, tells me that she expects him in a few days. Oh, how I have longed and pined for home, and mother, since I have been sick! All the home-sickness I have felt before was as nothing to it. But I hope to get the better of this weakness when I am able to take up my work once more.

July 1.

As I was sitting in the gallery this morning, who should come in but Mr. Penrose, whom I had not seen before since that unlucky day in the chapel. He looked pale and wretched enough, and I felt sorry for him.

"I am glad to see you up once more," said he, with something of a tremor in his voice. "I little thought what would be the end, when I called you into the chapel. If you had died"—

"You would doubtless have been much afflicted," said I, as he paused. "That would have been only natural, but even then, Mr. Penrose, you would have had no cause of self-reproach. Nobody would have been to blame—not even myself!"

"I would never have entered the desk again!" said he. "I would have sought some solitude—there are no convents now to retire to—and have given my life to fasting and penance forever after."

"Then you would have done a very wrong and foolish thing!" said I. "What if St. Paul had taken such a course? His crimes were committed of set purpose, yet did our Lord himself call him to the ministry, and that when he was upon the very errand of slaughter."

"I don't know that I ever thought of that," said he. "But you know Archbishop Abbot was deprived because he killed a man by accident when out hunting."

"I always thought it a very hard measure to the poor old gentleman," I said. "There was no malice in the act, and the archbishop did all in his power to make amends. My father was ever of the mind that if the Archbishop had been more of a courtier, his homicide would have troubled nobody."

Mr. Penrose looked a little grave upon this. I believe he thinks it little less than blasphemy to say a word against the present archbishop.

"But you see I was not killed, nor anything like it!" I continued, "so you may put off your purpose of retirement a little while."

"Do you feel quite yourself again?" he asked, anxiously.

"Why no, not altogether," I said. "I feel weak, and a little thing tires me, but I have no pain, and my head is quite clear. I had odd fancies while I was sick, Mr. Penrose. I remember them only dreamily, however, and hope to forget them altogether soon. I feel that I have much to be thankful for, both because my life was spared, and also for the care and kindness of all about me. It is not every poor girl, alone and among strangers, who meets with such friends."

"If Margaret had died, I would have died too!" said Betty, who had hitherto taken no part in the conversation.

"And so would I!" said Mr. Penrose; but Betty was not pleased.

"She is not *your* Margaret!" she retorted, with the pertness which I have not yet been able to cure: "I don't see any call that *you* would have to die!"

I could not help smiling, but seeing Mr. Penrose's color rise, I chid Lady Betty, and bade her ask pardon, which she did readily enough only rather spoiling it, by repeating, very decidedly, "But she is *not* your Margaret, Mr. Penrose! She is mine!"

"I wont have any quarrelling about me!" said I. "Come, my dear, we have sat here long enough, and here comes Mary to say that our dinner is ready."

For since I have begun to sit up and move about a little, I have taken my meals with my child, an arrangement which she likes marvellously.

"Shall we not see you at the table soon?" asked Mr. Penrose.

"As soon as Mrs. Judith permits," I said. "I am at her orders, you know. Thank you, Mr. Penrose, for coming to see me."

"Can I do nothing for you?" he asked.

"There is one thing, if I may venture to ask so much," I said. "Would you find time to go down and read a chapter now and then to Dame Yeo at the almshouse. I promised to do so, but she must think me strangely forgetful."

To my surprise he hesitated. "I would gladly do so," he answered, presently; "but I fear Doctor Parnell would think it an undue interference."

"I don't believe he would," said I. "He is a kind old man, and I believe he would be pleased with anything that pleased the old folks. At all events, you could speak to him about the matter. But do not do anything about it, if it is like to make any trouble."

"Oh, I will go!" said he, and, I rather think he did go this very afternoon.

July 3.

I felt so much better this morning that I coaxed Mrs. Judith to let me go out with Lady Betty into the wood. The day was lovely, and the whole air seemed full of the scent of hay. Lady Betty, who walks with more and more ease every day, ran about quite a good deal, and gathered wild flowers for me. Her little dog has done her a great deal of good in this respect, for she goes after him and joins in his play. My Lady came out while we were in the wood and sat down by me. After looking at, and highly commending my work, which I had brought in my hand, and kindly telling me not to tire my eyes over it, she began to talk about Lady Betty, who was at a distance gathering some plants which had taken her fancy.

"You have done wonders during the little time you have had her in charge," said she. "I could never have thought to see her move so freely—so much like another child. If she had gained naught in learning, I should owe you a debt of gratitude for all you have down for her health."

"You owe me nothing, my Lady," I said. "I have but done my duty, and I would gladly have done ten times more. It is I who am in your debt for all your goodness to me."

"Well, well, we wont dispute the matter!" said she, with her sweet, sad smile. "If only you can stay for a year or two—but I fear that will hardly be."

"I don't know why not, my Lady," I ventured to say. "Unless you tire of me, or I misbehave myself, which I trust not to do; I see no reason why I should not stay with Lady Betty as long as she needs a governess."

"Then you have yourself no desire to change

your condition—to be anywhere else?" she asked, looking at me in a searching way, with her great beautiful eyes, as if she would read my inmost thoughts.

"My Lady," said I, "I will tell you the simple truth. I would rather be at home with my mother, even in her little cottage, than here in Stanton Court, though here I am lodged and waited upon as I never was before. But as for any other place, I speak but simple sooth in saying, that since I cannot be at home, I would rather be here than anywhere else in the world. Every one is kind to me, and I love my Lady Betty dearly. I have no wish to change my condition."

"It is well said, sweetheart, and as much as I could ask," said my dear Lady. "I could not in reason ask you to prefer any other place to home. But suppose some one comes and proffers you a house and home of your own, what then?"

"That is too large a supposition for my poor imagination!" said I, smiling. "A poor plain parson's daughter, without beauty or dower, is not like to attract many suitors, I fancy. Besides, if I were as beautiful as Mrs. Corbet, or the Fair Dame herself, I see nobody."

"You are like the princess in the fairy tale, shut up in an enchanted castle!" said my Lady. "But you forget Mr. Penrose."

"Oh, he is nobody—so far as that goes!" said I. "He looks down upon me as an ignoramus and a person of no family, and besides he thinks me a Puritan!"

"What is a Puritan?" asked Lady Betty, coming up and leaning on my lap.

"That is more than I can tell you, my dear," said I; "unless it is a person who likes clear glass better than painted windows, and carven oak better than scarlet cloth and embroidery."

My Lady laughed and bade Betty see if she could find a clover with four leaves. When the child had set seriously about her search, she said to me, taking my hand, and speaking very earnestly:

"Margaret, will you make me a promise?"

"If I can, my Lady," I answered.

"Promise me then that you will not leave Betty for at least a year, whether I live or die. In the latter case I do believe the child would not be long behind her mother—certainly not,"—she said, with a strange look in her face—"if, as some say, the dead mother hath the power of calling the child after her. But promise me that you will remain with my child for at least a year."

"I promise you, my Lady!" said I, as soon as I could speak. "I will not leave Lady Betty for a year, at least, unless I am sent away."

"You may not find things always as pleasant as now," she went on to say. "My sister-in-law sometimes takes strange fancies, and she has great influence with her brother, though they are so very different. But promise me that you will not leave my child for at least a year, even," she added, "if the fairy prince should come for you!"

"The fairy prince is not likely to come, unless, indeed, my poor dear father's ship should come home at last," said I; "but if he does, I shall send him about his business. My dear Lady, I am so glad you are pleased with me," said I, with a silly gush of tears, which, however, I could not help. I suppose because I am so weak still.

She smoothed my hair with her lovely hands, and said many kind things, and I recovered myself presently, and begged her pardon.

"Tut tut," said she, lightly. "Tell me about your father's ship."

So I told her all about it, and how we feared it had been a total loss, and how my brother had been obliged to change all his plans, with much more—too much, I fear, for it was so pleasant to talk of home, and she listened so kindly, that I hardly knew when to leave off.

July 6.

Mr. Corbet has come back, and has brought me a great packet of letters and little keepsakes from the friends at home—so large a parcel that I fear it must have been inconvenient to him, but he made light of it.

Betty and I were out in the woods, as usual, she running about—for she can really run a little now—and I very busy with my pretty work, when Mr. Corbet came out of the side door and down to where I was sitting. Betty gave a cry of joy at seeing her cousin, whom she loves dearly, and with some reason, for he is ever kind and gentle with her. He caressed her, and gave her a pretty box of comfits he had brought, and then turned smiling to me.

"And Mrs. Merton must also have her box of comfits," said he, putting my precious packet into my hand. I am sure to bring my welcome, since I come from Chester and Saintswell."

"And did you really go to Saintswell?" I asked.

"I really did," he answered. "I stayed a week with my good friend, Mr. Carey, and made acquaintance with your honored mother, and with Master Jacky and his sisters, as well as with many other folk, old and young, gentle and simple. I should have been much flattered by their attentions, only I was forced to lay all to the account of my knowing the last news of dear Mistress Margaret."

I asked him many questions, as to dear mother's looks, and I know not what all, some of which I doubt he thought silly enough. I know I asked him whether the twins were grown.

"That I can hardly tell you, as I never saw them before; but 'tis not likely that they have changed a great deal in three months," said he.

"I can't think that I have been hardly three months away," said I. "It seems so long since I have seen any of them." And then I began with new questions, which he answered patiently enough.

He told me that Mr. Carey seemed to be much liked by all his people, though some of them thought his preaching not so plain and simple as my father's. He had even been taken by the twins to see the almshouses, and had been able to give dear old Goody Crump news of her sister, and of other folk she had known. The old woman had sent me her blessing, as had also Dame Higgins; the latter hoping that I had safely kept her precious medal.

"We shall have to begin watching you as a dangerous person," said he, smiling: "since you deal with such trinkets as medals blessed by the pope."

"I could not well refuse the old woman's gift," I said. "'Tis but a bit of tarnished silver, when all is said; and as to the pope's blessing, I fancy, as Goody Higgins said, if it does no good it can do no great harm—especially as I keep it with the stone old Esther gave me to keep off the witches."

"Do you believe in witches, Mrs. Merton?" asked Mr. Corbet.

"I never saw one," I answered. "We were happy in having none of those fearful troubles in our parish, which were so rife in this part of the country some years ago, and all our old women are very harmless folk. I believe Esther has her doubts of Goody Higgins, but that is only because the poor thing, being a papist, never goes to church. No, I don't think I have much belief in witches."

"Nor in ghosts?" he asked, smiling. "Are you

not just a little afraid of the Halting Knight, when the wind blows hard o' nights? Or have you never heard his story?"

"O yes, I have heard all about him," I answered. "I dare not say that I have not sometimes listened for his lame step in the gallery; but I don't think I am much afraid of him, after all. I don't think, to say the truth, that I have it in me to be very much afraid of such things."

After that we fell into a pleasant chat till it was time for Betty to go into the house. I have read my letters over and over—the long ones from dear mother and Richard, poor Jacky's short and somewhat blotted scroll, and the printed notes of the twins. I feel as if I had made a visit at home. So many little things can be told by word of mouth, which no one thinks of putting in a letter; and Mr. Corbet seems to have noticed everything, even to poor Punch, our three-legged, or rather three-footed cat, who lost his fore-paw in a rabbit-trap, and whom father would not have killed, but dressed the creature's wounds with his own hands, and nursed him till he got well.

He is a wonderful kind gentleman to take so much pains for me. I am so glad he and Richard took so to each other. It would seem but natural that they should, thinking so much alike on many ubjects; but one can never guess beforehand how such things will turn out.

Richard says he makes progress in his studies, and that Master Smith is kind and generous as ever. He still hears much of public affairs, and I can see that he does not like the complexion of them, and doth fear much trouble and discontent, arising from the high-handed proceedings of the Archbishop and the Star-chamber.

He writes me that Mr. Prynne, the barrister, an old friend of my father's, and one who hath been many times at our house since my remembrance, is in prison, and like to fare badly. He was always a bugbear to us children, with his sour, austere face, and his perpetual arguments with my father, wherein he was ofttimes so sharp and rude, that a less sweet-tempered man would have at the least declined his acquaintance; but my father always said there was much good in him, and I know that he was ever liberal in giving to the poor. I shall be sorry to hear of any great harm coming to him, poor man. It seems he hath writ a book concerning stage-plays, whereat the Court are much offended.

CHAPTER VI.

July 9.

AT her own earnest desire Lady Betty has began writing. She takes to it very handily, as indeed she does to most things. I never saw any child learn to read so fast. I was astonished thereat, till my Lady told me that it was in some sense rather a revival than a new acquisition of learning; that before her last long and dreadful illness, which lasted more than a year, Betty had known how to read in easy words pretty well; but that when she recovered her right senses, after many days of unconsciousness or raving, she seemed to have forgotten everything, even the names of those about her.

The dear child takes great pains to learn, as well to please me, as for learning's sake. Her health is certainly much better. She now moves with freedom and without pain (unless, which I have learned to guard against, she is on her feet too long at a time), sleeps soundly, and is far less whimsical about what she eats, so that she takes contentedly plain nourishing food. Her temper and spirits improve with her health. I rarely have to reprove her, and it is a long time since we have had a screaming bout, which I dread most of all. They distress my dear Lady, and make my Lord so angry if he chances to hear them; and he is not a man to hold any curb of measure or reason over his anger. Well! well! my Lord is my Lord, and I desire to pay him all due respect, but at times I cannot but wonder what ever my Lady married him for. 'Twas a love match, too, so Mrs. Judith says.

But as for my child, I have much to be thankful for in her continued improvement, and her affection and obedience to myself. And I am also thankful to my dear mother for using me early to the care of the young ones, and for her confidence in me, almost always telling me why she did thus and so with them. It will be her credit far more than my own, if Lady Betty recovers her health. The child's back can never be straightened, of course, but now that her face is filling up, and she is gaining color, and losing her unhealthy sallowness, she is really very pretty, and hath a great look of her mother's.

For myself, I must say that I have been far happier under this roof than I ever expected to be anywhere away from my home. Indeed, I don't know when I have been better off. I have had very few trials of temper (which were always my trouble when I lived with Felicia), and every one is kind to me—my dear honored Lady above all. As to Mr. Penrose's little pets, I don't value them a pin; especially since I know the real goodness of his heart. He hath been almost daily to read with Dame Yeo and old Master Dean, at the almshouses. But he seems like one who hath some great trouble on his mind. I wonder what it is?

July 18.

I am quite sure of one thing—namely, that Lady Jemima hath somewhat against me, and that ever since she returned from London. She treats me with studied coldness and indifference, never comes to my room, as she used to do, to ask me about my reading and my devotions, nor stops to chat in the hall, or the gardens. My Lady is just the same; but my Lord, I fancy, looks coldly on me, and throws out hints against Puritans, &c. Even Mr. Corbet does not come to see his cousin as often as he used to do. I cannot understand it, for I am sure I have done nothing to merit displeasure. Mr. Penrose alone is unchanged, and we have really had some pleasant talks together. He preaches every week in the chapel—sometimes very well, too—and I go to hear him; but I know not how it is, the more I hear, the more discouraged and downhearted I grow. I feel downright rebellious, sometimes. Mr. Penrose says it is fitting we should go mourning all our days on account of our sins, thankful that we have so much as a chance of salvation, but not building too much thereupon, lest we fall short after all, and all our good works be as nothing. He ought to know. He is a clergyman, and a good one, but I cannot feel satisfied.

July 22.

Well, the murder is out—at least a part of it. Lady Jemima has treated me more and more coldly all the time; and yesterday, being in my Lady's antechamber, mending and arranging of some laces too fine for Brewster's eyes, I heard Lady Jemima come in by the other door, in earnest conversation with my Lady, and talking so loud, that though I made a noise to announce my presence, she did not seem to heed in the least.

"You ought to send her away, Elizabeth!" I heard her say, in her emphatic way. "You ought not to keep her about the child a day longer!"

"I shall certainly do nothing of the sort, till I see better cause than I have yet seen," replied my Lady.

"Better cause!" repeated Lady Jemima, in that contemptuous tone of hers which always makes me angry, whether she speaks to me or not. "What better cause do you want than that the girl is a bitter Puritan—an Anabaptist, for aught I know, and will be sure to fill your child's mind with all sorts of poisonous notions about religion and government!"

"But I have no evidence that she is so Jemima, nor do I believe it. Margaret is regular, both at church and chapel. She is a clergyman's daughter, hath been well brought up, and the Bishop of Exeter told me himself that he thought I had made a happy choice. He saw Margaret at home, and was much pleased both with her and her brother."

Now, for the first time, I discovered that they were talking about me, for at first I thought it was Mary they meant, and I wondered how any one could think of calling her a Puritan. I knew I ought not to hear more, and as I was considering for a moment what to do, I heard Lady Jemima say, contemptuously:

"The Bishop of Exeter, indeed! He is a fitting person, truly! He is as much a Puritan as the worst of them."

"He is your spiritual pastor and Bishop, Jemima, and, as such, is entitled to your respect!" answered my Lady, more sharply than I had ever heard her speak to her sister, save once. "It is a wonderful thing to me, to see you and Mr. Penrose, professing to think so highly of the priestly office and authority, and yet losing no occasion to condemn and vilify your own Bishop. I have spoke my mind on it to Mr. Penrose, and I must say to you that such conduct is neither consistent nor becoming!"

Brewster coming in at this moment, and beginning to commend my work on the lace, put a stop to the conversation, and I escaped to my room, more angry than ever I was with Felicia at home, to think that Lady Jemima should be trying to undermine me with my Lady, and to separate me from my child. I was much perturbed all day, insomuch that I fear I was impatient with Betty even, for she asked me, rather plaintively, what was the matter; adding, "You are not angry with me, are you, Margaret?"

I kissed her, and had much ado not to burst out crying. However, I conquered myself, and told her that she was a good girl, and that I loved her dearly.

"I am sure I love you!" said she. "Aunt Jemima asked me if you were good to me, and I told her that you were just as good as ever you could be. But I am sure that something troubles you, if you are not vexed with me, for you go red and pale, and your voice does not sound natural."

"It is true, my dear, that something has happened to vex me, but you need not mind. I hope all will come right by and by. Come, now, I will teach you your task in the Catechism. You know you must be well learned in it that you may teach your little god-daughter by and by."

(I forgot to say, in the right place, that the babes were christened the other day, I standing as proxy for Lady Betty, and Mrs. Corbet for the other child, who is named for her. Mr. Corbet made the poor woman a handsome present, and the next day she brought the babes up to the Court, to Lady Betty's great delight.)

Betty did her lessons well, and enjoyed her walk

in the wood. I have got permission to try riding for her, and Thomas is training a fine steady donkey for her use, which she goes to see every day. Sitting in my usual place in the wood, while Betty played about, I could not but remember the conversation I had with my dear Lady, and wondered if she had even then foreseen this trouble. A few tears came to relieve me, as I remembered her kind words. Betty espied them, and came in great trouble to wipe them away.

"You must not cry, Margaret," said she, with quivering lips. "I can't bear to have you cry."

"Then I wont," said I, recovering myself. "There, see, the tears are all gone away."

"I am afraid they have only gone *inside*," said the dear child, regarding me wistfully. "I am afraid they will come out again by and by. You said, when I was ill the other day, that we might ask God to take our pains away, if He saw best. Why don't you ask Him to take your trouble away?"

"Why, so I will!" I answered her; and I did put up a petition then and there for grace against anger and uncharitableness. I could not but think it was heard, for I grew more calm in spirit, and was able to think what I had better do. Betty was very sober all day, and at night, she added to her prayers, of her own accord, "Please take away Margaret's trouble, and make her happy again." The dear little loyal soul! I am sure of her love, at all events.

It was a custom of my dear father's, when we did not have prayers in the church, after his voice began to fail, to say the Litany with his own family, every Wednesday and Friday; and I have kept up the custom of repeating the petitions on those days. As I did so that night, and especially at the prayer, "O God, Merciful Father," a wonderful quietness and peace seemed to come over met, and I felt like a grieved child hushed and quieted in its mother's arms. 'Twas as if an all but visible Presence filled and sanctified the room. When I had finished, I took up my Bible to read, as usual, and my eye lighted first on these words:

"If thy brother trespass against thee, go and tell him his fault between him and thee alone. If he shall hear thee, then thou hast gained thy brother."

"Surely," I thought, "this is the rule for me to follow. I will go at once to Lady Jemima, and lay the case before her fairly, and try to find out where the trouble lies."

No sooner said than done. I knew Lady Jemima would be in her room and up, for she never goes to rest early. So I went and knocked at her door, and she bade me enter. I had not been in her room since her return, and I noticed some changes. She hath put a great crucifix over her reading-desk, and taken away the cushion and mats before it, as if she used to kneel on the bare boards; and she hath a fine picture of the Assumption, as they call it—assumption, indeed!

'Tis to be hoped the Blessed Virgin knows not the use made of her name. Lady Jemima was sitting reading by her table, and as she looked up and saw who it was at the door, she said, sharply enough:

"Well, Mrs. Merton, what brings you hither at this time of night?"

"I desire to see your Ladyship alone," I answered; "and I knew that I should find you so at this time, therefore I took the liberty to come."

"Very well," said she, still very short. "What is your business? State it quickly, for I have no time to spend in idle talk."

"I would fain know your Ladyship's interpretation of this text," I said, putting into her hands the Bible I had brought with me, and pointing to the text in St. Matthew, I had just read.

She relaxed a little at my words, as I thought, and looked gratified; but colored scarlet as she looked at the text.

"What should it mean, save just what it says?" she asked, with asperity, yet displaying a certain uneasiness. "'If any person hath done you a wrong, go first to him alone, and tell him his fault in all kindness.' I see nothing hard to understand in that. You are trifling with me, Mrs. Merton!"

"By no means, Lady Jemima," said I; "I never was more in earnest in my life. 'Tis upon that very errand I have come, since you have not come to me; and I desire humbly to know what it is that you have so much against me, since your return."

"I have not said that I had anything against you," she answered. "Why should you think I have?"

"I would fain hope so," I answered her. "It would be lack of charity to think that you should treat me so unkindly, and strive to set my honored mistress against me, unless you had some cause for so doing."

"How do you know that I have tried to set my sister against you?" she asked.

"Because I heard you—much against my own will," I answered her; and then told her how it came about. "And I would fain know, my Lady, who hath so changed your mind toward me, or who hath traduced me to you?"

"Nobody has traduced you!" she said, shortly.

"But somebody has given you a bad character of me, I am sure," I said; "and I have a right, with all due respect, to ask who that person is."

"It is one who has known you ever since you were born," said Lady Jemima, "since you must know; one on whom you have heaped many injuries, even to the driving her forth of her own home, among strangers, but who still wishes you well. She hath told me naught of your unkindness toward herself, though I can gather enough; nor did she tell me anything directly, till I asked her."

"Felicia!" I exclaimed, enlightened all at once.

"I see it all now. Felicia has been poisoning your Ladyship's mind against me."

"My mind is not poisoned against you," she answered, coldly; "but I have learned enough of your rebellious temper, your disobedient carriage toward your parents, and your openly avowed heresies in religion, to make me aware that you are no fit companion for my brother's child. Felicia, as you disrespectfully call her, seems to me a most religious, and virtuous, and sweet young person, with a mind most open to receive the truth, and a most becoming modesty and deference,—a quality, Mrs. Merton, in which you yourself are very deficient, let me tell you. I saw some things in your conduct, even before I left home, which did not please me, and I am convinced that you are no fit person for your place."

"May I ask what those things were, my Lady?" I asked.

"Your flirting and coquetting with Mr. Penrose, for one thing," answered Lady Jemima. "Yes, you may laugh as you please, but I have seen what passed. You know he is all but vowed to celibacy, and it would be a fine triumph to your Puritan notions, to make him false to his profession."

"Lady Jemima," said I, feeling my cheeks flush in spite of me, "I know not why you call me a Puritan. I am an unworthy but faithful member of the Church of England. I love her ways, and desire her peace above all things; and whoever has told you to the contrary hath said falsely. Felicia was ever mine enemy, and hath made me all the trouble I have ever had in life, heretofore; and I believe she will not be content till she works my ruin."

"You misjudge her much, and with great want of charity," interrupted Lady Jemima. "She desires naught but your good, and 'twas to that end she spoke to me about you, beseeching me to have an eye to you, that you did not get into mischief, or make mischief for others. 'Tis you who have injured her. As for her, I believe she would not hurt a fly."

"I have known her nearly eighteen years, and your Ladyship not as many weeks," said I. "Which hath had the best opportunity of understanding her character?"

"I am not apt to be deceived in my estimate of character," answered Lady Jemima, stiffly. "I said to myself the first time I ever saw you, 'Here is one destined to make mischief,' and so you did, causing a misunderstanding between me and my sister the very first day you were in the house. But this is unprofitable," she added, catching herself up; "if you have no more to say, Mrs. Merton, I must pray you to retire, and leave me to my devotions."

"I will do so," I answered, "first taking the liberty to tell your Ladyship a rule given me by my Lord the Bishop of Exeter, at my coming to this place: 'Never to do anything upon which you cannot ask the blessing of God.' Doubtless your Ladyship will ask His blessing on your attempts to undermine and defame an orphan girl, who is striving with all her might to do her duty in that station to which it hath pleased God to call her."

So saying, I courtesied and shut the door. I thought she would have called me back, but she did not, and I returned to my room, feeling grieved, vexed, and discouraged, yet withal a little disposed to laugh.

"Flirt with Mr. Penrose!" quoth I. "I would as soon flirt with that red, yellow, and blue Saint Austin in the chapel window. How can she be so absurd!"

July 24.

It seems I did not improve matters by my appeal to Lady Jemima. She will hardly speak to me at all now, and I know she doth not cease to prejudice others against me. Even Mrs. Judith grows rather cool, or so I fancy, at least; only my Lady is just the same. I should not say *only*, for Mr. Penrose is even kinder than ever, and Mrs. Corbet and her son treat me with as much consideration as though I were a relation of the family. But I can't help feeling the change very much, for I was fond of Lady Jemima, though I used sometimes to be vexed with her meddling ways. Besides, I *know* that I have done my best since I came here, and any one may see how much the child has gained.

It is very hard, but I see no way but to bear it for the present, and that in silence. I cannot and will not trouble my dear Lady with any complaints, and I don't suppose she could help me, if I did. I have passed my promise to my Lady to stay for a year, unless I am sent away, and after all, my lot is not as hard as hers. As old Jane Betterton used to say at the end of her catalogue of troubles, to my father, "I hav'n't no old man to plague me, thank goodness!"

I remember once, when dear father was teaching us Latin (and a kinder teacher sure never any one had), my growing terribly discouraged, and thinking I never should learn. Father comforted, instead of chiding me, when I burst out crying over Cæsar, his Commentaries, and told me that I had only come to the *hard place*—that every one found just such a hard place in all serious undertakings, and if I would only do my best, and persevere, I should soon get past it, and find I had made a great step in advance; and so I did. I suppose I have now come to the hard place in my service, and if I can only live it over, I shall go on well again. If only I can be kept from wrong doing—but my natural temper is so warm, and I fear I have not made much progress in controlling it.

I find it hardest to forgive Felicia. Her conduct seems so wantonly malicious—unless, indeed, she has grown tired of Aunt Willson, and wants the place herself. How she must have flattered

Lady Jemima. I can see it all—how she hinted, and then drew back and let herself be questioned, and brought out her tale with seeming reluctance, and was so anxious all the time for my good. She is not at home to plague mother, that is one comfort, and she will never be able to hoodwink Aunt Willson, living, as she does, under the same roof.

Well, well! "'Tis all in the day's work!" as Dick says, and we must take the bitter with the sweet. Oh, Dick, only to put my head down on thy honest shoulder, and tell all my troubles!

July 25.

Mr. Penrose preached this evening in the chapel, on charity. "The greatest of these is charity."

He made a noble discourse, and spoke, methought, with some asperity of them that take up idle reports and are ready on the least evidence to believe evil of their fellows.

I dared not glance at Lady Jemima, but I saw Mrs. Judith look rather uneasy, and after chapel she was unusually kind to me, and asked me to sup with her in her room, which I did. I thought she had something on her mind she wished to say, and at last it came out.

"My dear, you are not a concealed Papist, are you?"

"I must be very carefully concealed if I am, Mrs. Judith," I answered, laughingly; "for I have never even found it out myself. Whatever put it in your head to think me a Papist?"

"Well, I will tell you," she answered, in a confidential tone; "though I am afraid you will be vexed. You see, when you were so very ill, I went one day to your cabinet to see if I could find any smelling-salts or the like, and there, lying with some other trinkets, I saw a silver medal with a picture of the Virgin thereon."

"Yes," I answered, as she paused; "I know what you mean. A poor old woman at home gave it me for a keepsake."

"Well, that was not all," continued Mrs. Judith. "I put my hand back in the recess to take up a bottle I saw there, and I suppose I touched a spring, for a door opened at the back, and there lay a rosary and crucifix, and a little carven stone image of some saint or other."

"I know nothing about that," I answered, surprised enough. "I did not know there was any such door. The things must have been there a very long time, I think. Did you take them out, Mrs. Judith?"

"Not I, Mistress Merton!" answered the dear old woman. "I had no call to be prying into your secrets, if you have any. So I just laid matters as they were before, and locked the cabinet, that no one else should meddle. But oh, my dear, you are not a Papist nor a Puritan, are you?"

I could not help laughing, but stopped, as I saw the tears in the old lady's eyes.

"Dearest Mrs. Judith," said I, "I begin to

think that I must be just in the right place, since Lady Jemima calls me a Puritan, and you think me a Papist. But I solemnly assure you I am neither Papist nor Puritan, Anabaptist nor Turk, nor do I worship the sun and moon, as Doctor Parnell says the old heathens used to do on the great barrow up on the moor. I am just a simple Churchwoman, as all my family have been. But Mrs. Judith, if you are so startled at seeing a little medal in my cabinet, what do you think of some other rooms in the house, and of the pictures Mr. Penrose has just put up in the chapel?"

"I like them not, my dear,—I like them not," said Mrs. Judith, shaking her head, solemnly. "It looks too much like bringing back the old religion for denying of which my grandfather died bravely at the stake. But I am so glad you are not a Papist! Do have some of this junket, now do, my dear heart! I made it with my own hands, and the clotted cream is an inch thick on the top."

I was in no ways averse to the junket, and so all was well once more between Mrs. Judith and me. I cannot but note here what a different spirit in the two! Lady Jemima telling every one she can get to listen to her of the great discovery she fancies she has made to my disadvantage—Mrs. Judith locking up my cabinet, lest some one else should see what she had seen and I be injured thereby.

I have been examining this said cabinet, and have found, not only the rosary and the little marble saint, but several other small matters, none of them of any great value, save a rose noble of King Henry's day. I carried them all to my Lady, but she bade me keep them if I liked, so I set the saint on the top of my cabinet. 'Tis a fair little image, carven in alabaster, perfect, but somewhat yellow with time, and represents a young maid with spindle and distaff, and and a lamb by her side. Mr. Penrose says it is meant for St. Agnes, and has promised to find out her history for me. Poor little lady, she hath had a long and dark imprisonment; if, as my Lady supposes, she has been hid there since the early days of King James; but she looks very smiling. Lady Betty will have it that she is Una, with her milk-white lamb, about which I have read to her in "Spencer his Fairy Queen."

July 26.

I can see that Mr. Penrose's sermon has done me no good with Lady Jemima, and only hurt himself with her. They were talking together a long time this morning, in the garden, and parted evidently ill-pleased with each other—I could see thus much from my window.

This has been a great day for Betty. She has taken her first ride on the donkey, Thomas leading him, and I walking by her side. I held her at first, as she seemed rather timid, and I wanted her by no means to have a fright; but presently she gained more confidence and would ride alone. We did not go far the first day, for I did not wish her to be overtired, but she enjoyed herself wonderfully. Mr. Corbet joined us as we were returning up the avenue, and taking Thomas's place, led the donkey himself. He told me a great piece of news— namely, that the Bishop is coming here within a short time. Now I shall see whether he will remember me, or whether, as Felicia said, he has never given me a thought. Mr. Corbet looked grave and disturbed, and made somewhat absent answers to Betty's questions, which she remarking, he roused himself to be more attentive.

"Some day, perhaps, Margaret and I shall come down to your house to see you, Cousin Walter," said Lady Betty. "I should love to see Corby-End, wouldn't you, Margaret?"

"And Corby-End would love to see you," answered Mr. Corbet: "but maybe Mrs. Merton would find the walk long."

"O no!" I answered. "I have been used to long walks, and I often walk down to the Parsonage."

"Have you ever been down to the cliff?" asked Mr. Corbet.

I told him that I had not; that I was rather frightened at the steepness of the path, and the roaring of the waterfall so near.

"It looks more dangerous than it really is," said Mr. Corbet. "The little children from the Cove come up every day to school. 'Tis a hard walk for them, and but for seeming to interfere with Mrs. Ellenwood, I would set up a dame school down there for the little lads and maids. But I believe I should have few willing pupils. The children are all devoted to their present mistress, who is indeed an admirable person. But you must go down there some day, Mrs. Merton, and make acquaintance with my old friend, Uncle Jan Lee and his family. They are well worth knowing.'

At supper time, Mr. Corbet being present, my Lord asked him if he had seen Doctor Parnell, adding that to him the old man seemed failing.

"I see that he is so, and I am very sorry," answered Mr. Corbet. "There are few better men than he. I would all parish clergymen were like him."

"So would not I, though I like the old man well enough," replied my Lord. "He is too stiff-necked for me, and I like not his opposing of the Sunday sports on the Green. The King and the Archbishop have approved them, and what is good enough for his betters might, one would think, be good enough for him."

"However, the Archbishop does not sanction them by his example," said Mr. Corbet.

Thereupon ensued an argument on Sunday games in general, in which Mr. Corbet seemed to me to have much the best of it, he keeping cool, while my Lord grew very warm, and said the same thing over and over, not without some oaths better left out. Catching Mr. Corbet's eye, I ventured to glance toward my Lady, who I saw was uneasy, as she always is when there is danger of one of my Lord's tantrums. He took the hint at once, and smilingly changed the subject, by asking my Lord if he had heard, I know not what wonderful tale of a stag lately killed by Sir Thomas Fulton. My Lord opened on the scent of the stag directly, and so all ended well. Mr. Penrose was not present, nor Lady Jemima.

After supper Mr. Corbet came to me as I was passing through the hall, and said:

"Thank you, Mrs. Merton, for the hint."

"I fear you must think me too bold!" I answered, feeling my cheeks flush scarlet: "but a little thing disturbs my Lady now-a-days."

"I shall never think you aught but what you are," said he; "but tell me, how does this matter strike you?"

I told him that I thought as he did—that such sports, even when harmless in themselves, were ill-suited to the Lord's day, which was needed for religious improvement, and meditation, and added that my father used to say that if masters were so anxious for the poor to have a holiday, it would be far better to give them time for recreation during the week, than thus to run the risk of driving out in the afternoon all the religious impressions made in the morning. Just as I was saying good-night, my Lord came into the hall.

"So, Master Watty, the Puritan, you have found some one to agree with your strait-laced notions!" said he. "Mrs. Merton, I dare say, can give you text for text and groan for groan. Come, Mrs. Merton, let us have a specimen of your power. Give us a text!"

"I can think of but one at this minute, my Lord," I answered, I fear not in the meekest tone, "and that is this: 'Judge not, that ye be not judged!'"

"Well put, Mistress Presician!" said my Lord, with a great laugh. "I see there is something within that can strike fire, after all. But I bid you beware, Walter. You are poaching on another man's manor."

I waited to hear no more, but escaped and went to my child. I wish they would let me sup with her all the time. I suppose I shall do so next week, when the Bishop comes to stay.

July 29.

This day we were returning up one of the paths in the chase. Betty had taken quite a long ride, and was full of the wonderful things she had seen, especially of the ruins of the old abbey. She was talking with great animation, when, at a turn in the road, we met my Lord. One can never be sure of his mood, and I am always rather uneasy when Betty encounters her father, but he was in high good humor this day, having been angling and met with great success.

"Hey-day! whom have we here?" he exclaimed. "Surely this bold horse-woman, or donkey-woman, can never be Betty! Why, what change has come over you, child? Hold up your head and let me look at you!"

Smiling and blushing, Lady Betty held up her head. She did really look wonderfully pretty.

"Why, the fairies have been at work with you, Betty!" said my Lord. "I never in all my life saw such a change! But can you walk as well as ride?"

"O yes, papa!" answered the child. "I can run a little, too, and I have learned to read and to write, and I sleep almost all night, now. I did not hear the clock strike but twice last night."

"But what is it?" questioned my Lord. "What medicines have you given her?"

I told him that I had given no medicines except change of air, exercise, and amusement; that I had in fact treated Lady Betty just as my mother had treated her own younger children, and I hoped with like good results. I added that I thought, unless she had some new drawback, Lady Betty might yet grow up to be a healthy woman. He muttered somewhat to himself, and then turned to Betty again, asking her about her ride, and telling her she should have a pony some day.

"I did not think you could sit so straight," said he. Betty straightened up still more at the words and looked so much pleased, that I think my Lord's heart was touched. He kissed her, a thing I never saw him do before, told her to be a good maid, and get well as fast as she could; and then turning to me, he said, with real feeling and dignity :

"I thank you heartily, Mrs. Margaret Merton, for what you have done for the child, and you shall find that I do. I could not have thought such a change would be wrought in so short a time. It was a good day, as my Lady says, that brought you to us. Only mind," he added, relapsing into his usual manner, "mind you teach her none of your new-light notions. I will not have her made a Puritan, no, not if she never sets foot to ground again."

"What is a Puritan, papa?" asked Lady Betty.

"A Puritan, child? How shall I tell you? A Puritan is one who sings naught but Psalms through his nose, and wears his hair cropped close, and is always turning up his eyes, and hates king and church, and thinks a play-book, or a romance, or a dance round the May-pole, worse than the devil himself."

"Then I am sure Margaret is not a Puritan!" said Betty, eagerly; "for she sings me all sorts of merry songs, and not through her nose at all, and she has beautiful long hair, almost down to her feet, and she makes me say a prayer for the king and queen every day. And she is teaching me the Catechism, and she does not hate all romances or play-books, for she has 'The Fairy Queen,' and some of Mr. Shakespeare's plays in her room, and she read one to me, all about Puck and Titania, and some poor men that played a play before the Duke—what is its name, Margaret?"

"'The Midsummer Night's Dream,'" I told her.

"And she can dance beside, for she showed me how her mother taught her to dance the Corants," continued Betty, eagerly. "So, you see, she cannot be a Puritan!"

"Argued point by point, like a good advocate," said my Lord, laughing. "Well, well, child, you do well to speak up for your friend. I dare say it is all nonsense what your aunt says."

And with that he bade us good morning, and went on his way whistling.

August 1.

Dear good Doctor Parnell died this morning, just at sunrise. He has been ailing for some days, but it was only yesterday that they thought him near his end. Mr. Corbet and Mr. Penrose sat up with him all night. He did not sleep much, but spoke many times, sometimes of his sister, whom he solemnly commended to Mr. Corbet's care, sometimes of the parish, and again of the joys of heaven, where he seemed, Mr. Penrose said, to feel himself already translated. He thought of everybody, and even sent me, by Mr Penrose, his parting blessing, and a little book of devotions.

He died just as the sun was rising, commending his soul to God, without any appearance of fear or anxiety. Mr. Penrose, telling me the story, was affected even to tears, and I wept with him, feeling that I had lost a friend.

I went down to-day to bid him a last farewell, and to see Mistress Parnell. She is as it were stunned by the blow. She said to me:

"I am several years older than my brother and I had arranged everything for my leaving him; but I never once thought of his going first and leaving me. Ah well, I am thankful that in the course of nature I cannot be long behind him. Mr. Penrose is a good young man, and I think he will be kind to the poor folks."

"Mr. Penrose!" said I; and then it came out that my Lord had promised the living to Mr. Penrose. It is a great piece of preferment for so young a man, the living being a very good one; and I am glad he is so well provided for.

My Lord joked with him a little, at supper, and said somewhat about a mistress for the parsonage; at which Lady Jemima said hotly enough, that Mr. Penrose was not a marrying priest. He cast a glance at her, as if he were not over well-pleased by her interference, and said, very soberly, that he counted not the house his own, so long as the corpse of its former master lay under its roof, and therefore he had no need to take any order about a mistress for the same as yet; whereat my Lady smiled approvingly, and my Lord seemed somewhat dashed. I thought it was very prettily said of him, for my part. I wish he had a good sensible wife. He would not have nearly so many absurd quiddities if he were married.

August 4.

Doctor Parnell was buried this day—in the churchyard, as he desired, and in a spot which he himself selected long ago. Mistress Parnell told me afterward it was by the side of a young lady, a cousin of the Mrs. Corbet that then was, who died more than forty years ago. It seems there were some love passages between them, but she being caught in a heavy storm of rain, took a quick consumption and died, her lover attending her, and cheering her last moments by his prayers. Since that time he would never hear of taking a wife, though some of good family were proposed to him, he being accounted rich; but he would have none of them, though he was a great promoter of marriage in the parish, and always made the brides a present. Methought a pretty story of constancy.

August 6.

Here is a change of affairs with a witness! Mr. Penrose has made up his mind with respect to a mistress for the parsonage, and upon whom should his choice fall but on my unworthy self. I never was so astounded in all my life, as when my Lady told me (for he broke the matter to her in the first place); and I told her I thought she must be mistaken, that he must have meant somebody else.

"I hardly know who else he could mean, unless you think Lady Jemima was the person," answered my Lady, smiling. "Besides, he was quite too explicit, and too much in earnest to leave room for a mistake. 'Tis your own little self he wants, sweetheart, and nobody else.'

"Then, my Lady, 'his want must be his master,' as they say in our country," I said. "I cannot marry Mr. Penrose."

"Bethink you this is a grave matter," said my Lady. "Here, sit you down and let us talk it over reasonably."

We were talking in her closet, and I sat down, not on the chair beside her, but on a hassock at her feet. I was glad of the permission, for what with excitement and some other feeling, I know not what, I trembled from head to foot.

"Bethink you well; this is a grave matter,' repeated my Lady. "Mr. Penrose is an excellent man, and a gentleman. He hath now a good living, and you will have such a settlement for life as belongs to few at your age."

"I know it, my Lady," I answered, as she seemed to pause for a reply. "I know all that, and that it is an offer far above my deserts, but I cannot marry him."

"But, sweetheart, have you never given Mr. Penrose cause to think that you would marry him—at the least that you were not averse to him?" said my Lady.

"No, madam, that I have not, I am sure," I

answered, eagerly. "How could I, when I no more expected such an offer from him, than from St. Thomas of Canterbury, in the chancel window? I never even thought of such a thing, till Lady Jemima accused me of flirting with him; and since then I have seen Mr. Penrose hardly at all. Indeed, my Lady, I have given him no reason, and he is a coxcomb if he says I have!"

"Gently, gently!" said my Lady, laughingly (which she does but rarely). "Why, what a little pepper-pot it is, after all! Mr. Penrose neither said nor hinted aught of the kind, so you need not be so hot against him. 'Tis no insult, sure, for a good gentleman to wish to marry you."

"I beg your pardon, my Lady," I faltered. And then, like a great baby, I burst out crying, and sobbed, "O mother, mother! I want my own mother!" Instead of chiding me, as I deserved, my dear Lady laid my head against her knee, and kissed and soothed me, till I was able to recover some self-control. Then she asked me again, what objection I had to Mr. Penrose.

"I don't know that I have any particular objection, my Lady, only that he is Mr. Penrose," I answered. "I liked him well enough till he wanted to marry me, and now I cannot bear him. Beside, my Lady, I cannot leave you and Lady Betty. I am promised to you for a year, at least. Oh, my Lady, don't turn against me and send me away! Indeed, the stories about me are not true. I am no Puritan, and"—I found the tears were coming again, so I checked myself and said no more.

"I have no wish to get rid of you, Margaret," answered my Lady, gravely and kindly. "I have seen no fault in you myself, and I pay no heed to idle tales. 'Tis true I have written to your Aunt Willson about the matter, but only that I might have the better means of defending you. It is my most earnest wish that you should continue my child's governess as long as she wants one. But, at the same time, I would not selfishly stand in the way of your prosperity. I know it is not as pleasant to you here, as it has been, and it will be still less so if I am taken away. You may never have such another offer, and I want you to do what is best for yourself."

"I cannot marry Mr. Penrose, my Lady, if I should never have another offer in all my life," I answered. "I have no wish but to live with you, and take care of Lady Betty; and if things are not quite so pleasant now, I dare say they will come round again, and if they do not, why I must expect some trouble as well as other folk. 'Tis all in the day's work!' as brother Richard says."

"But would not brother Richard say that ''twas in the day's work' to marry and settle when so good an offer came in your way?" asked my Lady.

"No, madam, I think not," I answered. "Richard gave up all his own plans in life, that he might help dear mother, and I came here to do the same thing. I am sure he would say I ought to consider her more than myself."

"But, see you not, sweetheart, that this marriage would put you in a better position to help your mother than you are now?" argued my Lady. "What with his place as chaplain, which he is still to keep, and his living, Mr. Penrose will be well to do, and he is like to rise, holding as he does in all things with the Archbishop, who is all powerful now-a-days. He will be able greatly to help your mother and the younger children."

"Able is one thing, and willing is another, my Lady!" I answered. "'Tis not every man who would wish to be burdened with his wife's family, nor should I like to ask my husband to support my mother. I would rather do it myself."

"I am afraid you are very proud, Margaret," said my Lady, shaking her head.

"Perhaps so, my Lady," I answered. "But I pray you, dear Lady, do not urge me farther. I am greatly beholden to Mr. Penrose for his offer," (I am afraid this was a fib. I did not feel beholden to him at all, but very much as if I should love to box his ears for him;) "but I never can marry him in the world."

"Well, well, you shall not be urged," said my Lady. "I will tell him what you say, but I feel sure he will not be satisfied without talking to yourself. And, Margaret, let me add one thing more. My Lord hath gotten hold of this matter—through no good-will of mine, but by Mr. Penrose's bad management; and 'tis like he may rally you upon it. Do not you get angry if he does, but laugh in your turn. Learn to rule that fire within, and it will save you a great deal of trouble, my little one."

She bent and kissed me as she spoke, and I kissed her beautiful hand. "Oh, my dear Lady!" I said, out of the fulness of my heart, "if I could only do anything to return or requite your goodness to me!"

"Then I will tell you what you may do," said she, smiling. "I am going to spend the day at Corby-End with my cousins, and you may take the opportunity to look over all my laces and lay out those which need repairing. The work is too fine for Brewster's eyes, and I know you love to do it. Bring Betty in here and let her superintend the operation."

I knew Betty would be delighted with the change, and I was glad to hear that I need not meet my Lord for one day, at least.

So Betty and I spent the morning very comfortably, and I got quite cooled down over the laces, and was able to look at the matter reasonably. I am ashamed now to think how foolishly I behaved, and how absurd it was in me to be so angry with poor Mr. Penrose. I am sure it was kind of him to think of me. All the same, I would never marry him if there were not another man in all the world. I only hope he will take my Lady's word for it, and not desire to see me himself.

August 8.

It turned out as my Lady said. Mr. Penrose would not be satisfied without talking with me himself, and trying to move my resolution. He used many arguments, as the advantage to my family, my having such a pleasant home near to my Lady, chances of usefulness in the parish, and so on, till at last I lost patience a little, and said:

"Mr. Penrose, you are but wasting your breath. If I loved you as I am sure a woman ought to love the man she marries, I should need none of these persuasions, and as I love you not, they are all thrown away."

"You think, then, that I could not make you happy?" said he. "I know I am faulty, and that you have often seen me peevish; but I would do my best, Margaret."

"I don't doubt you would," I answered him. "As for your faults, if I loved you at all, I know I should love you none the less for them, but perhaps all the more. But I have seen married life—only from the outside, 'tis true—and I am sure the trials of temper which come in the happiest marriage, would be too much for me, unless I—Well, the whole of the matter is, Mr. Penrose, I cannot think of it. I am sorry if I have been to blame; but I do assure you solemnly, that till my Lady broke it to me, I no more thought of your wanting me, than I did of being Queen of England."

"You have not been to blame," said Mr. Penrose, abruptly. "Nothing is to be blamed but my own miserable folly in thinking that one such as you could ever fancy such a lout as I am."

"Now you are just as far the other way," said I. "You are quite my equal in every respect, and very much my superior in most things. I am greatly honored by your regard, and do really wish that I could return it. You must see that I should have everything to gain, if I did, and therefore you should allow that my refusal is disinterested. Besides, even if I did, there is another lion in the way. I have promised my Lady, in the most solemn manner, not to leave Lady Betty for at least a year."

I was sorry I said as much, for he caught at it directly.

"Then you will wait that time before coming to a final decision. You will let me try to change your mind. I promise you that you shall not be urged or annoyed in any way. Only wait a year before quite deciding."

"I do not feel that a year will make the least difference," said I, feeling vexed at him and at myself. "I wish you would put the matter out of your head, and marry somebody else."

"I shall never marry anybody else," said he, flushing up. "It may be this disappointment is a punishment laid upon me for entertaining the notion of marriage at all. I suppose Lady Jemima would say so."

"Never mind Lady Jemima, but follow your own

good sense, Mr. Penrose," said I. "Do you think if marriage had been such a sin, so many of the apostles would have married? I hope to see you well settled with a wife yet, and as happy as you deserve to be in your own family. Then I will come and see you, and be Aunt Margaret to every one, though Lady Betty says aunts are always cross."

He smiled faintly, kissed my hand, and went away looking very crestfallen, and I went back to my room, and had a good cry, partly because I was sorry for him, partly, I believe, because I was a little sorry for myself. He is a good man, that I am sure of, and a gentleman bred as well as born, which is more than one can say for some folks; and the parsonage is so nice, and then it would be so pleasant to have a home to which I could ask dear mother. I shall never have another so good a chance of settling in life to advantage.

But after all, I feel that I never can bring my mind to marry Mr. Penrose. I could as soon sell myself for a slave. And I should not make him happy, either. I feel sure that all the good would die out of me, and all the evil increase tenfold. I could never ask God's blessing on such a marriage.

When I went back to Lady Betty I found her in tears, and Mary in vain trying to pacify her. It seems the story of Mr. Penrose's offer has gone all through the household (thanks, I must say, to his own awkwardness in the matter), and Mary, who, with her good qualities, is somewhat of a gossip, had been telling Betty, thinking, to be sure, the child would be delighted. As soon as I came near, Betty threw her arms round my neck, and sobbed out, "O Margaret, don't go away and leave me! I shall die if you do!"

"But, Lady Betty, Mrs. Merton will be no farther away than the parsonage, and you can ride down to see her on your donkey," said Mary.

"I wont!" cried Betty, in something of her old tone. "I will never go near the parsonage!"

"You had better wait till you are asked, my dear!" said I, a little sharply. "If you do not go thither till you go to see me, it will be a long time first. Mary, you would do much better to be about your work, than to be gossipping about my affairs. You have made the bed very ill, and the hangings are all in strings, nor have you put away your Lady's clothes, nor dusted properly. And you, Lady Betty, have neglected your lesson to hear and fret yourself over this idle matter. If you do so again, I shall set you a double task."

Dick used to say, laughing, that I could be awfully dignified when I chose, and I suppose I was so now, for poor Mary looked very much scared, and began to make apologies; but I cut her short.

"I wish to hear no more," said I. "Do your work over, and do it properly, and another time remember that my affairs are not yours. Lady Betty, you can bring your book into the gallery, and learn your lesson there, till this room is fit for you!"

Lady Betty took her book and followed me, meekly enough. As I closed the door, I heard Mary say to herself, in a tone of wonder:

"O dear! Then she don't mean to have the parson, after all!"

I set a chair for Betty in her favorite window, and took my place beside her with my embroidery. After a little Lady Betty said, timidly, "You are not vexed with me, are you, Margaret?"

"Yes, I am!" I answered. "'Twas not like a little lady to let Mary gossip to you about me and Mr. Penrose. My Lady, your mother, would be ill-pleased if she knew you had done such a thing. I shall not tell her, but you must never do so again. Come now, learn your lesson, and then we will go out into the chase."

Mr. Corbet joined us in the chase. I think he must have seen that something was the matter, but he made no allusion to it; on the contrary, he began telling Betty stories of his travels and the wonders he hath seen, and soon effectually diverted not only her but myself. He hath been to America two or three times, and hath seen the place whither so many colonists are now going. He says it is a fair land and fertile enough, but that the winters are long and severe, and the perils many, both from savages and wild beasts. Yet more and more people go thither every year, and he thinks that in time the settlement may be one of considerable importance.

"What sort of people go thither?" I asked him.

"Mostly people of substance and good character," he answered. "None of very high rank, that I have heard of, but many gentlemen have gone from this country, and more substantial yeomen and tradesmen; but all of the sort called Puritans. A good many of the descendants of the French Huguenots have also joined them, driven out by this new edict concerning their worship, and obliging them to conform. The Court is doing here what Mazarin hath done in France, namely, sending away the wealth and industry of the country to enrich foreign lands. However, in this case, it may turn to good in the end, for I believe the trade to North America will in time grow so great as to be valuable to the mother country."

"Think you that the Church of England will be benefited by these extreme measures?" I ventured to ask him.

"So far from it, that she hath need to pray that she may be delivered from the foes of her own household," said he. "But that I believe her to be founded on the rock of Divine Truth, I should despair of her cause, and think the dark ages were coming back again."

"Yet the Archbishop professes a great hatred of popery!" I said. "They say he hath refused a cardinal's hat more than once."

"The Archbishop thinks mayhap that he would

rather be King of Brentford than Lackey in London!" said Mr. Corbet, dryly. "What signifies lacking the name, if we have all the worst errors of the thing? I would as soon have an Italian Pope as an English one, and the Star Chamber seems like to rival the Inquisition in its cruelties. But we will talk no more of these grave matters now," he added, seeing Betty's eyes wide open. "I wonder if she ever heard the story of how Will Atkins and I saved the Indian woman's babe from the lion?"

Betty had never heard the tale, and "did seriously her ear incline," like Desdemona in the play. If she were older—but she is only a child, and it can do no harm. Only for her misfortune it would be a good marriage—but then Mr. Corbet is past thirty—nearer forty, I should say. He tells a story better than any one I ever heard, neither speaking too much of himself nor affecting a false modesty. He hath read and reflected much, as well as seen a great deal of the world; but Mrs. Judith says the Corbets are naturally scholars. The families have been so much mixed up with intermarriages and constant intercourse, that I should think it would be hard to tell which was Corbet and which was Stanton.

When the tale of the lion was ended ('tis not a true lion, either, Mr. Corbet says, but a much smaller, though very fierce beast), I told Betty it was time to go in, and Mr. Corbet took his leave.

I dined in the nursery, but went down to supper,

where I had to meet my Lord's jokes, as I expected, but he was in a good humor, and more inclined, I thought, to be merry at his sister's expense than at mine, reminding her of what she had said about Mr Penrose not being a marrying priest, and telling her that her turn would come next; whereat she was very angry, which only led him on to tease her the more. Then he turned to me, and swore I was a fool not to have the parson, adding that he would have put the parsonage in good order for me, but he would not touch it for Mr. Penrose. It was good enough for a bachelor.

"Perhaps Margaret may think better of it," said my Lady. "She is but young, and she is promised to me for a year at least. There is no time lost. She is not yet eighteen."

"Nay, that is not fair—to keep the poor fish on your hook so long, Margaret!" said my Lord. "Either land him or let him go."

"No fear of her landing him!" remarked Lady Jemima, with a sneer. "She is angling for higher game. She fishes for salmon, not for trout."

I felt my face grow scarlet, but I would not say a word. My Lord looked from one to another.

"What do you mean?" he asked, wonderingly.

"Mr. Corbet finds the chase wondrous attractive of mornings!" returned Lady Jemima, with another sneer. "He is very fond of poor Betty's society, now-a-days. 'Birds of a feather flock together,' they say!"

"So! I take your meaning," said my Lord. "Is that true, Mrs. Merton, that you are setting your cap at my cousin, and think Corby-End at present, and Stanton Court in reversion, mayhap, better than Stanton Parsonage? Is that Jem's meaning?"

"What Lady Jemima means she can perhaps explain herself;" said I, rising from the table. "Meantime I must beg your Ladyship's permission to retire, and henceforth to take my meals with Lady Betty in the nursery, or with Mrs. Judith. There at least I shall be safe from insult!"

My Lord stared a moment, and then burst out into one of his great laughs.

"Gad-a-mercy, what a firebrand it is!" said he, as soon as he could speak: "who could think gentle Mrs. Merton could look so like a queen of tragedy! Nay, nay, sit you down, my maid, and finish your supper, and nobody shall affront you. What, then! I must have my joke, you know, and, if Wat did make love to you under pretext of caring for the child, it would not be the first time such a thing has chanced. Many a long dull sermon have I sat out under my wife's uncle the Bishop, that I might have the pleasure of sitting next her, and reading from the same book. Come now, sit down again, and care you not for my jokes nor for sister Jem's sour grapes!"

"You are blind, brother, utterly blind!" said Lady Jemima, as I resumed my seat, feeling rather ashamed of my outburst.

"And you are spiteful, Jem!" retorted my Lord. "You need not grudge every other woman a sweetheart because you have none!"

It was now Lady Jemima's turn to leave the table, which she did, and the room too, slamming the door with some force behind her. My Lord laughed again, and fell to talking to my Lady of the days of their first acquaintance at King James' Court. After supper he challenged me to play backgammon with him, and so I did. He was very kind, and even courtly, as he knows how to be well enough; only at my going away, he detained me, and said, very seriously:

"One word, my maid. Do not you lose your heart to Mr. Corbet. He is the next heir to the Earldom, and like to be lord of all, should my Lady miscarry, which heaven forbid, and he must marry according to his rank. I believe not my sister's words have anything in them, but 'forewarned is forearmed,' you know. You are a good girl, I truly believe, and my Lady loves and trusts you, and if for no other reason, I would be loth to have any trouble arise."

"You need not fear me, my Lord," I answered. "I am but a poor governess, 'tis true, but I am a gentlewoman born and bred, as much so in my station as Lady Jemima in hers, and I do not think I am like to forget what is due to myself, even if I did not remember my duty to your Lordship's family."

"'Tis well said," answered my Lord, seeming no

way displeased by my frankness. "I like your spirit. As for Penrose, you shall not be teased about him. He is a good fellow, and I should be well pleased to see him fitted with as good a wife as yourself; besides that I can't but enjoy the joke of the thing; but 'tis early times yet, and he can afford to wait. Come, you bear me no malice, do you?"

I never liked my Lord so well, and was very willing to part good friends with him. As for Lady Jemima, I can hardly think of her with patience, much less forgive her. Yet I must, or what will become of me?

When I put Lady Betty to bed, she put her arms round my neck and whispered in my ear:

"Please don't be angry, Margaret, but you wont marry Mr. Penrose, will you?"

"I will marry the man in the moon, and go and live with him upon green cheese, if I hear another word about the matter," said I; "or I will run away in the first ship to America, paint my face all over red stripes, and wed the king of the Neponsets."

Betty laughed, and so did I, but my heart hath been heavy enough since. Here is Betty deprived of one of her greatest pleasures (and she has few enough, poor child), that of hearing her cousin's tales and playing with him, and all mine own ease and comfort spoiled, all because of Lady Jemima's spiteful words—for spiteful they were. Ah me! My day's work is like to be a hard one—too hard, I fear, for my strength.

CHAPTER VII.

August 10

THE Bishop hath really come, and I have seen him and heard him preach. He was to arrive yesterday, and for three or four days, Mrs. Judith has been as busy as a bee, making up extra beds, airing rooms, and superintending the cooking of all sorts of nice things. I had myself the honor of making some almond tarts after dear mother's own receipt, which turned out very well.

Well, the Bishop came at last, and with no such great retinue, either—only his necessary servants, his chaplain and secretary. Betty and I peeped out of the window and saw him alight. I think Betty was rather disappointed, for she said gravely: "I should never have taken him for a Bishop. He looks just like any other clergyman, for aught I see."

My Lady would have me go down to supper, which I had not expected or exactly wished to do, knowing that I should have to sit next Mr. Penrose. However, my Lady's least wish is law to me, so I dressed myself all in my best, and went down. Mr. Penrose, however, sat farther up the table than his old seat, and so I was put next the Bishop's chaplain, a very handsome, modest young man, who hardly opened his lips. His name I believe is Tailor, and the Bishop thinks him a person of much promise. The Bishop sat near the head of the table, at my Lady's right hand. I saw him looking down the table, and as he caught my eye he bowed to me and smiled, yet without speaking at that moment. Mr. Corbet, who sat near me, looked surprised. I have never said anything about my former acquaintance with my Lord to any one but my Lady and Lady Jemima, and I believe the latter thought I made more of the matter than there really was, for she too looked surprised, and then scornful. In a little pause of the conversation, the Bishop said to my Lady:

"I am glad to meet at your table, a young friend of mine, Mrs. Merton. Mistress Margaret Merton, I hope you are in good health," he added, turning to me.

I answered as well as I could, though feeling rather embarrassed at having the eyes of all the table turned upon me. He then asked after the health of my mother and brother, and said he would see me again. There is an indescribable charm in his voice and manner. He is wonderfully polished and courtly, yet with no appearance of insincerity, or an effort to please. Even Lady Jemima, who has a fixed prejudice against him, and who had come down looking as black and as stiff as one of the clipped yews in the garden, relaxed and became quite gracious under his influence.

Lady Betty had for some time been begging that she might go to chapel when the Bishop came, and my Lord being in high good humor to-day, I ventured to ask permission. He hesitated a little, but finally said:

"Yes, if she likes. I suppose she will have to show sometime. After all 'tis not her fault, poor little thing, and she may improve with time."

"She is much improved now," I said, feeling, God forgive me, a kind of disgust for him—a father ashamed of his own unfortunate daughter.

"Do you think she will ever be straight again?" he asked, eagerly. "I was surprised to see her sit up so well the other day."

"I do not think her back-bone can ever come straight again," I answered; "but she grows stronger every day, and the deformity will be less noticeable. I am not sure, but I think she is growing taller also, and your Lordship must allow that she has a beautiful face. She would be observed anywhere."

"That is true, too," he said. "I noticed it the other day. Well, well, do the best you can for her, Margaret, and let her have her way in this, since her heart is set upon it. It would be natural enough for her to take to religion, wouldn't it?"

I told him I thought it was natural enough for any one, especially any one in affliction.

"That's because you are a woman," he answered, tapping my cheek, as he does sometimes, but not in any offensive way. I will do my Lord the justice to say, that loud and careless, and hectoring as he often is, he is polite to the point of chivalry to every woman about the house or place, aye, and respectful, too. "Here, wait a moment."

He turned from me and began searching in his cabinet, and presently brought out a book splendidly bound in gold and blue velvet, though somewhat faded.

"Here, give this to Bess, with my love," said he. "It was her grandame's book, given her by the queen that then was, and I have always meant the child to have it. Tell her her father sends it, and bids her be as good as her grandame was."

I was more pleased than if he had given it to myself, for I knew that such a message and token of remembrance from her father, would make the poor child happy for a week. She worships her father with a devotion which I must say he neither understands nor deserves.

We looked the book over together, and were delighted to find on the fly-leaf, the bold, plain writing of the great queen herself. It seems Lady Stanton was her god-daughter.

Well, at the due time, or rather a little before it, Thomas carried my little lady down and set her in a comfortable corner, and I took my place beside her, as my Lady had told me.

"Why do you not take your usual seat, Mrs. Merton?" asked Lady Jemima, who was placing some flowers on the high altar, as she calls the communion table.

I told her that my Lady had desired me to sit by Lady Betty.

"You had better take your usual place," said she. "I will myself sit by Lady Betty, and see that she behaves properly."

I knew that this would never do in the world.

"With submission, Lady Jemima, I think it best to obey my Lady's orders," said I, as respectfully as I knew how. "She will not be pleased if I do not." And to avoid any further words, I took my place directly, and knelt down to say my prayer, so that she could not decently interrupt me. The company came in directly, and, with our own servants, made a good congregation. Lady Betty was as good and reverent as a child could be, only she did not kneel, which was not her fault.

The Bishop's chaplain read prayers without any of the extravagant gestures of devotion which Mr. Penrose is apt to use, but as my father used to do, and with a voice so full, so musical, and withal so devout and reverent, that it was a pleasure only to listen, and would have been had he read in a foreign tongue. The Bishop spoke a few words of exhortation on a text from the Psalms.

When prayers were over, I whispered Lady Betty to sit still till Thomas came for her. As I stood by her, partly screening her from observation, the Bishop drew near. He was talking with my Lady, and at first did not see me, but presently turned round, and smiled as his eye met mine.

"Will you not present me to your little daughter, madam?" he said to my Lady, who presented Lady Betty, and then me, in due form. He sat down by the child, and spoke kindly to her, asking her if she loved coming to church.

"I like it very much," answered Betty, who does not know what shyness means. "I never came before, and I asked mamma to let me to-night, because I wished to see you, and hear you."

His Lordship smiled, and said it was a pretty compliment. "But I think you would like to come every day, would you not?"

"Yes, when my back does not ache," said Betty; "but I wanted to hear you because Margaret told me about you, and how kind you had been to her and her mother. I love Margaret, and I love everybody that is kind to her."

"Why, that's well said, my daughter," returned the Bishop. "You do well to love Mistress Merton, who deserves your regard. I doubt not but she is a good governess, for she has been a dutiful daughter, and a kind sister, as I know."

These praises were very sweet to me, and all the more as Lady Jemima stood by and heard them. She looked very scornful, and presently asked the Bishop, rather pointedly, if he knew my kinswoman, Mistress Felicia Merton. He looked surprised, and said he believed he saw her in church with the family, but that was all.

"No doubt she was cleverly kept in the background," murmured Lady Jemima, not so low but I heard her, and so did the Bishop also, I am sure, from the way he glanced at her, as he said:

"My first meeting with Mrs. Merton and her brother was purely accidental and fortuitous. I came across them in the church, and having been uncivil enough to listen to their conversation, was so much interested in it as to desire to improve the acquaintance. I had afterwards some dealings with their mother in the way of business, and now I think of it, I saw a young gentlewoman, whom Mistress Merton presented to me as her husband's sister. If I mistake not, your mother told me she was not going to remain with her."

I told him no, she had gone to live with an aunt in London, Mrs. Willson by name.

"What!" said his Lordship; "not my old acquaintance Mrs. Willson, widow of the bookseller and stationer, living near St. Paul's churchyard?"

I told him my aunt's husband had been a bookseller, and that she had still an interest in the business, and lived I knew near St. Paul's; and added that she had been very generous, not only to Felicia, but to all the family.

"I know the good woman well," said the Bishop, "for good she is in every sense of the word. We must talk over our mutual friends, Mrs. Merton. I will see you again."

I can see that every one thinks it a great matter that I should receive so much notice from the Bishop. Mrs. Judith would know the whole story, and she will tell good Mistress Parnell, so I shall be illustrated.

Since I have been out of doors so much with Lady Betty, I have left off my morning walks, but this morning, I know not why, I felt as if one would do me good, so I took my hood, and went out into the chase. The morning was fine, and everything was pleasant, but I felt I know not what, of heaviness and discouragement.

"Sure 'tis very hard to have such an enemy as Lady Jemima, and that for no fault of mine own that I know of," I thought. It is Felicia's doing, to begin with, but she has no right to judge me on such slight evidence, nor to treat me as she does. Every time I try to set matters straight between us, I only make them worse. I have no one of whom I can ask advice either, now that Doctor Parnell is dead, and Mr. Penrose has raised up such a bar between us. If only I could see Mrs. Corbet alone, she might help me; but then she is one of the family, and it might only make trouble.

As I was thinking thus, walking with mine eyes on the ground, I almost ran against somebody coming in the opposite direction, and looking up, I saw the Bishop before me.

"Why, this is well," said he, with his kindly smile. "So you too love the early morning. But methinks your roses are not as blooming as when we met before. I trust all is well with you?"

I told him that I was quite well in health, and that my Lady was very kind to me, and I thought I had satisfied her so far.

"But," said he, smiling, and then seemed to be waiting for me to say more; then, as I did not, he continued himself:

"But you have found, I suppose, that things do not go on without rubs in courts and castles, more than in rectories and cottages?"

"I suppose there must be rubs everywhere," said I. "'Tis all in the day's work.'"

"Not of course," said my Lord. "We make a good many rubs for ourselves, which do not come into our day's work at all."

"I don't really know that I have made any of my rubs for myself," said I, considering a little, "unless it was about"—and then I stopped, and felt my face grow scarlet, for I was just going to speak of Mr. Penrose.

"Well," said the Bishop, as I paused—"except what? Except in tempting poor Mr. Penrose away from his vocation, as they say abroad among the Papists. Truly that was no great sin. They talk about arguments for and against the celibacy of the clergy," he added, more to himself than to me. "Truly, I have ever found the meeting and acquaintance of a comely maiden, better than any logic in that matter."

"How did you know?" I asked, in utter amazement, forgetting, I am afraid, the respect due to his Lordship.

Oh, a little bird told me. But now I must tell you all, or you will be fancying more than there is. Sit you down, if you have a little time. I should like to talk with you about that and other matters."

We sat down together on a rude seat which stood well sheltered by a thicket of holly, and he went on talking as he might have done to his own daughter.

"My Lord told me last night that Mr. Penrose was looking for a wife, and Lady Jemima said he had not looked very far, or very high, or some such phrase. Then Mr. Tailor asked my opinion about priests marrying." He paused, and I suppose I looked curious.

"And 'what then,' you are looking," he said, with a laugh which it did me good to hear, it was so clear and genial, yet with nothing coarse or rude about it. "Marry then, I told my young friend that if what was sauce for the goose was sauce for the gander, as our old saw hath it, I thought the dressing that did for the bishop might suit the curate well enough, and that I hoped to see each of them fitted with as good a wife as I had myself. Then—I am betraying no confidence in this matter, sweetheart, for I told Mr.

Penrose that I should speak to you about the matter—Mr. Penrose came to me in private, and told me that he had asked you to be his wife, but you had put him off for a year, on account of a promise you had made my Lady; but my Lady was willing to let you off your promise in such a case, and my Lord was also favorable, and he begged my good offices with you. There, you have the whole story."

"My Lord," said I, "Mr. Penrose is under some strange mistake. I never said or hinted that I would marry him at the end of the year, or at any other time."

"Understand me! He did not say positively that you did so promise," said his Lordship. "He only told me that you had put him off till that time before he should speak again. He told me that you had behaved most honorably with him, with a great deal to your praise, which I need not repeat, and then, with a great deal of humility, he did ask me, if I thought right, to speak with you on the matter. So now I have fullfilled my word in so speaking; and what do you say thereto?"

"Only what I have said before, my Lord," I answered, trying to speak calmly. "Mr. Penrose is a good young gentleman, and I know the match to be far above my deserts; but I can never marry him, if he waited ten years instead of one."

"But your mind may change in a year," said my Lord.

"I do not believe it will, and I do not want it to change," I answered. "I *know* I shall never want to marry him."

"But why?" asked the Bishop.

"Because," I answered, "I know how I feel now. I like Mr. Penrose very well as a friend and neighbor; but the minute I think of marrying him, I perfectly hate him, and feel as though I would walk to the Land's End to get out of hearing of his name."

"That would be going out of the river into the sea," said the Bishop, laughing again at my vehemence. "You would meet with plenty of Penroses between here and the Land's End. Ah, well! I see my poor chaplain's cake is dough, and though I like him well, I would not have it otherwise, so long as you feel so. I would not have you marry for interest, my maiden. Wedded life is a lovely and a holy thing where love is, but where it is not, there is confusion and every evil work. And then, you are but young to settle in life. I am sorry for Mr. Penrose, though. He is a good young man."

"Indeed he is!" I answered, warmly. "And that made me so sorry to have this come up, because I liked him so well; and now we can be naught but strangers. I wish he would fall in love with somebody else."

"'Tis not unlikely your wish may be gratified!" said my Lord, dryly; "but let him pass for the present. My Lady tells me that your little pupil has improved wonderfully under your hands, and that she is much pleased with your management."

"I am very glad," I answered. "My Lady does me more than justice. I do not think that Lady Betty has learned so very much, but her health has improved, and with it her spirits and temper. She is so bright, 'tis but a pleasure to teach her."

"And now for yourself," said the Bishop, with a penetrating, but kindly look. "How have you fared? Do you remember the promise I exacted from you that day in the church?"

I told him that I had never forgotten it, and that I believed I had kept it every day; and added that I had read half through the volume he gave me.

"That is well!" said he, seeming pleased. "And have you not found these things a help to you?"

"They have been a help," said I; "and also a comfort; but I know not how it is, I seem to gain no ground, or what I gain one day I lose the next. I have tried to be good, indeed I have!" I continued, feeling the tears very near my eyes, but determined, if I could, to keep them back; "but I do not succeed, and I sometimes fear that I shall never reach heaven at last. When I first came here, Lady Jemima was very kind to me; and gave me rules about devotions and fasting, and so on; but I cannot keep to them because my time is not my own, nor my strength either, and my Lady was not pleased when I gave up my hour of recreation to sew on Lady Jemima's work for the poor. Then I am conscious of so many failings every day that I am afraid "—I had to stop here and look very steadfastly through the tears.

"I understand," said the Bishop. "My dear maiden, do you not see wherein your trouble lies? You have undertaken something which is not in your day's work at all, and which therefore is too much for your strength. You are trying to purchase eternal life by your own works and deservings, whereas it has already been bought for you, and the whole price paid by another, so that to you it is offered as a free gift. The *gift* of God—observe, daughter, the *gift* of God is eternal life, through Jesus Christ our Lord."

I looked at him, but I could not speak—such a light seemed all at once to flash upon me. He went on. I cannot tell all he said; only he made it plain to me from many places of Scripture, that nothing we could do, could save ourselves. That God had appointed another way, easy and plain, namely, faith in His dear Son, whom He had sent to die for our sins and to rise for our justification. That He, by His one oblation of Himself, once offered, had made a full, sufficient, and perfect atonement and satisfaction for the sins of the whole world, and that I should make that atonement mine, and receive all its benefits, the moment I should come to Him in faith and humility, giving myself to Him, and asking God for His sake to receive me.

"But what becomes of good works?" I asked.

"They are of the utmost value!" he replied. "They show our sincerity to ourselves and to the world, for one thing; and they are a part of the work our Heavenly Father has given us to do; not as task-work to slaves, to be sharply exacted and grudgingly paid, but as work laid out for good and loving children, that they may both improve themselves thereby, and also help on His plans for the good of all. Tell me, sweetheart, which is best—to make garments for an old woman because she is in need and because she is one of God's creatures whom He loves, or because clothing the poor is one of the corporal works of mercy, and you are laying up just so much merit thereby?"

"The first, of course," I answered. "'Love makes easy service,' dear mother used to say. But, my Lord, you say that I have only to believe that this sacrifice was made for me—that I have but to believe and be saved."

"Well," he said, kindly.

"Then I may know that I am saved *now*—because I can certainly know that I believe now, as well as I can know anything."

"Well, why not?" he repeated. "Is not the knowledge pleasant—to feel that you are the beloved child of God, and an heir to everlasting life?"

"So pleasant," I replied, "that I see not what

becomes of Mr. Penrose's saying that it behoves us to walk softly and mournfully all our days, in the bitterness of our souls. It seems to me that there is no room for it."

"Ah, my dear maiden," said the Bishop, smiling somewhat sadly, "we shall have sorrow enough, never fear—quite as much as is good for us, without seeking or making any. I wonder if Mr. Penrose ever thought that with all the commands to rejoice, to be exceeding glad, to rejoice evermore, and so on, there is not one single direct command to mourn, in the New Testament. I would have you go on your way rejoicing. I would have you gather every flower which your Father plants in your path, and take delight in every innocent pleasure, because 'tis a gift from His hand. And even when trouble comes, as come it does to all, I would have you rejoice because you are in the hand of One who never afflicts willingly, and who is bound, by all His attributes, to bring you safely through."

Much more he said, but this is what I remember best—what I am sure I shall never forget as long as I live. I have felt all day as though a great burden which I had been trying to carry, but which was beyond my strength, had been suddenly lifted off, and I had been told to go on my way without it.

When I came in, my Lady asked me if I had heard any good news, that my face was so bright.

The Bishop preached for us in the chapel this

evening. There was a great congregation—all the Fultons, and many other neighboring gentry, besides Mrs. Corbet and her son, all of whom were entertained at supper afterward. Lady Betty sat in her corner, only somewhat more out of sight than before, and I by her. The Bishop's text was out of the third of St. John's Gospel—"Whoso believeth on Him shall not perish, but have everlasting life." I shall never forget it while I live—so clear and plain was it, so full of beauty, and delivered with such eloquence, yet so expressed as that the youngest and simplest person present could take in somewhat of the doctrine.

I saw many looks exchanged, mostly of approval, though Lady Jemima was evidently ill-pleased, and I thought Mr. Penrose somewhat dubious. As for my Lord, he slept through most of it, as he does at all sermons.

I did not go to the supper table, but Lady Betty and I supped sumptuously in Mrs. Judith's room afterward—a great delight to the child, to whom every change is a treat. Mrs. Corbet came in to speak to her, and spent an hour with us talking about the sermon, which, she said, had made her young again. Mr. Corbet was here, but I did not see him, save for a moment, as he came to speak to me in the chapel. Poor Mr. Penrose looks very pale and downcast, but did give me a very kindly greeting, and a message from Mistress Parnell, whom he has begged to remain in the rectory and keep his house for him.

"I thought you would have one of your sisters," said I, when he told me this bit of news.

"Perhaps I shall, by-and-by," he answered; "but they find enough to do at home, and it seems a pity Mistress Parnell should leave the roof which hath sheltered her so long. So I have even begged her to stay, and she hath consented to do so, instead of going to her niece at Bristol. Will you not come and see her sometimes?"

Then, as I hesitated, he added, "Believe me, Margaret, I will annoy you with no more importunities. I see that there is no use in it, and I will spare myself the humiliation and you the pain, of asking what can never be given."

He spoke with much kindness, but with dignity, and without a tinge of pique or offence; and then added, smiling somewhat sadly, "You know you are to be Aunt Margaret by-and-by, so you had best begin on Mistress Parnell."

"Oh, I shall come," said I. I never was so near liking him as at that last minute. If it were not —but there it is. Nobody knows or guesses—there is one comfort. O yes! there are a great many comforts. What a long story I have made of the matter!

August 15.

The good Bishop has gone, but I might say that his spirit abides with us still, everything seems to go on so pleasantly and peacefully. My Lord has been away for a few days, but is to return to-morrow. My Lady keeps her room a good deal, looking over papers, &c., and has spent more than her usual time in the nursery, to the delight of both Betty and myself. This morning she brought me a letter from Aunt Willson, which came in one to herself. She showed me the last. It is short, and to the purpose, saying much that is kind of me and mine, and thanking her Ladyship for her goodness to me. Her note to me was the same, only adding, at the end, that she hoped I should have no more trouble made by the schemes of one that should be nameless.

Only Lady Jemima will not be pacified toward me. She stopped me in the garden the other day, and told me she had had a letter from Felicia, who sent me her forgiveness for the ill offices I had been trying to do her, but which had failed; as she hoped, for my own sake, all my plans of that sort might do.

"So do I," said I. "If I ever make any plans for mischief, I trust they will fail. As yet I have made none, nor done any one ill offices. Whether any one has done them for me, is quite another matter."

"Beware!" said she, solemnly. "You are so set up with pride, because of the Bishop's ill-judged notice of you, and because my Lady takes your part, that you can see no danger; but beware! There is One that sees and judges."

"I rejoice to think there is, and to Him I commit myself and my cause." And with that I left her. It is strange how prejudiced she hath become.

Mr. Corbet rarely joins Betty in her walks and rides now, and the poor child is very much grieved, and thinks cousin Walter has grown strangely remiss. I fancy some one—my Lady, perhaps—has spoken to him. It is just as well. I only wish he had not begun it. And yet—I don't know that I do, either.

August 17.

I said the last time I wrote that things were going on pleasantly; but since then we have had a grand explosion, the effects of which are felt even yet. It came about in this wise.

My Lord came home the day before yesterday, bringing with him a guest—Lord Saville, a court gallant, and I know not what relative of my Lady's. Never was anything so fine as this gallant, with his satin trunks and hose, his shoes with roses of gold lace and brilliants, his jewelled hatband, and I know not what else of bravery in the gayest colors—nay, I verily believe he painted his face, at least his eyebrows. For my part I cannot think so much finery becoming a man. Mr. Corbet, in his plain dark cloth and trimmed hair, looks ten times the gentleman that this lovelocked and perfumed court popinjay does.

Well, he was at the supper-table, of course, and Mr. Corbet and Mr. Penrose also. One of Sir Thomas Fulton's daughters is here visiting Lady

Jemima, and she was the only lady guest. It fell out that my Lord began speaking of Mr. Prynne, and of Lilburne, and now for the first time I heard of the barbarous sentence—the branding and cropping of the former gentleman—for a gentleman he is, and of as good blood as my Lord himself. My Lord swore with many oaths, as his way is, that the canting beggar was rightly served, and he would like to see them all served with the same sauce.

"It would be a great dish that should hold them," said Mr. Corbet, dryly; "and would need to be made very strong."

"You are right, sir," said Lord Saville. "The faction increases wonderfully, in spite of the Archbishop, who is a jolly Churchman. They say that Mr. Prynne received wonderful tokens of kindness and sympathy on his way to prison, and that money was showered on his wife, but she would not take it. Marry, that is the wonderful part of the tale."

They should all be served alike, my Lord swore, and said he would like to hear one of his household or dependents say a word in favor of the sour, vinegar-faced hypocrite or his abettors. My Lady looked at me, and I read in her glance what would have kept me quiet but for Lady Jemima's interference. She saw my disturbed countenance, as she sees everything, and said, in her most sarcastic tone:

"Mrs. Merton, you need not look so distressed.

I dare say my brother will make an exception in your favor, if you are desirous of pleading the cause of your kinsman."

How she knew Mr. Prynne was my kinsman I cannot guess, unless Felicia told her.

All eyes were turned on me at once.

"What!" exclaimed my Lord. "That canting scoundrel Margaret's kinsman! I do not believe it! Speak up, Margaret, and deny it; or say, at the least, that you do not take the part of such an execrable villain. Say that he hath had his deserts, or at least some small part of them, and I shall be content. Speak out!" he cried, seeing that I hesitated, and smiting the table with his fist till the dishes rang.

"Since I must needs speak, then, my Lord," said I, "Mr. Prynne *is* my kinsman, and hath often been at our house in my father's life-time; and then I am sure he was an honest gentleman, though somewhat sour and austere. What he has now done, I know not, save that he hath printed a book inveighing against stage plays; but sure it must have been a greater crime than that to merit so barbarous a sentence."

"Barbarous! Do you say barbarous?" exclaimed my Lord, in tones that trembled with passion, while Lord Saville looked on with an expression of contemptuous amusement.

"I did say so, my Lord," I answered, for my own spirit was up by this time. "Branding and cropping do seem to me barbarous punishments, and unworthy a Christian age: and I cannot understand how a Christian prelate could sit by when such sentence was given, and not protest against it."

"He was so far from protesting, that he was the very head and front of the matter," said Mr. Corbet.

"And am I to hear this?" said my Lord, fairly glaring at me. "Elizabeth, do you hear this—this chit brave me at mine own board?"

"Margaret said nothing till she was pressed," answered my Lady, more loftily than her wont.

"And you dare to take the part of this fellow!" said my Lord to me.

"How can you be surprised, brother?" asked Lady Jemima, scornfully. "'Birds of a feather flock together,' you know."

"But you don't mean it, Margaret," said my Lord: "you do not mean to take the part of this crop-eared scoundrel and own him for your kinsman? You don't mean to say"—

"I did not mean to say anything, my Lord, and should not, unless it had been forced upon me," said I, as he paused for breath, and seemed to expect some answer; "but what I have said, I cannot unsay. Mr. Prynne *is* my kinsman, and he has been kind to my mother since my father's death. What ill he may have done I cannot say, but if it is no more than writing a book against plays and play-houses, I must say that the sentence seems to me a very severe and barbarous one, and most unworthy of a Christian prelate." I said this, I am conscious, with some emphasis and heat, for it seemed to me that I was being very unfairly treated both by my Lord and Lady Jemima, and it did not make me any cooler to see that Lord Saville was amusing himself with the whole affair. But here I received support, though I can hardly say assistance, from a very unexpected quarter.

"I am with you, Mistress Merton, said Mr. Penrose (who had hitherto been quite silent), in his clear, precise voice. "I have always hitherto loved and revered the Archbishop, but I cannot approve his course in this matter. It seems to me far worse than the homicide for which Archbishop Abbot was deprived. I have seen Mr. Prynne's book. I have also seen two or three plays, when I was last in London:" (and withal he blushed like a girl,) "and though I like not at all Mr. Prynne's spirit, and believe him to be guilty of dangerous errors in doctrine, I think what he says of the practises of plays and players too well deserved. I am ashamed when I remember the play which I saw played before the king."

"And what was that play, Mr. Chaplain, an it like you?" asked my Lord Saville.

"It was called, if I mistake not, 'The Gamester,'" answered Mr. Penrose.

"I would have you to know, sir, that the plot of that play was furnished to Mr. Shirley the poet by his Majesty's own hands," said Lord Saville, arrogantly, and as if to bear down all before him: "I myself heard the king say it was the best play he had seen in seven years."

"So much the worse," said Mr. Penrose, shortly. "I could not have believed it of his Majesty."

With that my Lord exploded in a new fury. He put no bounds to his language, but called Mr. Penrose all the opprobrious epithets he could muster, and reproached him with the benefits which had been bestowed upon him in language which I am sure he would not have dared to bestow upon an equal. It was enough to make one ashamed of ever having been in a passion, to see what a pitiful spectacle this man made of himself. Mr. Penrose sat quite still till my Lord paused, from sheer inability to say another word. Then he said, rising from the table, as he spoke:

"My Lord, it has been your pleasure to insult at your own table, and before your servants, a gentleman whose birth is as good as your own, and whose family was known and distinguished, when yours was still in obscurity. My profession, if nothing else, forbids me to demand of you the satisfaction which one gentleman owes to another in such a case. I am your debtor, 'tis true, but I am also a gentleman, and a clergyman of the Church of England, and as such entitled to speak my mind. I return upon your hands the benefits with which you reproach me, and which you have rendered more bitter than gall, by your insults. I will be no man's lackey, though I be forced to drudge for my daily bread like any plowman. I here resign both the chaplaincy and the benefice which you have given me, thanking you for any courtesy you have shown me hitherto." And with that he rose from the table, bowed to my Lady and the rest, and took his hat to leave the room.

"I will walk with you, Mr. Penrose," said Mr. Corbet, also rising. "Give you good-night, fair ladies." And they left the hall.

I could not have believed it was in the little man to look and speak as he did, with so much calmness and dignity. Even the allusion to his own family (which, he being a Cornishman, is, of course, a good deal older than Adam), sat gracefully enough upon him. My Lord was actually silenced, and had the grace to look ashamed. My Lady prevented any more words by rising from the table, and of course all of us did the same. As we passed out of the hall, I heard Lady Jemima say to my Lady:

"Well, Sister Elizabeth, what think you of the storm your immaculate Mrs. Merton has raised? Is she not a fit person to have charge of your daughter's education?"

She spoke in the tone of sarcastic contempt, which she always uses to or about me. My Lady answered more sharply than I ever heard her speak:

"It was yourself, Jemima, who raised the storm, as most storms in this house are raised, by your impertinent meddling. Margaret would not have spoken but for your drawing my Lord's attention upon her."

"Oh, of course, it was all my fault," Lady Jemima began, but my Lady interrupted her:

"It *was* all your fault! You are constantly tormenting the child for no other reason than because she dares to have a mind of her own. But I have had enough of it; and have long borne with your impertinent interference in household affairs, your contradicting of my orders, upsetting my arrangements, and taking the words out of my mouth at mine own table: but I will have it no longer. The next time you make such a piece of mischief you leave the house, or I do!"

"Well, I must say!"—Lady Jemima began, but my Lady cut her short:

"I will hear no more!" said she, sharply. "I am wearied and fretted to death now. Margaret, why do you not go to the nursery?"

I might have said that I was only waiting for her to give me room to pass; but I saw well that my Lady was driven past her patience, and no wonder: so I courtesied and made my escape by the way of Mrs. Judith's room.

I did not know what to do, for my Lord had bid me quit the house the next day, and I had nowhere to go. I had money enough owing me to take me home, but I knew not how to get there, and I had no friend to whom I could apply, unless it were the Bishop. I could hardly calm myself

to think of anything for a time; but at last, by
dint of walking in the gallery, which I did for an
hour, and by schooling myself to do my usual
reading, I found myself in a condition to consider
matters quietly. I never felt any more unhappy
in my life, and regretted twenty times that I had
not stayed in the nursery with my child; but there
was no use in that. Besides the disgrace which
had been put upon me, and the triumph which
that disgrace would afford to mine enemies, my
heart was broken at the thought that I must leave
my child to a stranger, just at the time when she
was like to need me most, and have all my work
for her undone. Lady Jemima is mine enemy,
though I know she would not own herself so. She
persecutes me, as my Lady says, because I think
for myself instead of following her. As for my
Lord, I care not so much for him.

Well, I could do nothing that night—so much
was plain—and the next day might bring cooler
councils. So I looked in upon my child, as I
usually do the last thing, and then said my prayers.
I know not whether I did entirely forgive Lady
Jemima, but I know I tried faithfully to do so. I
confess I cried myself to sleep, but I did go to
sleep at last, and slept well, with sweet dreams of
walking in pleasant green fields, in good company.
Methought that a deep river seemed to divide us
for a time, which I could not cross because of the
child who was with me; but at last, I know not
how, my Lady brought us together again, and

then, taking Betty by her hand, she smiled lovingly upon us and seemed to float away. I awoke not a little comforted, though 'twas but a dream.

I thought I would do nothing good or bad till I saw my Lady, so I dressed Lady Betty, as usual, (though she has learned to help herself a great deal,) heard her say her prayers, and gave her her breakfast. I then went to my room for my work-basket, where I met my Lady. She looked pale and tired, but greeted me kindly, as usual, and asked me some questions about Betty's lessons. I answered her, and added that I had thought it best to go on as usual till I saw her and received her commands.

"You have said nothing to Betty, I hope?" said my Lady. I told her I had not.

"That is well!" said she. "Margaret, have you the patience to let matters stand as they are for a few days, and do nothing?"

"Surely, my Lady, if you desire it," I answered. "I would do more than that for you."

"I know I ask a good deal," she continued. "I know the position is a painful one, but I hope things may be mended."

"My Lady," said I, thinking it was time for me to speak, "I can bear all things for your sake and for Lady Betty's. I have been turning the matter over in my own mind—I mean what chanced last night—and truly I see not what I could have done differently from that I did. Mr. Prynne is my kinsman, and, as I said, he has been kind to us;

and had my dear father taken his advice, it would
have fared the better with us at this time. I
would not have spoken unless I had been called
upon, but being so called upon, it does seem to
me that I should have been base and ungrateful
not to speak up for my cousin."

My Lady sighed. "I know, Margaret. I do not
blame you. I know my Lord was somewhat hot
and hasty, and he was provoked with Mr. Penrose
for his uncalled-for words."

Somewhat hot and hasty, indeed! But he is
her husband, and, as I once heard dear father say,
a woman must be somewhat more than an angel
to be just where her husband is concerned.

"But rest you quiet, sweetheart!" continued my
Lady. "Let the storm go by! At the worst, I
will see that you are taken good care of, but I
trust not to lose you. It will be my great comfort,
under my approaching trial, to know that Betty is
in such good hands."

After such words from my Lady, I could not
doubt what my duty was. So I said I would go
on just as usual, only praying her leave to absent
myself from table, which she granted, saying that
Betty and I might dine either by ourselves or with
Mrs. Judith. I knew Betty would choose the
latter, and said so; whereat she bade me inform
Mrs. Judith of the arrangement. I went to her
room for the purpose, and found her busy blanch-
ing and shredding almonds, stoning dates and
raisins, and so forth, for the dinner. She would

not let me stay to help her, however, as I would have done, but saying that I looked pale, and the fresh air would do me good, she filled my pocket with spiced comfits and sent me away to walk.

The day has passed quietly enough. I have been careful to keep out of my Lord's way, and also to keep Lady Betty out of his sight, for 'tis the way of grand and magnanimous natures like his to revenge their humors on little and weak creatures. Marry, they now and then find themselves mistaken, as my Lord did with Mr. Penrose last night. How grand and dignified the little man was! My Lord has gotten himself into a scrape there, and I am wicked enough to be glad of it. It seems that the presentation to the living belongs to both houses in such wise that my Lord has it one time and Mr. Corbet the next; so by Mr. Penrose's resignation last night the next presentation is Mr. Corbet's. I do hope he will reinstate Mr. Penrose, and I think he will, for he was clearly pleased last night.

August 20.

Things still go on quietly enough in the family. My Lord has said nothing to me, good or bad, but I fancy he hath made some sort of apology to Mr. Penrose, from something I saw passing between them in the garden this morning, and from the fact that Mr. Penrose read prayers in the chapel this evening. He made a short but earnest lecture on the text, "The temple of God is holy, which

temple ye are;" and spoke most forcibly and
beautifully on the point of purity, not only of life
but of mind, carrying out the figure, and likening
the man who entertained unclean and impure
thoughts in his mind, to one who should feast
boon companions in the sanctuary of the church,
and make the sacred vessels themselves the in-
struments of his debauchery.

Methought my Lord looked a little uneasy, but
Lord Saville kept his usual sneering composure.
The latter gallant favored me with a low reverence—I suppose in the usual Court mode; but I
would not so much as let him know that I saw
him. His very look is an insult. I made my
reverence to Lady Jemima, in passing, but did not
speak to her, nor she to me. I have tried hard to
forgive her, and I hope I have done so, in some
measure, for I would not, as Mr. Penrose would
say, bring sword and dagger into God's sanctuary.

I thought of the sermon all the evening. Surely
if a very awful, 'tis also a marvellous comforting
thought—that abiding of the Spirit in our hearts!

Mistress Parnell walked up with Mr. Penrose,
and was loud in his praises afterwards, when we
were at supper together in Mrs. Judith's room;
saying, with tears, that he was like a son or
younger brother to her, constantly seeking what
he may do to please her, and studying her comfort
in every way.

"Ah, Margaret, Margaret!" said the old lady,

"I doubt you are throwing away what can never be gotten back again."

"I don't know but I am; but there is no help for it. If I had never seen anybody else—but that *if* is as wide as the ocean. There is no ship to cross it.

Betty, dear child, is as good and loving as a child can be. She has taken double pains with her learning of late, and makes wonderful progress. This day, after sitting long and silent over her sewing—she is making an apron for Goody Yeo—she said to me:

"Margaret, you know Latin, don't you?"

I told her I did know some Latin, and one day I would read her some pretty tales out of Virgil, his Enead.

"Will you teach me Latin?" she asked, wistfully.

"That must be as my Lady says," I answered; "but, my love, why do you wish to learn Latin?"

"Because," said she, "My little brother will have to learn it some day, I suppose, and if I know it, I can teach it to him."

"Suppose your little brother should turn out a little sister?" said I, smiling.

"Oh, but I hope he will not!" she answered; "you know papa likes boys best!"

Betty rarely shows a spark of her old heat or perverseness, and if she does, it makes her very unhappy, and she will not rest until she has asked and received forgiveness. I sometimes think her character is ripening too fast, and that such deep feelings in a child forebode an early death; and yet, why should I say fear? 'Twould be a blessed thing for her. Her life is not like to be a happy one.

August 21.

Another explosion, and by my means, though not by my fault. I only wish all the consequences had fallen on myself. I should find it easier to forgive the author than I do now.

It chanced on this wise. I have kept Betty out of the way as much as possible, but the morning was so fine that I could not resist her entreaties for a ride, and we went as far as the Abbey ruin, which Betty has always wished to see, and which, from its stillness and loneliness, hath been a favorite haunt of mine own. I had no thought of meeting any one, for none of the family ever came thither; so we let the donkey graze at his will while we wandered about and spelled out the inscriptions on the stones, I translating the Latin for Lady Betty's benefit. There was no danger of Jack's straying far, for he loves Betty with all the force of his donkeyish nature, and will come prancing and flinging in most ludicrous sort to meet her, whenever she comes near.

Well, as I said, we were spelling out the inscriptions, and Betty was much interested in the tomb of Abbot Ignatius, when we heard my Lord's voice, and presently he and Lord Saville came from behind the wall of the ruined refectory. Now,

Betty loves her father's very shadow, and before I could hinder her, she had run to meet him, with a cry of delight.

"Hallo!" exclaimed my Lord Saville. "What little mundrake have we here? Are your grounds haunted with dwarfs and pixies, my Lord?"

My Lord's brow turned black as thunder.

"This is my daughter, my Lord!" said he, in a lofty tone: but Lord Saville was by no means overawed.

"I crave your pardon!" said he, carelessly: "I knew you had a daughter, but I thought her to have died long since;" and with that he turned away.

"What are you doing here, Bess?" asked my Lord, harshly.

"I—I—only came—I don't know!" answered Betty, flushing and stammering, as she is apt to do when startled.

"Mrs. Merton, since you pretend to have the government of the child, methinks you might at least keep her out of sight!" said my Lord, turning the vials of his wrath on me. "'Tis surely misfortune enough to be the father of such a changeling, without having her paraded to shame me at every turn! I think the devil himself served her alive, to vex me. I would she had died at her birth, like her brothers yonder," he added, muttering between his teeth.

I don't suppose he meant she should hear him, but she did. She drew herself up as I should not have supposed possible, and looking her father in the face with her flashing black eyes, she said:

"God made me, my Lord!" Then turning to me, she said, with as much dignity as ever I saw, "Margaret, we will go home!"

Felicia used to say sometimes that if I could command the lightning her life would not be safe. I am sure my Lord's would not have been at that moment. I am ashamed to write it, but I do think I could have killed him. I could not trust myself to speak to him. To make the matter worse, Betty's little dog ran between his legs and nearly upset him. With a curse he kicked the poor beast violently out of his way, and against a stone, where he lay stunned for a moment. This was too much, and Betty burst into passionate tears and lamentations. "Oh, my dear dog! Oh, what shall I do!"

"Hush, hush!" said I. "The dog is not dead! See, he moves now!" I set her on her donkey, and put into her arms poor Gill, who was beginning to make a feeble whining, and so we went away, leaving my Lord looking foolish enough. I thought all day the poor beast would die, but he is better to-night. Betty never said one word all the way home, and she has moped all day. I have not told my Lady, and shall not. My Lord met me in the hall to-night, and said something about a game of backgammon, but I would not understand, and passed him with only a reverence. Maybe I am wrong, but I dared not trust myself with him. Since we are to order ourselves reverently to our betters, 'tis to be wished that our betters were a little better!

August 23.

The poor little dog is dead! We nursed it up as well as we could, and I hoped it would get well, but it died last night, after two or three hours of great suffering. It was pitiful to see the poor little wretch, how in its greatest agonies it would look up in answer to Betty's voice, and make a feeble effort to wag its tail. The poor child was broken-hearted, and no wonder. I thought to have a sad time with her; and so indeed I did, but not as I expected. There was no screaming, none of the violence she has shown heretofore, but deep, distressful sobbing, which seemed to shake her poor thin frame all to pieces. It was not only the loss of the dog, her only playfellow, though that was enough; but that "papa" should have done it. I had at last to come to my final argument, which I keep in reserve when all else fails to quiet her.

"My love, you will make yourself sick!" I said: "and that will distress my Lady, and perhaps make her sick as well."

"I *am* sick!" said the poor thing, sobbing; "I am sick of *being* at all. Everything is so hard for me. I wish I had never been made! Oh, Margaret, why do you suppose that I was made?"

"To be happy in heaven forever!" I said. "That is what we were all made for."

"Then I wish I had gone there when I was born!" said she. "I think it is a very hard road to get there!"

"It is a hard road to many beside you, my dear one," I answered. "Think how hard it was made to the poor men Mr. Corbet told us of, who were shut up for years and years in the dungeons of the Inquisition, only to be burned at last, because they would not deny the truth."

"But why should it be so?" asked Betty.

"That I cannot tell you," I answered. But, Betty, don't think all the time of the hardness of the road. Think of what is at the end thereof, and how you may help those who are going the same way; and perhaps turn some back who are travelling in the opposite direction. If you live and grow up, you will have a great many chances of doing good, both to men's souls and their bodies. There are your little god-daughters down at the Cove, and the children in the school, and as you grow older, more people still."

She seemed a little comforted, and to divert her still farther, I told her of Goody Yeo's granddaughter, who needed a petticoat, which she might make for her. At last she ceased crying, and allowed me to loosen her dress and lay her down to rest. I thought she was asleep, when she roused herself and asked me:

"Margaret, what sort of a man was your father?"

I told her he was a good man, and much beloved by all who knew him.

"If you had had a little dog he would not have killed it," said she. "If you had been crooked and sickly, he would not have wished you were dead!"

"My love," said I, "you think too hardly of your father. He did not mean to kill the dog."

"He did not mean to break my heart, either," said this strange child; "and yet he has done both, and they can't be cured because he did not mean to do it. It was not the saying so—it was the thinking so."

"I don't think he meant it, either," I answered. "People often say a great deal more than they mean. The other day, when Mary broke your china image by accident, you told her that she was an awkward clod, and you wished she was a thousand miles off; yet I am sure you would be very sorry to have her go even ten miles away, would you not?"

She was silent at this, and seemed to be turning the matter over in her mind. When Mary came in, shortly after, Betty roused up and called her.

"Mary," said she, "I am very sorry that I was so cross with you about breaking the china image. I said I wished you a thousand miles away, and it was not true. I would not have you go away for anything, and I will never say such wicked things again."

"Bless your dear, tender heart!" said Mary,

kissing the hand Betty held out to her. "I thought nothing of it, my lambkin. I knew you were only angry, and we all say more than we mean at such times."

"I will try never to be angry again," said Betty. "Margaret, will you ask Thomas to bury my poor dog near to our seat in the wood, and to mark the place? I should like to have Thomas do it, because he was always fond of poor Gill."

I promised that it should be done as she desired, and leaving her with Mary, with a charge not to talk, but to lie still and try to sleep, I carried the poor little beast down to the stable, and asked Thomas to bury him. As he was smoothing the turf over the little grave, my Lord came along.

"Hullo, what are you doing here?" he asked.

"Burying my little lady's dog," answered Thomas, shortly. He hath been here since the time of my Lord's father, and is apt to say his say to every one about the place, my Lord included.

"Why, what ailed the dog?" asked my Lord.

"You ought to know, if anybody did, I should say," was the surly answer. "The poor whelp had half his ribs broken. More shame for them as used a dumb beast so—or a Christian either," he muttered to himself. "There, Mistress Morton, that is done as well as if old Sexton himself had had the job; and I'll beg Dick Gardener for some of his double *vilets*, to plant over him." So saying, he shouldered his spade and stalked off.

To do my Lord justice, he did look heartily ashamed and sorry.

"Well, well," said he. "I never meant to hurt the dog, I am sure. I suppose Bess is screaming herself into fits about it."

I told him Lady Betty was very unhappy, but that she had not screamed at all, only cried bitterly.

"Well, well, I am sorry," he said again. "Give my love to Bess, and tell her I did not mean to kill him. I will get her another, if I have to search the country for it."

I was glad to hear him say so, and gave his message to Betty, though I did not say he meant to get her another dog. I knew she would not take kindly to the notion just yet, and, besides, it might be only another disappointment. She was very much comforted, and is beginning to be quite cheerful again, though I hear a deep sigh now and then.

And here I must say that I am conscious of never having done justice to my dear father so long as he lived. He had his faults, no doubt, the chief of which were an over-sanguine disposition, which made every new scheme look absolutely desirable and feasible, and a too lavish use of money while he had it; but never was a pleasanter man to live with. He was always so genial and kindly: so sunny and cheerful, not by fits and starts, but steadily, and at all times. If mother were disappointed in her calculations—if some favorite dish were spoiled, or some book or paper mislaid, he was always the one to laugh it off and make everything pleasant again.

Dear mother had her sorrows and cares, 'tis true; but I think she was a happy woman, after all. Father was such a help to her, and he was such a *safe* man to live with. It was like walking on the firm, solid ground, instead of upon treacherous ice, or over a mine; like sailing on the open sea instead of among rocks and quicksands, where one must be all the time on the lookout, and after all some sudden gust or unsuspected current may make all one's caution of no avail. I fancy it is this constant observing of her husband's humors which has made my Lady so silent and self-restrained in company, even at her own table, and which makes many people think her stiff and cold. She is like another person here in the nursery, or with Mrs. Corbet.

And yet my Lord hath many excellent qualities. He is generous to a fault, and I am sure he would spare neither time nor gold to procure for my Lady anything he thought she would like. He is brave too, and would venture his life without a thought, if even the poorest fisher lad were in danger; as he did, they tell me, in the storm last winter. I am the last one to judge him hardly, for I know my own failings in that line, and how often I have said or done in a minute of provocation what I would have given a great deal to undo again. I am sure my Lord is not malicious. He would never lay such a trap for any one as Lady Jemima did for me the other day, nor would he persevere in a course of tormenting, day after day, or take advantage of a time when one was feeling unhappy or annoyed about something else, to say the most aggravating thing he could think of. But there! I said I would never think of Felicia if I could help it.

CHAPTER VIII.

September 3.

SOMETHING has happened since I wrote last, which, though it makes no seeming change in my outward circumstances, has changed my whole life, so that I seem to myself to be living in another world. Mr. Corbet hath asked me to be his wife.

It chanced on this wise. I had been down to see Goody Yeo and carry her the petticoat Betty had been making for her grandchild. Betty was to have gone herself, but the day was damp, and I thought it not safe for her to go out. I would have kept the petticoat till next day, but Betty would not hear of that, so I wrapped myself in my cloak and went down to the village. It cleared up before my return, and I thought I would come back by the ravine, which is ever a favorite walk of mine, from its lonely stillness. The servants rarely use the path, from I know not what superstition of a ghost which haunts it. There is a ghost, or a dobby, or a pixy, or some such creature in every corner of the place, it seems to me.

Well, as I was lingering a little by the spring, and looking into its clear depths, where the water boils up from a large and seemingly deep cleft in the rocks, I was startled by a voice, and looking up, I beheld Lord Saville. I have hated the man since the first time I ever saw him. His very look is an insult: especially when he tries to look fascinating and amiable.

"So the fair Margaret is admiring her own beauty in the mirror of the spring!" said he. "Are you not afraid of exciting the jealousy of the naiad of the fountain? Nay, be not in such haste"—for I would have passed him, with only a greeting, but he stepped into the narrow path and would not let me go by. "Surely you will not be so cruel as not to vouchsafe one word to your most humble admirer!"

"I understand no court compliments, my Lord!" said I, trying to speak coldly and calmly, though I was in a fever of indignation. "I am but a simple country maid. I pray you to let me pass!"

He would not, however, but went on in the same strain of fulsome flattery, and said things which I will not write here. Seeing that I could not pass him, I turned to go back to the village; but a single stride brought him to my side.

"Not so fast, fair lady!" said he. "You are the rightful captive of my bow and spear, and do not escape so easily. What! It was another cavalier you were waiting for!"

"I was waiting for nobody!" said I. "I was on

my way home about my own business and my Lady's."

He laughed in his impudent, jeering fashion, and saying something about pretty Puritan airs and graces, attempted to put his arm round my waist. Then all the old Merton temper flashed up in me in an instant, and I am ashamed to say, I turned upon him and slapped his face so soundly as to leave the prints of my fingers on his pink cheeks. Nay, I verily believe I made his nose bleed. I am sure my own palm smarted for an hour after. He withdrew his arm with an oath, which sounded much more genuine than his compliments, and clapped his hand to his face. I burst from him, and running down the path, half blind with shame and anger, I ran right into Mr. Corbet's arms, who was coming up the coomb, followed by his dogs.

"Margaret!" he exclaimed, in amazement, and well he might, for my dress was disordered, and I dare say I looked like a fury. "What is the matter? What has so discomposed you?"

For the moment I saw him I felt myself safe, and, like a fool, I burst into tears, and cried as Betty herself might have done. In the midst of my distress, and while he was trying to soothe me, and get some sense out of me, Lord Saville made his appearance.

"So!" said he, "Oriana hath found her Amadis, it seems. Doubtless the fair dame knew her knight was in hearing when she resisted with such ferocious virtue. 'Tis an old trick, but it may do for the west country."

"My Lord!" said Walter—I may call him so here—"if you say another word or offer another affront to this lady, I will put you over the cliff yonder, and give you a worse wetting than old Norman Leslie did in Paris, when he laid your face downward in the gutter for sneering at his Scotch accent."

Lord Saville grew pale with rage. "You shall answer this!" said he. "You shall give me the satisfaction of a gentleman!"

"The satisfaction of a gentleman is due to gentlemen!" answered Walter. "Nay, never grind your teeth at me, I know you well!" and with that he said some words in Italian, at which Lord Saville blenched as if he had been struck.

"Allow me to see you home, Mistress Merton!" said Walter, and putting the courtier aside, as if he had been an intrusive dog, he passed him and led me toward home.

"Sit down a moment," said he, kindly, seeing that I trembled so that I could hardly stand. "You are quite overcome."

"I am very silly," I stammered; "but oh, nobody ever spoke so to me before."

"'Tis not worth minding," said Mr. Corbet. "How did it chance?"

I told him, as well as I could, though I would not repeat all that Lord Saville said to me.

"Aye, he is a fine specimen of a Court gallant,"

said Mr. Corbet, bitterly. "'Tis such as he, ruffling in his fine clothes and spending money and compliments, that are alienating men's hearts from the king, and raising among sober, hard-working people in London, such hatred toward the Court party, as I fear will bear bloody fruit ere long."

"But surely," said I, "the King cannot approve him?"

"The King, sweetheart, sees with his wife's eyes, and hears with her ears: and Lord Saville is mighty great with the Queen and her party. But are you enough recovered to go home? I was on my way to my Lady with a message from my mother, which concerns you. I am obliged to go to Bristol for a week, on public business, and my mother means to beg you and Betty to keep her company for the time. It will be a change for the child, and for you also, and my mother will be much pleased."

I was glad of the chance for such a change of air and scene for Betty, who was still rather drooping, and not sorry for my own sake to go away for a little time.

"I think you will find our old house a pleasant one, though it is nothing so grand as the Court," continued Walter. "I want you to learn to love it, for my sake."

Perhaps he might have said more, but at that moment he met Mrs. Priscilla Fulton, who has been staying in the house: so leaving me with her, Walter went straight to my Lady.

"I have been looking for you," said Mrs. Fulton, who is always very gracious to me and everybody: "my Lady says you are a famous knitter, and I want you to teach me the stitches. Is that asking too much of your good nature Mrs. Merton?"

"Surely not, madam," I answered. "I will do so with pleasure." So we went up to the nursery, and really had a very nice time over our knitting. She is a very pleasant young lady. In the midst thereof came my Lady with a note in her hand, and calling me out of the room, she imparted its contents to me, and asked me how I should like to make a visit to Corby-End? I told her that I should like it very well, and that I thought the change would do Betty good. So it was settled. Mr. Corbet went to Bristol next day, and Betty and I to Corby-End, where we are now. 'Tis a beautiful old house—far more to my mind than Stanton Court, with all its grandeur. Betty is delighted, though she was a little homesick the first night, and cried for her mother. She goes with Madam to see and feed the fowls and calves, and seems to be gaining strength every day.

But I am a long time coming to the gist of my story. Only three days after Walter went away, we were sitting by the fire late one evening, after Betty had gone to bed (for Madam uses a little fire now the evenings are growing cool and damp), when we heard some one ride up the road, and presently Walter entered in his riding suit, splashed with mud, and looking so distressed that his mother started up in alarm.

"Walter, my son, what brings you back so soon? And surely you have heard some bad news?"

"Aye, that have I, mother—evil and bitter news," said he, gravely. "Mother, Sir John Elliot is dead."

"Alas! alas! Is he gone, the good and brave man?" said Mrs. Corbet. "Did he die at home?"

"Not so! He died in prison—in the Tower, whence he had vainly prayed to be removed. The King hath even refused to his orphan children the poor comfort of paying the last rites to their father's body, which is thrust into a hole, like a dog's. The brave good man hath been denied that mercy he ever showed, even to his enemies. Alas, my brother!" And with that he covered his face and wept like a child. 'Tis a terrible thing to see a strong, self-restrained man weep. He controlled himself in a moment, however, and sat silently looking at the fire.

"But how did you hear?" asked his mother, presently. He told her that he had met in Exeter a messenger with letters from London, and that he must himself go up to town next day but one. "I must see what can be done for those children. Maybe something can be saved for them," said he; "and I must see and consult with our friends. I think the King is utterly mad. At the rate things are going, the Court will leave us neither King nor Church before another five years. We are fallen on evil days, and the worst is, one knows not which side to take."

"If only one need take neither side," said Madam, sighing. "But I well know that cannot be. 'Tis a woeful thing that the King should be so ill advised. But are you sure that Sir John's body was refused to his family? I can scarce believe it."*

"So Mr. Hampden writes me," returned Walter, taking a letter from his pocket; "and he is not a man to speak at random. Here is what he says:

"'Sir John petitioned again and again that he might be set at liberty, to regain his health, injured by the close and bad air of his prison, but the King's only answer was that the petition was not humble enough. At last he died, and his son begged most humbly that he might have liberty to carry his father's body into Cornwall, there to be buried with his ancestors. His Majesty wrote at the foot of the petition:

"'Let Sir John Elliot's body be buried in the church of the parish where he died,' and accordingly our friend's corpse was thrust into an obscure corner of the Tower church. This is the end of an honorable and just man, after ten years' languishing in prison, and that for no fault save that of upholding valiantly the constitutional liberties of the House of Commons. The Court party make no secret of their exultation, but the

---

* I here take a slight liberty with history. Sir John Elliot died in 1632. The circumstances were as related above.

King's real friends are in great dismay; and for mine own part I see not any good end possible.'"

"Mr. Hampden writes very moderately," remarked Madam.

"'Tis ever his way to say less than he feels," replied Walter. "The others are hot enough. But I am forgetting my trust," he added, turning to me with a grave smile. "My grief makes me but a faithless messenger. I have letters for you, Mrs. Merton, which Mrs. Carey received in a packet from her son, and prayed me to deliver."

So saying he took out a packet and put it into my hands.

"And I am forgetting, too," said his mother; "you have had no supper."

"I have tasted nothing since morning, save a cold morsel at Dame Howell's, where we stopped to feed the horses," replied Walter.

"Margaret, will you order supper?" asked Madam. "You see," she added, smiling, as I rose to obey, "I treat you as a daughter."

I could have boxed my own ears worse than I did my Lord Saville's for the burning blush which mantled my face at these simple words. Mr. Corbet smiled in his sudden fashion, which makes me always think of the shining out of the sun from behind a cloud, and repeated some lines of poetry in Italian, for which I was none the wiser. I ordered his supper (and I might have spared the pains, for old Mrs. Prudence had it already prepared, and was nowise pleased, I could see, at my interference), and then escaped to my room to read my letters.

They were both pleasant and painful. Mother and the children are well, and everything goes on comfortably at home. Mother says that many of the farmers and neighboring gentry have sent her presents of fruit, honey, and the like, as they used to do when my father was alive; and she hath wool and flax enough to keep her wheel going in all her spare minutes. Eunice hath learned to spin flax, and sends me a sample of her thread, which is very fair, but Lois cannot manage it. However, she hath learned to write nicely, and my mother says Jacky is growing a good boy, and a great help to her, and does well at his books. Richard has an increase of wages, and is in great liking with his master. The disagreeable part is that Felicia has written to mother, saying she has heard a very bad account of me from one of the ladies of the family, and begs mother to advise me to hold my tongue and keep to my own place, with other such matters. Mother says she does not regard the news, knowing so well the quarter from whence it comes, but I can see that it troubles her.

The next day we were all busy in preparing for Walter's journey to London. Betty was made happy by being allowed to help make some gingerbread and biscuits. The servants all pet her and make much of her, and she goes about the house freely wherever she likes, and is as one of the family, which is a great deal better than being confined to one room. I fear she will feel the change greatly when she goes home again.

A little before sunset I was in the garden, whither Madam had sent me to gather some early apples for supper, when Walter joined me.

"I fear my mother lays too much upon you," said he, bending down with his strong arm the bough I was striving to reach.

"Not at all," I answered. "It makes me feel happy to be going freely about house again, and helping in household matters. If I only had my wheel, I should feel myself quite at home."

"So would I have you feel," said Walter, earnestly. "I would have you look upon this house as your home, and my mother as your mother. All that I have to give is yours if you will but take it. Margaret, will you be my wife, and a daughter to my mother?"

I hardly know what I said, but he went on speaking.

"I am not a fit mate for you in many respects," said he. "You are a fresh young maid, and I am a middle-aged man, worn and browned by much travel, and many wars by sea and land—too grave and sober, mayhap, to please a maiden's fancy; but I love you, and I believe, with God's blessing, I can make you happy!"

"And your mother—and your friends—and my Lord!" I stammered.

"My mother will be well pleased with what

pleases me, and she also loves you for your own sake," he rejoined. "As for my Lord, it is no concern of his, that I know of!"

"But as the head of your house and family," I said.

"He is no more the head of my family than I am of his!" was Mr. Corbet's reply. "For the matter of that, the house of Corbet is older than that of Stanton, and lived on their own lands when the Stantons were unheard of. Don't you know the rhyme:

> 'Corby of Corby sat at home,
> When Stanton of Stanton hither did come.'

'Tis true, I am the next heir to the title at present, but I covet it not, and should rejoice heartily if my Lady had half a dozen boys to-morrow."

"So would not I," I could not help saying. "One would be quite enough!"

"Well, perhaps so. But, at all events, Margaret, I owe no duty to my Lord, in that respect."

I cannot tell all he said, but at last he made me confess that I loved him.

"Good!" said he, kissing my hand. "That is all I ask or need. And now, when shall we be married?"

I felt my face flush like fire.

"Not for a long time yet!" I answered him: "I have solemnly promised my dear Lady to stay with Lady Betty for at least a year, unless I am turned away, and I do not think that will happen, for from something my Lord let fall, I know he has promised my Lady not to interfere."

Walter looked annoyed, and his brow darkened. "When was this promise made?" he asked.

I told him it was at the time of the affair with Mr. Penrose.

"But my cousin would surely release you in such a case as this!" said Walter. "She is the most unselfish of mortals."

"I suppose she would, and therefore she must not ever be asked to do so," I replied. "I know well my duty to her and to Betty, and I should feel that I was making an ill-beginning, should I fail in that regard."

"But do you not also owe something to me?" he asked.

"Much!" I answered. "So much, that were it to do again I should not make such a promise; but having made it, when I had everything to gain thereby, I dare not break it, now that such a course would be to my advantage. I would not have the matter even mentioned, till the trying time is past. There is sure to be a storm, and such a scene as that of the other night is as much as her life is worth."

I cannot write all the arguments he used. We talked till Madam herself sent to call us in to supper.

"I bring you a daughter, mother!" said Walter, as we went into Madam's room, where she sat alone; "a dutiful daughter, but also an obstinate one. I trust to you to bring her to reason."

Madam folded me in her arms, and gave me her blessing most heartily. But when she heard the matter in dispute, she took my part, and said I was right; and after a time Walter yielded so far as to consent that the matter should rest till after Hallow-mass, by which time we hoped all would be happily over.

"Margaret must have the approval of her own mother and brother, as well as my Lady's, under whose care and authority she is at present," said Madam: "and though, as my son says, he owes no obedience to my Lord in this or any other matter, yet, for Margaret's sake, as well as our own, I would have no broils or disagreements. In these troublous times, family bonds should be drawn as closely as may be. Let matters rest as they are till Walter's return."

So it was all settled. I called Betty, who was helping Mrs. Prudence in the still-room, and we sat down quietly to supper. Afterward, and when Betty was gone to bed, Walter and I sat over the fire, talking for a long time, Madam being in her chamber.

"You will go and see my Aunt Willson in London, will you not?" I asked. "She is a good woman, though somewhat rough in her manners, and hath been very kind to me;" and then, suddenly remembering Felicia, I checked myself and wished I had not spoken.

"You have another kinswoman staying with her, have you not?" he asked; "a young lady who is very much engaged in Lady Jemima's scheme of the nunnery?"

That was news to me, but I said yes, my father's sister lived with Mrs. Willson.

"I heard of her from Lady Jemima," continued Walter: "you are not in my Lady Abbess' good books, Margaret, I can tell you."

"I know that, only too well," said I. "She has been prejudiced against me, and nothing I can do or say pleases her. I am very sorry, for I was fond of her, and she began by being very kind to me in her way."

"She has a great deal of good in her," remarked Walter; "but she is wholly governed by her imagination, and she can see no good in anybody who differs from her. After all, I think the root of her fault lies in her overweening estimate of herself, which makes it a crime in her eyes for any one to cross or oppose her."

So we talked till Madam herself sent us to bed. Walter went away early next morning, promising to write me under cover to his mother. The day after to-morrow Betty and I return home. I must say I dread it. My life here has been so pleasant and homelike; so free from any dread of giving offence; so full of quiet and homely pleasures. I have been to church, and so has Betty, and she has also had the supreme pleasure of visiting the school, and distributing to the girls with her own hands the buns she helped to make. The school is wonderfully effective, Madam tells me, and has been the greatest blessing to the children of the village.

Mistress Ellenwood has been here many years, and is now teaching the children of those who were her pupils when she first came hither. I have also been down to the Cove, where I heard the tale of Madam's persecutions, as a witch, many years ago, and made the acquaintance of Uncle Jan Lee, the fisherman, who had the chief hand in rescuing her from the mob. He seldom goes out now, and has no need to do so, for his son and nephew (who is also his son-in-law) provide for him handsomely. The latter, Will Atkins by name, is an officer on board the same ship as Walter, and much honored for his bravery and seamanship.

Aside from the great happiness it has brought me, I am heartily glad, for Betty's sake, that we made this visit. She has had her little world wonderfully enlarged thereby. She has been into the cottages and seen how the poor folks live : she has actually taken a little month old babe on her lap, and seen it dressed and suckled ; she has seen cows milked and poultry fed.

My Lord met us one day as we were coming from Goody Yeo's cottage. I knew not what would happen, but he only asked where we had been, and when he heard, laughed and patted her cheek, and called her "Little Dame Bountiful," and then, putting his hand in his pocket, gave her a handful of pence to bestow on her pets. It is a pity he will ever give place to the evil spirit, as he does at times. He is so very gracious and pleasant when he is his better self.

September 7.

We are at home again, and have fallen quite back into our old ways. Not quite, either. Betty is much more active, goes about the house and grounds, and has persuaded Mrs. Judith to give her some share in feeding the poultry. We found a pleasant surprise awaiting us at our return. Betty's room had been cleaned, and all now hung with fresh, pretty tapestry, representing scenes from the Morte d'Arthur, and a little room next, hitherto used as a lumber-room, hath been cleared out and fitted up as a sitting-room for her and myself. Here I found standing a pretty carved spinning-wheel and a basket of fine flax, and Betty a still greater surprise—a beautiful little dog, as like poor Gill as two peas, which at our approach sprang from his cushion, and began fawning around her feet, and looking up in her face as though he would entreat her favor. Betty looked at him and then at me, and then stooping down to pat him, she burst into tears.

"See how kind my Lord has been!" said I. "He told me he would get you another dog, if one could be found."

"It was very good in papa, and it is a very pretty dog," said Betty, sobbing; "but I shall never love him as I did poor Gill."

I did not think it worth while to argue that point, knowing that the dog would make his own way, but told her she should write a letter of thanks to my Lord. She took to the notion at once, and after some trouble made a very fai copy of a note of thanks, which I carried to my Lord at supper-time. He was pleased, and said 'twas very well done, and a credit both to Bess and to me.

"But did she really write it herself?" he asked.

"Of course not," interrupted Lady Jemima. "I wonder you cannot see that 'tis all Mrs. Morton's own work, from first to last."

"You are mistaken, madam," I answered. "I did indeed put the idea into Lady Betty's mind, but both words and handwriting are all her own. I never gave her any help, save to tell her how to spell the words."

"And very well done it is," said my Lord; "and you may tell Bess I am heartily glad she likes the dog. And I thank you too, Mrs. Margaret, for taking so much pains with the child, as I believe you do. You must not mind if I am hasty now and then. 'Tis only my way."

"I wonder you can be so deceived, brother!" said Lady Jemima.

"Tut, tut!" he answered, more gravely than he is wont to speak. "I have eyes in my head, I warrant you. See you not that the words and the writing are all those of a child? But never mind her, Margaret," he added, relapsing into his usual careless tone. "She is in an ill-humor. She has dismissed her fine court suitor with a flea in his ear, and now she is sorry, as all women are when a lover takes them at their word—eh, Margaret?"

From which words of my Lord's, and from what Mrs. Judith told me, I learned that Lord Saville was a suitor for the hand of Lady Jemima. It seems she has a good fortune of her own, and though she must be older than Lord Saville, she is a handsome woman still, or would be, if she dressed like other women of quality. But I am glad to say she would none of him, but sent him packing with but little ceremony. She is full of her notion of a kind of nunnery, which she means to establish at a house she has near Exeter, and has engaged several ladies to join with her, one of which, it seems, is Felicia. They will have a peaceful household, no doubt. She is very earnest with Mrs. Priscilla Fulton to join her also, but it seems the latter is not yet decided.

I cannot feel right about keeping this matter secret from my Lady. She stands, as Madam said, in the place of a mother to me, and she has been so very kind. I think I must tell her all about it, happen what may. I told Madam Corbet so this afternoon. She smiled, and said:

"I knew it would come to that, dear heart, and I think you are right. She may, perhaps, be ill-pleased at first, but she is the most reasonable of creatures. But, now, suppose I undertake the commission for you?"

"Oh, I should be so thankful!" I exclaimed. "Surely no poor girl was ever so blessed with kind friends as I am."

"Well, well! I hope you will never want them, my love," said Madam, kissing me. "But, Margaret, I think we will confine our confidence to my Lady. It need go no farther, at present. Not that I am ashamed or unwilling to let the whole world know what wife my son hath chosen, but coming events may change the aspect of matters, and for all our sakes, but especially for Elizabeth's, I would fain avoid a storm. Are you still resolved to abide your year's waiting?"

"I am, unless matters should greatly change," said I. "It seems to me one of the cases where a man sweareth to his neighbor and disappointeth him not, though it were to his own hindrance. I promised my Lady in the most solemn manner not to leave Lady Betty for at least a year, and I do not think that I have any right to break that promise, because it would be greatly to my advantage to do so. It does seem to me that the first thing to be thought of is our duty. The rest is of little consequence in comparison to that."

This little conversation took place in our sitting-room, Betty being out with Mrs. Judith feeding the fowls, in which they both take as much interest as though they were human beings. (I often wonder that Mrs. Judith can allow any of her subjects to be killed; she thinks so much of them. I believe she feels it a great hardship that they cannot have the freedom of the place, and she can hardly forgive Dick Gardener for stoning an old hen out of the garden, where she was making herself much at home among his gillyflowers. Richard used to say at home it was father's and my maxim that "A cat could do no wrong;" and I believe Mrs. Judith applies the same to her hens. Thus much, by the way.)

We were interrupted by Mrs. Fulton coming in with her knitting, about which she is much engaged. She had gotten into difficulties, and I asked her to sit down by me and do several rows, that I might overlook her. This same knitting of Mrs. Priscy's has made us well acquainted, and her visits are ever a pleasure both to Betty and me; but I don't think Lady Jemima is at all pleased with them.

After the knitting was rectified and going on well again, Mrs. Priscy began talking about Lady Jemima's nunnery, which is no longer any secret. She was quite full of enthusiasm about the matter, and thought it such a beautiful fancy for women to vow themselves to God's service, retire from the world, and occupy themselves with good works, such as nursing the sick and bringing up children.

Madam Corbet smiled. "But, dear heart, why should one retire from the world to do all these things? Tell me, Priscilla, how many children hath your own good mother brought up?"

"Sixteen," answered Mrs. Priscy, smiling.

"And, withal, she hath done not a little nursing, hath she not?"

"Indeed she hath!" answered Mrs. Priscy, with animation. "You know, Madam, my Gaffer, my father's father, was with us all the latter years of his life, when he was very feeble both in mind and body, and needed as much care as a babe and then there was poor little Amy, and my brother, who was wounded at Rochelle, and lingered on a year, besides the care of the little ones. Yes, indeed, my mother has had her share of nursing."

"And, with all that, she has found time not only to read the Scriptures and other good books herself, but to instruct her children in the same," continued Madam. "Moreover she has done what lay in her power to promote the innocent happiness of all about her."

"Yes, indeed she has," answered Mrs. Priscilla, with tears in her eyes, and a rising color, which made her, methought, prettier than ever. "Oh, Madam, nobody knows nor ever will know how much good my dear honored mother hath done in the world!"

"And all this without any ostentatious retirement from the world—any conventual robes, to say to every one, 'See how much better I am than you!' any vows but those of her baptism," said Mrs. Corbet, smiling.

Mrs. Priscilla smiled and blushed in her turn.

"That is true!" said she. "I am sure no nun ever did any more; but yet"—

"But yet all this was done in the station wherein

she was placed by God, and following out the duty to which God hath called her, instead of placing herself in one which He hath never appointed, and for which He hath given no directions!" said Mrs. Corbet. "In His word we find abundance of councils and commands to wives, husbands, widows, servants, and children, and the like, but not one that I can remember to nuns!"

"And to bishops and ministers," said Mrs. Priscy.

"Yes—that they should be the husband of one wife!" I could not help saying, whereat they both laughed, and Mrs. Priscy blushed. (I think she hath a fancy for Mr. Penrose. I wish he would take a liking to her. I am sure she would make him an excellent wife.)

"But all women do not wish to marry, or have not the chance to do so," said Mrs. Priscilla. "What would you have them do?"

"Whatever Providence brings in their way," answered Mrs. Corbet. "If they are in earnest about wishing to serve Him, they are not like to go begging for work. Look at Mistress Ellenwood, our excellent schoolmistress. Where will you find a life more useful and devoted than hers?"

"But still there seems something so noble in devoting oneself, body and soul, to His service!" remarked Mrs. Priscilla; "in vowing all one's energies to His work!"

"Well, my dear one, have you not already vowed as much at your baptism?" asked Madam.

"Tell me, now, what were those things which your sponsors then promised for you?"

Mrs. Priscy repeated according to the Catechism:

"'First, that I should renounce the devil and all his works, the vain pomp and glory of the world, and all the sinful lusts of the flesh: secondly, that I should believe all the articles of the Christian faith: thirdly, that I should keep God's holy will and commandments, and walk in the same all the days of my life.'"

"You see these promises cover a great deal of ground," said Mrs. Corbet. "You engage nothing less than absolute obedience and giving up of yourself to God all your life long. Now tell me, having promised all to begin with, what can any other vows add to the force of these?"

"But it seems as though it would be so much easier," said Mrs. Priscilla—"so much easier, I mean, to serve Him in retirement, away from the distractions of the world and all the temptations and interruptions of every-day life."

"Then it seems it is your own ease you are seeking, after all!" said Madam, with a penetrating look.

Mrs. Priscy blushed, but made no answer.

"I believe, however, that you make a great mistake in thinking so!" continued Madam. "I believe you would find that you had only exchanged the great world for a very narrow one, with which the flesh and the devil have as much commerce as with the other. I have heard in years past a great deal about convent life from my grandame, who brought me up, and who was herself bred in one of the best religious houses of this country, and I do not believe that life within the convent walls is, as a general thing, either holier or happier than ordinary family life."

The conversation was here interrupted by the entrance of Betty, in a state of great excitement, with a red-breast, which she had found lying on the ground with a broken wing. Launce (so she hath called her new dog, being short for Launcelot in the Morte d' Arthur) was as much excited as herself, and the small tempest diverted and broke up the conversation. After the red-breast was comfortably accommodated in a cage which I found for him, and Betty had gone to put her dress to rights and wash her face, Madam rose and said she would go see her cousin, and Lady Jemima came to seek Mrs. Priscilla. I called Betty to her lessons, which she now does regularly every day; but I am afraid I was rather absent-minded and distracted; for while Betty was repeating the verses I had set her to learn, she stopped, and said, rather sharply, "Margaret, you are not paying attention. I have said it wrong twice, and you have taken no notice at all!"

"Then if you have said it wrong twice, you had better take the book and learn it over!" I answered her gravely, handing her back the book; whereat she looked so blank that I could not forbear laughing.

"Come!" said I; "begin again, and we will both try to do better."

So I compelled myself to attend, and we finished the lessons prosperously. At night, after Betty had gone to bed, my Lady sent for me to come to her room. I did so, I must confess, with fear and trembling, for though I knew not that I had done anything wrong, I could not tell how my Lady might take the matter; and, for all she is so gentle and kind, or perhaps I should say because she is so gentle and kind, I dread her anger far more than I do my Lord's tantrums.

I found her alone, sitting in her great chair, and looking thoughtfully at the fire on the hearth. My Lady, like Madam, will have a fire when she pleases, without waiting till Michaelmas, according to the old rule; and, indeed, I can see no sense in going cold because it is one time of the year rather than another. So there was a little fire of pine cones and sticks blazing on the hearth, and my Lady sat before it. She beckoned me to take a low seat by her side, and I did so, in silence, waiting for her to begin.

"So," said she, presently: "I have been hearing of fine doings between you and grave Cousin Walter, whom every one thought to have a head too full of public matters to meddle in love-making. What think you I shall say to you, maiden?"

"I am sure you will say nothing but what is right and kind, my Lady, I answered, taking courage from her tone. "I begged Madam to tell you, because I felt that I ought not to have any secrets from you."

"So my cousin said, and so far it was well done: but, Margaret, ought you to have promised yourself to any man, much more a member of mine own family, without asking me?"

"I did not, my Lady," I answered her, eagerly "I told Mr. Corbet I was bound to be ruled by you, and I could not marry without your consent: and I said I would not leave you for a year, at all events, because I had promised to abide with Lady Betty for that space of time, whatever might happen."

"Why, that was well," said my Lady; "but, sweetheart, a year is a long time. I fear you are laying out for yourself a hard piece of work—harder than you will have strength to perform."

"I think not, my Lady," I said. "It is my duty to be faithful to my word and to you, and I am sure that I shall have strength given me to do it. Beside that, I do not think it will be as hard now as it has been heretofore."

"I suppose it was this same regard for Master Walter, which so hardened your heart against poor Mr. Penrose," said my Lady, after a little silence.

"I think not, altogether, my Lady," I answered. "I don't think I should have cared to marry Mr. Penrose, even though I had never seen Mr. Corbet; though, I confess, I never knew what Mr. Corbet was to me till then."

"So Jemima was right, after all," continued my Lady: "right, I mean, in thinking that your mind was fixed elsewhere. Not that I accuse you of using any art or coquetry, so you need not flush so angrily," she added, patting my cheek: "Marry, it needs no coquetry in the candle, to make the moths fly into it. Well, Margaret, I know not what to say to this matter. My cousin hath a right to please himself; and though you are somewhat too young for him, I believe he hath chosen wisely. His mother, I can see, is well pleased, and I suppose yours will hardly make any objection. Walter is a good man, though grave and sombre at times, but I believe he will make you a good husband. I think you, too, have made a wise choice."

"If it please you, my Lady, I do not feel as if I had made any choice," said I. "I cannot think that one goes to work to choose a husband or wife as one does a horse or a new gown. It seems to me as if those things should be ordered by Providence. I am sure I never chose to care for Mr. Corbet. It came upon me unawares, and I was as much surprised when I found it out as any one could be."

"And suppose Mr. Corbet had not cared for you, what then?" asked my Lady. "Would you then have gone on mourning all your days, or would you have turned your affections on another object?"

"Neither, I think, my Lady," I answered. "I

do not think a woman is to throw away her life, because she cannot have her own way, and marry the man she loves, like a petted child, which flings away its bread, because it cannot have sweetmeat thereon. And I think to marry the man one did not love to spite the man one did love, would be more foolish still. I think, in such a case, I should try to take up my cross and bear it as long as God saw fit, and seek to find my comfort in helping and comforting others, and in doing, as best I could, the work which was given me to do—in doing my duty in that state to which He was pleased to call me."

"You are wondrous fond of that word 'duty,'" said my Lady.

"I am," I answered. "It seems to me the bravest and best word in the world. Our feelings change with every wind that blows, and we are wondrous apt to be mistaken about them; but one's duty is usually plain, if not always easy."

"You are a wondrous sensible girl for your age, Margaret," said my Lady.

"I will write to them at home that you say so, my Lady!" I answered, laughing. "'Twill be greater news than the other."

"But the grand difficulty is to come," said my Lady. "What think you my Lord will say? You know that Walter is the heir, and is like to succeed to title and all, as things stand at present. Then, should ought miscarry with me, or should my

Lord die without male issue, you would stand in my shoes and be Lady Stanton."

"God forbid!" said I, as fervently as I felt. "We both hope that may be changed after Michaelmas, and I thought matters might rest till then."

"Perhaps that will be the best way," said my Lady, after some consideration, "though I love not secrets in the house. But, Margaret, bethink you whether with that matter on your mind, you will be able to do your duty by my child? Will not her interests suffer? And will you be content to meet Walter as a stranger, or only as you have done heretofore?"

"As to Lady Betty, I believe I have never yet neglected her, even when I have had the most on my mind," said I. "You are the best judge of that, my Lady. Have you seen any reason to be dissatisfied with me?"

"Surely not, sweetheart, but quite the contrary," said my Lady, kindly. "The child is wonderfully improved, and seems to gain health and strength every day. You would be like to hear of it, if I saw any fault."

"I hope so," said I: "and as to the rest, it must be as it happens. Mr. Corbet will be away in London for a month or more, and by that time we shall see what will be the state of things."

My Lady kissed me at parting, and so the matter ended. I do not believe I shall neglect my duty to Betty. I love the child more and more every day.

September 14.

Madam Corbet has given me a beautiful present —namely, a gold locket containing a fair likeness of her son, which he had painted when he was abroad in the Low Countries. It has a gold chain attached, and I wear it round my neck under my kerchief.

Having a chance to send to Exeter this day by Mr. Penrose, I have written a long letter to mother, for Mrs. Carey to send with her own to her son. But this writing is cold work. I would I could kneel down by her and tell her all.

The sick robin is getting well, and is very tame and playful, perching on Launce's back and plucking at his ears, to Betty's great delight, more than to the poor dog's, but he takes all patiently, as he would anything which pleased his mistress. He has fairly made good his entrance into her heart, and I believe she loves him quite as well as ever she did Gill, though she will not own as much. I can see that her father's hasty words still rankle in her heart, though she never speaks of them directly.

Yesterday eve, going down into the kitchen, I found all the servants looking on with great interest at a charm old Dame Penberthy was preparing, to learn whether the new-comer was to be boy or girl. She had found a stone with a hole therein, which she was suspending by a string, and with many ceremonies, over the door; and the first person who enters in the morning, whether man or woman, tells the sex of the babe. I told her of our old country charm to the same effect, made by burning a blade bone of mutton; and as they had one for supper, she must needs try that also. The maids would have had her hang her charms over some other door, because they said Peggy the milkwoman was always the first one to enter the kitchen; but she said no, it must needs be the kitchen door, and no other.

"What is the use of the pebble with a hole in it?" asked Thomas, who is an old soldier, and a bit of a Sadducee, I should fancy. "Why would not any other stone do as well?"

"Because it wont!" answered the dame, shortly. "How can I tell why, any more than why one who finds four-leaved clovers should always be lucky?"

"Then should I be the luckiest person in the world!" said I, "for I am always finding them."

"And so you are, and will be!" answered the old dame, looking earnestly in my face. "'Tis written on your very forehead. Any one may see that you have brought luck to this house, and so you will to any house you enter."

"Many thanks, dame, for the prediction!" said I. "Methinks I shall never want happiness myself, in that case. But now I want to ask a favor of you. I know there is no hand equal to yours in clear-starching, and I want you to wash and do up for me the robe I have been working for my Lady."

"That I will—that I will, dear heart!" said the old woman, "and I hope I may live to do as much for yourself, on the like joyful occasion!"

I made my escape at this, but as I left the room, I heard Anne say, "That will you not, dame. Mrs. Margaret scorns her suitor, and will have none of him, though 'twould be a fine match for her."

"When the right one comes, she will not scorn him!" Dame Penberthy answered; "she is no common maid to snap at a lover like a trout at a fly. She will marry well, I promise you, though she will see trouble first."

This morning Mary told me, with great glee, that the first person who came into the kitchen was Roger, my Lord's groom; and I was silly enough to be pleased likewise; but Mrs. Brewster was vexed, and said that trying such spells was unlucky, and would bring ill-hap on child and mother. I am sure I hope not.

CHAPTER IX.

September 15.

E have heard nothing from Walter yet, though it is full time. I cannot help feeling uneasy.

Yesterday we had a visit from a travelling bookseller, well known, as I learn, in these parts. He seemed a man of more than ordinary intelligence, and much gravity, and even austerity of deportment.

"Well, Master Blanchard," said my Lord, greeting him heartily; "what new play-books or romances have you brought us this time?"

"Truly, but few new ones, my Lord," answered Master Blanchard. "I like not the books of that kind lately printed, so well as to make myself very busy in spreading them abroad."

"I thought the Archbishop very careful in the matter of licensing books," remarked my Lady.

"He is," answered the old man, dryly. "He hath forbid the reprinting of 'Fox, his Book of Martyrs,' and of the works of Bishop Jewell, as well as of the 'Practise of Piety,' a book which has gone through no less than thirty-six editions!"

"By my faith that is being particular with a vengeance!" exclaimed my Lord. "Methinks if all we hear be true, his grace might find other things to forbid than the Practise of Piety. Why, my own mother used and loved that book next to her Bible. I believe between the Papists and the Puritans, the world hath gone stark mad."

"It will be madder yet, or I am much mistaken," said Master Blanchard. "I have good store of paper and blank-books, if you need them, my Lord, and some new music-books, and cards of patterns, and the like, for the ladies."

We were all purchasers. I bought a new blank-book and some paper, and my Lady gave me a silver pen and a pretty fashioned inkstand. Betty would needs buy a Bible and Prayer-book, as christening gifts for her god-child. Lady Jemima turned over the books of devotion and selected two or three, though she made a very disapproving face over some that she found there.

"But I cannot but think you are misinformed, Master Blanchard," said my Lady. "Why should the Archbishop forbid the printing of the Book of Martyrs?"

"That is a question asked by many people, my Lady," answered the old merchant. "I only know the fact in the case. 'Tis certain the books are to be printed no more, and they have risen in price in consequence. Folks say it is all the Queen's doing, but of that I know nothing."

"It was an evil chance that gave us a Papist Queen!" said my Lord. "I say nothing against the Lady herself, but 'twas a great pity."

"It gives the Papists great confidence," said Master Blanchard. "They are holding up their heads everywhere, and boasting of their favor with the King, and of the great things they will do hereafter. For mine own part I would as soon have an Italian Pope as an English. But least said soonest mended. I have Master Shakespeare's Plays and some of Ben Johnson's, my Lord, if you choose any of them."

I shall value my "Practise of Piety" more than ever, now I know that the printing thereof is forbidden. I have begun to read it over again this very night.

September 18.

We have had another travelling merchant, but of quite a different sort from Master Blanchard. This was a sharp, alert, and withal somewhat sly-looking little man, profuse of his bows and compliments, who brought ribbons, laces, and all sorts of trinkets and perfumes. My Lord, who is in high good humor about these days, would buy us each a fairing, and he gave me a little ivory and gilt box for sweetmeats—a pretty and convenient toy.

"Now must you have it filled," said the pedler,

and taking it from my hand, and first laying in the bottom a piece of white paper, as it seemed, he poured the box full of colored and perfumed comfits; and then closing the lid, he put it back into my hand with a look of intelligence which I did not at all understand.

The mystery has explained itself since, in a very disagreeable manner. I was going down to see a little lame girl in the village, and thinking to please the child, I poured all the comfits out of my box on the table, and was about to take the paper in the bottom to wrap some of them in, when looking at it, I discovered that it was a letter, and addressed to myself. Very much astonished, I opened it, and found it to be a regular love-letter, written in the most ornate and flowing style, and treating of broken hearts, flames, Cupid's arrows, and the like, bewailing my cruelty to the sender, and promising, if I would reconsider the matter, to make it more to my advantage than anything that had ever happened to me. Should I consent, I was to send my answer by the bearer, who was in the secret, and all should be managed with the greatest discretion. This precious epistle was signed "E. S." I was absolutely stunned for the moment, and knew not what to do; but presently resolving, I carried the letter directly to my Lady, in her own room, and begged her to read it, telling her at the same time how it had come into my hands.

"This is very strange," said my Lady, her cheek

flushing as it does when she is displeased. "Have you any idea as to the writer?"

"I have," said I; "but as I do not know for certain, and have moreover no wish to know, perhaps I had better not mention him."

"Do you mean Lord Saville?" asked my Lady, and as I assented; "why should you think of him? Had he ought to say to you when he was here?"

I told her what had chanced at the spring.

"And what did you say to him?" asked my Lady, something sharply. "I fear you must have given him some encouragement, or he would not have ventured to write."

"I boxed his ears soundly, if that be any encouragement," I answered, forgetting, I am afraid, the respect due to my Lady in my vexation: "I only wish I had boxed them harder still."

"So that was the history of his swollen cheek," said my Lady, much amused. "Truly I think you left not much to be desired in that way. And how did you escape from this modern Amadis?"

I told her the farther history of the encounter, adding that I should have spoken to her before, only that I did not like to annoy her.

"Well, well! I see no fault to find with your conduct, on the whole," said my Lady: "though 'twas rather a rustical way of defending yourself. However, I hardly know what you could have done. I am heartily sorry for the whole matter—sorry that you should have been annoyed—that my kinsman should have no more respect for me than to attempt an intrigue with one of my family, and specially sorry, that Walter should have made an enemy of him. Despite his gay and careless manner, he hath a sullen and revengeful temper, and is like to be a dangerous foe. I think you had best keep quiet at home, Margaret, till this man leaves the neighborhood. As for this precious missive, we will give it to the flames. You will make a good wife, sweetheart, if you are as frank and open with your husband as you have ever been with me."

So I have kept close house ever since, having a good excuse in the great rains. I am confident I saw the pedler in the avenue last night, and as I was going to bed, a pebble rattled against my casement more than once.

I would not go near it, and Ban, the great mastiff, scenting some disturbance, came barking and baying round the corner in such savage sort, that the intruder, whoever he was, beat a hasty retreat. I begged of the cook a good bone for the old dog this morning, and carried it to him with my own hands.

September 19.

I ventured this morning to go down and see Jenny Lee; and walking on to Corby-End, whom should I meet in the wood near the wicket-gate, but this same pedler. I would not stop, however, though he called to me, and even followed me on the path, asking me in a fawning tone whether I had no word for him.

"You are turning your back on your own good fortune, my pretty lady," he said. "Could you but see the lodging and apparel that awaits you, you would change your tone. I pray you give me a word for my master."

"I will give you this word, not for your master, but yourself," said I, at last. "If you ever dare to accost me again, I will tell my Lord and Mr. Penrose of your practises, and have you set in the village stocks for a vagrant and mischief-maker, as you are."

The fellow was silent, and slunk out of sight. As soon as I got home I threw all his comfits in the fire, not knowing what charms might be contained in them, though, I believe, a pure loving heart that trusts in God, may set all charms and enchantments at defiance.

It is very strange that we hear nothing from Walter.

September 28.

I must write, if I cannot speak. Oh that I dared tell the whole to my Lady, or to Madam Corbet, my second mother!

This morning I went down to the Cove to carry some comforts to a sick woman Mr. Penrose had been telling my Lady of, and after I had finished my visit to her, I turned into Jan Lee's cottage. I knocked, and the door was opened to me by Will

Atkins, who greeted me with such a perturbed and anxious countenance as made me exclaim at once:

"O Will, have you any news of Walter,—of Mr. Corbet?"

"In sooth, I fear so, and that none of the best, madam," answered Will. "Come in, if you please, and give us your advice how we shall deal with the matter."

He gave me a chair as he spoke, and I sat down, with a curious feeling of being in a kind of dream.

"I was over at Exeter yesterday," said Will, "and there whom should I meet but Tom Andrews, who you remember went away with Mr. Corbet. At first, I could get naught out of him, save that some great misfortune had happened to Walter; so dazed and muddled was he. But by questioning him, I at last made out that his master had been set upon one night, as he drew near to Salisbury, by a party of highwaymen, and, as he believed, murdered."

"You are too hasty, son Will!" exclaimed old Jan, rising from his seat. "The young lady is fainting."

"No, no!" I exclaimed, putting him back with my hand; "I am not fainting. Let me hear all, I beseech you! No one has a better right than I."

Will then went on with his tale. He said he had questioned and cross-questioned the man, and had at last discovered that Tom did not stay to see the end of the fray, but had hastened to save his own neck, and had then been ashamed to show himself. He told a great story of the number and strength of the assailants, and was quite sure that Mr. Corbet and John must have gone down among them.

"And now the question is, what shall we do with this tale?" concluded Will. "I shall myself ride post at once toward London and try to discover the truth or falsehood of Tom's story, which I do not half believe. What shall we do in the mean time about Madam and my Lady? The story may not be true, and then they would have all the alarm and suspense for nothing, and it would be ill for my Lady."

"You are right!" said I. "She must not know it—but how to keep it from her, and from his mother! Have you told any one here?"

"Nobody," answered Will. "I have but just now come home, and was consulting with my father as to the best way of dealing with the matter. He is disposed to treat the whole as an idle tale, made up by Tom to shield himself, and believes that Walter hath dismissed him for some misdemeanor."

"Master Watty never should have taken him," said the old man, "and so I told him. 'Tis a poor rascal and comes of a poor stock, but Watty must needs try to make a man of him. 'Tis always his way, ever trying to make whistles out of pigs' tails!"

"I will make him whistle to purpose, if he has

put such a lie upon us," answered Will, grimly; "but I fear there is more in the matter than mere lying. That fine lord who was here last month was no friend to Walter. They have crossed each other's path more than once before this last time, and it would be quite in his way to hire bravos or highwaymen to execute the vengeance he dare not attempt himself. He hath lived in Italy long enough to learn all their tricks. But we lose time in talking."

"What do you mean to do?" I asked, still with the same strange, dreamy feeling, as if the matter concerned somebody else and not myself.

"I shall take horse at once, and ride toward Salisbury," answered Will Atkins. "I can easily find out by inquiring at the inns whether Mr. Corbet hath been there within a month. He is well-known on the road, and always uses the same houses."

"But you will not go alone?" I said.

"No, David Lee will ride with me, I am sure, and I must go to him for a horse."

"And for money. Have you money enough?" I asked, putting my hand in my pocket. It is curious to me now to consider how cool I was. I seemed to think of everything at once.

"I have a plenty for my purpose, Madam," answered Will. "But you look very pale, and your hand trembles," he added, as a blink of sun shone in on my face.

"I fear the keeping this matter a secret, will be a task beyond your strength!"

"No, no!" I answered, hastily. "I can do whatever is necessary. I shall have help, I am sure."

"Aye, that she will!" said old Jan. "I can see it in her face. They call women the weaker vessels, but they ever seem to me the stronger, when there is anything to be borne. But 'tis hard the burden should be laid upon her, poor young maid!

Will looked at me with such a penetrating yet puzzled glance, that I thought best to tell him all, knowing that Walter hath no nearer or warmer friend than this his foster-brother and old playmate.

"I am betrothed to Mr. Corbet," said I; "we do not make the matter public as yet, but his mother and my Lady are in the secret. You see, I have the best right to know everything, and to help" —

But here, for the first time, I broke down, and sobbed hysterically.

No woman could be more tender in her ministrations than the old sailor, and when I recovered myself, which I did presently, he opened some secret nook and brought out a bottle of wine, of which he would have me take a glass, and indeed I was glad to do so.

"My Lord hath none such in his cellars," said he, with some pride.

"'Tis Canary, which hath made the voyage to South America. Marry, the Bishop who carried it over to St. Jago for his own drinking, little guessed whose palate it would regale!"

'Tis strange to myself how I remember and write down all these trifles. I seem to find therein a kind of comfort and relief.

My Lady noticed my pale looks at supper, and asked me if my head ached again, for ever since the fall of the candlestick, I have been subject to hard headaches. I told her it did, which was true enough, and she bade me go to rest early, and not rise in the morning unless I felt able. But I cannot rest. Oh that I had some one to whom I could tell all! And so I have. Faithless that I am, is there not One who knows all, who has promised help and comfort according to our needs, and in whose all-powerful hands my Walter is, and must be safe, wherever he is. He cannot go out of God's sight. We are both His children, and love Him, and so all things must needs be well with him, however hard and bitter they may seem now. Oh, how thankful I am that I have learned before this great trouble came upon me to regard my Maker, no longer as a hard taskmaster, exacting so much for so much, but as a kind, tender, loving Father.

"He that spared not His own Son"—His own Son!

Feast of St. Michael. September 29.

I have been to church to-day, and feel wondrously comforted and soothed thereby. It seemed at first as if I could not go—as if my service would be only a mockery, and a lip-service: but Betty wished to go, and I knew what my duty was. She hath become very fond of going to church, and my Lord no longer puts any obstacle in the way.

Her deformity is not nearly so noticeable now that she is stronger and sits up straighter, and she grows pretty every day, while her aptness and quick replies make her an amusing companion, even to her father. I think he will end with being very fond of her, unless some new influence should come in the way. I earnestly hope so, for the poor child loves him with an intensity painful to see, and far more than he deserves. It is a different kind of affection from the quiet, trustful love she bestows on her mother, and in a somewhat less degree, on me. Any chance careless word of his—and there are plenty of them—cuts her to the heart; and any instance of thoughtfulness or affection makes her happy for all day. My Lord is fond of chess; though, with reverence be it said, he is about the worst player I ever saw, and I have to play my best to ensure his beating me now and then: and I am teaching Betty to play. The more of a companion she can be to him, the better for her in the event of anything happening to my Lady.

There was but a small congregation in church, as usually happens on a holiday. Lady Jemima was there, kneeling on the stone floor, and did not even look up as we came in. Madam Corbet was also present, as indeed she never misses a church service, and old Mistress Parnell. It was pretty to see Mr. Penrose hand the old lady to her place before going into the vestry. Mrs. Priscilla Fulton was present, and, methought, Mr. Penrose did send a glance in that direction.

I found the service as ever, so now in my greatest need, wonderfully soothing and comforting. The words seemed just what I needed—more to the purpose than any words of mine own could be. They always seem to me to be hallowed, and as it were perfumed by the devotions of all the thousands who have used them in the ages past. I am sure no prayers composed on the spur of the moment, such as they say the Puritans are wont to use, would be as grateful to me as these. I could not be sure that another and a stranger would express my wants—nay, he might, even as poor Mr. Prynne used, I know—say what would seem to me downright irreverent and untrue. I should have to hear, and in a manner criticise every sentence, before joining in it. Of course this does not apply to private prayer, though even there I find myself constantly falling back on the well-known and familiar psalms and collects, especially when my feelings are most strongly excited. I must begin to teach Betty the collects.

I could not forbear weeping during the prayers, but my tears were a relief, and I rose up feeling much more hopeful than when I went to church. Mr. Penrose read the whole of the invitation to the Communion, on Sunday. I wish it were old Doctor Parnell. Then indeed I could go to him and open my grief; but I cannot, for many reasons, make a confidant of Mr. Penrose. O that dear mother were within my reach! Sure 'tis a hard fate which sends a young maid away from her mother, at my age. And yet I ought not to say so, considering the many kind friends I have met here. Then, too, I should not have known Walter. However this matter may turn, I shall always rejoice and be thankful that we understood each other before he left home. How much worse would the suspense be to me now, if I did not feel sure that he loves me and thinks of me, wherever he is.

Lady Jemima never rose from her knees during the whole service; and just at the end she fainted and sunk down on the floor. We got her into the air, and by-and-by she revived, only to burst into hysterical tears and sobs. I was glad the rectory was close by, where she could take refuge from gazers. It turned out presently that she had eaten nothing since noon the day before. I would have had her ride home on Betty's donkey, but she refused, yet with more kindness than she hath lately shown me, saying that the walk would do her good.

She appeared at supper, as usual, though she looked pale and worn. "Brother," said she, presently, "when do you mean to have a new chaplain?"

"Not at all, as I know of!" said my Lord: "why should I? Penrose is a good fellow enough, for all his crotchets, and a gentleman beside. You thought there was nobody like him when he first came here."

"He hath changed very much since he came here," answered Lady Jemima. "He is not the same man at all, and I have no trust in him. I want a spiritual guide and director—one in whom I can place confidence."

"That is to say, you want a guide who will be guided by you!" said my Lord, shrewdly. "What is the use of a spiritual director if you only mean to be guided by him just so long as your notions happen to square with his own?

"But if by a man in whom you can place confidence, you mean one who will not fall in love with Margaret, I had best look out for one who hath a handsome young wife of his own. Here hath been Basil Champernoun, with his grave face, asking me about the young lady's family, and so forth. I doubt he is looking out for a stepmother to those black girls of his, and I dare say Wat Corbet, with his Puritan ways, will be the next, if indeed he hath not fallen under the enchantment already!"

Lady Jemima shot at me a glance of absolute fire, but did not speak, while my Lady said, gently:

"It is hardly fair to put Margaret to the blush in this way, my Lord. I am sure nobody could be more circumspect than she, or take less pains to attract admiration."

"Oh, she does not care!" answered my Lord, carelessly. "She knows my ways. Sure 'tis no shame for a maiden to have admirers, especially when she is, as you truly say, so circumspect and prudent as Margaret. I verily think she cares more for Betty's little finger than for all of them."

So all ended well. But, as I recalled the look that Lady Jemima bestowed upon me, I cannot but wonder whether she herself hath any thought of Walter. I am sure she hath something on her mind which makes her very unhappy.

October 1.

My Lady sent me down early this morning to ask Mrs. Corbet for a pattern. I found her rejoicing over letters from Walter, sent from about Illchester, where he had stopped a day to see some friends of Sir John Elliott's and his own. They were gravely cheerful, as usual, and there was one for me, which I put in my bosom unread. I dared not trust myself to read it under his mother's eye when I thought it might be, perhaps, the last of him that I should ever see. She asked me kindly of my health, and on my telling her that my head troubled me again, she pressed on me a little flask of distilled and rectified vinegar, very pungent and refreshing, as well as a bottle of some strong sweet water, wherewith to bathe my temples and forehead. If she knew what I know—but I am glad she does not. I should suffer none the less because she suffered the more. Coming home, I found the church door open, so I went in and spent a few minutes quietly in prayer, and in reading the ninetieth and ninty-first psalms. I wish it were the custom here, as they say it is abroad, to keep the church always open. Surely many, especially of the poor, who have no place of retirement at home, would gladly resort thither now and then for devotion. Methinks there is something in the very air of the place which disposes one to a quiet and worshipping frame of mind.

When I got home, and could be alone, I read my letter—a long one, full of goodness and love—how precious none can tell. Oh, could I but certainly know that he was safe and well!

Lady Jemima met me in the gallery, and after passing me, she came back and said, abruptly enough:

"You have been down to Corby-End, I hear. Have they any news of Walter—of Mr. Corbet?"

"His mother had letters this morning, written at Illchester, my Lady," I answered. "Mr. Corbet was well when he wrote, but the letters have been a long time on the way."

"Aye, no doubt you know all about the matter!" said she, with a kind of scornful bitterness. Then with a sudden change of tone, "Margaret, tell me what you do to make everybody like you?"

"I don't think I do anything, madam," I answered: "and besides every one does not like me.

You yourself are my enemy, though I know not why, for I have never willingly or knowingly injured you: yet you are ready to believe every evil report about me, and to put the worst construction on all I say or do—or have done, for that matter."

She colored deeply. "You are too free!" said she, austerely. "You forget yourself very much when you speak thus to me."

"I beg your pardon, madam!" I answered. "I meant not to be so. You asked the question, and I answered it."

"Well, well, let it pass!" she said, impatiently. "What is this I hear from my brother about Mr. Champernoun and yourself?"

"I have heard nothing more about the matter," I replied. "I think it was only one of my Lord's jests. Mr. Champernoun hath never seen me except in church, and when the Bishop was here, and I have never so much as exchanged a word with him."

"He is an excellent man, and it would be a match far above anything you have a right to expect," she continued: "and you might make yourself very useful as stepdame to his little daughters. I advise you to accept his offer!"

"Time enough for that when he makes it, my Lady!" I answered, laughing in spite of my vexation. "For me, I am quite content as I am for the present. I do not believe Mr. Champernoun ever thought of such a thing!" With which I made my escape.

Betty's tame robin flew away this morning.

She shed some tears at first, but finally said it was natural the poor bird should love the woods and fields best, adding, sadly enough, "I am sure I would fly away, if I could."

"And leave me?" I asked.

"No, I would take you with me!" she said: "and I would not fly away to stay either, but would come back after a while—after I had seen the world."

"Perhaps your bird may come back," said I; and sure enough, at sunset, the little creature came pecking at the casement, and being let in, flew to his favorite place on Betty's shoulder, and showed great joy at seeing her again. I was as well pleased as the child to see the truant return. I believe I had made a kind of omen of it.

I dreamed last night of a great fall of snow, and telling my dream to Dame Yeo, she tells me that snow out of season means trouble without reason, and shows that I am or soon shall be fretting myself about some matter without cause. I am sure I hope it is so, but I am no great believer in dreams.

October 3.

This day brought me two letters, or rather three—one from Dick enclosing a note from dear mother. They are all well at home, though mother says there is fever in the place, and that two have died out of Robert Smith's family. She also tells me, what I am sorry to hear, that Sir Peter Beaumont hath prosecuted John Edwards for holding a conventicle in his house.

It seems several of the neighbors have been in the habit of assembling there to worship, at which time they prayed and spoke to each other on religious subjects, but all in a quiet way. Mr. Carey would have nothing to do with the matter, and was much vexed at Sir Peter's taking it up, saying that it was the next way to make the thing popular, to make martyrs of the promoters thereof: and sure enough the parish is in arms about it, some taking one side and some the other. I am very sorry. We were all so quiet and peaceable in my dear father's time. Methinks Sir Peter would better show his zeal for religion and the church, by leaving off drinking and swearing, and some other worse matters, than by hunting out prayer meetings and the like. I remember John Edwards was a very strict Calvinist, and he and my father used to have many arguments, but they always ended pleasantly, however much heat John Edwards might fall into.

My father never lost his temper, which I fancy gave him somewhat the advantage. At any rate John Edwards was a good friend to us, and always remembered us when his Warden pears were gathered, we having none of that sort. I am heartily sorry for this trouble which hath befallen him.

My other letter I did not at all understand, at the first. It purported to be from a lady of quality residing near Exeter, who said she had heard of me by Mrs. Carey, and wishing to engage me at a liberal salary—twice as much as I have here—to act as companion to herself and her daughter, promising to treat me in all respects as an equal. If I consented to come, she said, she desired I would not mention the affair to my Lady, between whom and the writer there was an old feud, arising out of family matters, and who would be sure to prejudice me against her; but I was to ask leave to go to Exeter on some errand of mine own, where I would be met and conducted to the gentlewoman's house.

I thought this a very dishonorable way of proceeding, and what of itself would be enough to set me against the author of the letter, but I thought of nothing more till all at once it did seem to me that the writing was familiar. It happened that I had preserved the cover of Lord Saville's first letter to me, and on comparing the hands, they were clearly the same, though the last was a little disguised. Then I carried the letter at once to my Lady.

"Margaret," said she, after she had read it through, "this letter is not genuine. I know no such gentlewoman as the person signing it, nor do I think it to be in a woman's hand."

"Nor I, my Lady," said I, "for the best of reasons:" and with that I showed her the cover of the other letter. "I believe it to be a wicked trap; but it is very hard"— And then my voice failed me and I burst into tears. It did seem very hard that with all my other troubles, I should be so persecuted: and though sure of mine own innocence and right dealing, I could not but feel very much humbled and degraded in mine own eyes.

"It *is* very hard!" said my Lady, "and it must be stopped. I will myself write to my kinsman and see if this persecution cannot be put an end to at once. You have done well in showing me this letter, Margaret, and you will always do well so long as you are thus open and truthful."

Then she asked me about my other letter, and was kindly interested, as usual, in my news from home: but seeing me still sad, she kissed me, and bade me not to fret over the other matter, saying that all would come right in time.

"Unless I see you more cheerful," said she, smiling somewhat sadly, "I must perforce release you from your engagement and marry you and Walter out of hand so soon as he returns. I like not these long engagements."

Oh, how my heart sank, as my dear Lady said these kind words.

"You are not looking well yourself, my Lady," said I, feeling as if I must say something, and indeed she was not.

"I am not well," she answered, wearily. "My head is heavy, and I have a sinking of the spirits, such as I never felt before in all my life. I do not sleep well, and I dream constantly of my mother and of my dead children. It is well that I have no real cause of trouble or anxiety," she added. "I think I should sink under it, if I had."

Oh, how glad I was that I had borne my burden myself alone. Hard as it has been, and is, I am thankful that I have had the strength to keep it all to myself. I believe the alarm and suspense might have made all the difference to my Lady. And 'tis certain I have been wonderfully helped. Never in all my life have I had such a sense of the nearness of God and of His goodness and love to me, as during this trouble. I have felt—I say it with all reverence—such a freedom with Him—such an ability to go to Him, not only with all my trouble and anxiety, but with all my fretfulness, and rebellion, and impatience, yea and faithlessness, for I have been very faithless at some times.

October 6.

"Sorrow may endure for a night, but joy cometh in the morning." For two or three days, life hath seemed to me merely an intolerable burden. It was as if I had carried my load till my strength was spent to the last ounce, and I must lay it down or die. I could scarce attend to my ordinary duties or collect myself enough to answer a simple question; and I felt so irritable and fretful that I longed to shut myself up and see or speak to no one. Doubtless it was well for me that I could not do so, but had my work to occupy me even more than usual; for Betty herself hath not been well, and hath shown more of her old exacting and fractious spirit than I have seen in a long time. Last night I said to her, "Lady Betty, cannot you help being so peevish and fretful? Do you know you almost wear me out?"

"Do I?" asked the child, as if surprised. "I did not know I was peevish, Margaret; but I feel so tired and uncomfortable."

"And so do I feel tired and uncomfortable," I answered; "and I have a headache, beside; but you would not like me to be as unkind to you as you are to me. Such conduct does not make you feel any better, does it?"

"I don't know," she said, pondering, instead of saying yes or no at once, as any other child would. "Sometimes I think it does. But then that would not be any excuse, would it, Margaret?"

"I think not," said I. "Beside that I don't believe it does you any good. The more you allow yourself to speak crossly and impatiently, the easier it is to be cross and impatient next time."

"Well, I will try to be good," she answered, drawing a long breath; but oh, Margaret, you don't know how hard it is!"

"Indeed I do, sweetheart!" I said, kissing her upturned face. "I'll tell you what, I don't believe it is one bit harder for you than it is for me."

She seemed a little comforted at that, and presently went to sleep, and I escaped to my room, feeling almost desperate. I was ready to say with the wicked man in the Scripture, "What profit shall we have if we pray unto Him!" my prayers of late had seemed so destitute of any real devotion, and had seemed to bring me so little help. Still I knew it was not right to neglect them, however I might feel; so, it being Friday night, I said the Litany, as my custom is. At the prayer "for all who travel by land or water," I surprised myself by bursting into tears and weeping freely, and my heart seemed to be a little lightened of the intolerable weight which lay upon it.

I slept well, and arose feeling somewhat refreshed in body, and under a strange calmness of spirit, such as I never felt under any trouble before. I seemed, without any effort of mine own, to be settled upon the ground of God's unchanging love, and to be made sure that all would be well, however He should see fit to order the matter.

After breakfast my Lady came in to stay with Betty, bringing her work, and telling me to go out for a long walk, to refresh myself. I was only too glad to do so, and bent my steps to Corby-End. As I entered Madam's room, I found her just opening a great packet of letters, while Will Atkins stood at the side of the fire. The first look at his face told me that he brought naught but good news, which Madam confirmed, looking up with her sweet smile at the moment of my entrance, and saying:

"You see I am well employed, dear heart. I have at last news from London of my runaway boy!"

The sudden relief overcame me, as the trouble had never done, and I sank down and swooned clear away—a thing I never did in all my life before. When I opened mine eyes again, I was lying on the couch, and Prudence was fussing over me with hartshorn and burnt feathers, and what not.

She is better now!" said Madam's tender voice: "leave her to me, good Prudence, and by and by bring some little refreshment."

When Prudence was gone, I raised my head, and said, dreamily enough, I believe, for I was still bewildered: "Did Will bring news from Walter—from London. Was he not killed, after all?"

"Killed!" said Madam. "No, dear love! What put that fancy in your head? Walter is safe and well, and sends you a packet by Will. Come now, and be a brave maid, and we will see what he says."

I gathered together my scattered senses at this, perceiving that Madam had not yet heard the story. After saying how glad he was to see Will, and to have his company to London, Walter went on to add :

"But I am sorry he should have been so misled by that miserable coward, Tom Andrews, as to come on such a bootless errand ; and sorry, above all, that my dearest Margaret should have had to bear such a burden of anxiety."

"What means that?" said Madam, pausing, and ooking perplexed.

"Perhaps we shall see, if we read on," I answered. So she read on :

"It was true, indeed, as Andrews told Will, that I was set upon near Salisbury by a party of villains, but as Andrews ran away at the very beginning of the fray, he had no chance to see how it ended. We were the better armed and mounted, and though they outnumbered us, we soon beat them off, with the gift to one of them, at least, of a broken arm. I would not say it publicly, but I verily believe the man I shot was the Italian who was lately in attendance on one who shall be nameless, at Stanton Court. However, I have spoiled his sport for one while, I fancy. Pray convey news to Margaret at once, my dear mother. Poor maid, how she hath been suffering all this time, though I doubt not her stout heart hath kept her up through all."

"And so you have been going about all this time, bearing this heavy burden all alone!" said Madam: "and all to save me from bootless anxiety! Dear heart, how could you do so?"

"It seemed my duty," I answered. "Your anxiety would not have relieved mine, and I feared the news reaching my Lady's ears. She is far from well, and a little matter might make a difference with her."

"But all alone!" said Madam, again, "and a young maid like you!"

"Not quite alone," I answered, smiling. "Alone, I could never have endured it."

She clasped me in her arms, kissing and weeping over me, and calling me her dear, brave maid, her dear stout-hearted, good daughter, with many other kind words, more than I deserved, but which made me very happy, nevertheless. Then we finished reading the letter, which was long and very interesting, containing much public news, and that not of a pleasant kind; but I could not let it make me unhappy.

Madam would have me eat and drink before I left her, and I was glad to do so, for I had not broken my fast that day. I could not forbear opening my letter and glancing at it as I walked home, through the wood; and so doing, I ran against Mr. Penrose, who was coming down the path.

"Good news wont keep, eh, Mrs. Margaret!" said he, smiling at my confusion. "I wish you joy of your letters from home!"

He is much more free and brotherly with me than he used to be, for which I am very glad. I can't but think Priscilla Fulton hath something to do with this change. I did not think it needful to tell him that my letters were not from home.

As I was going on, he called me back; much to my annoyance. 'Twas to ask me whether I had ever held any conversation with Dame Yeo on religious matters? I told him how I had read to her, and that we had talked over what I had read, adding, what was quite true, that she had cheered me up, and done me a great deal of good.

He shook his head. "I know not what to say," said he. "I cannot but fear she is in a very dangerous way."

"Why?" I asked, surprised; "she always seemed to me one of the best Christians in the world."

"I fear she is guilty of the sin of presumption!" said he. "She says she knows her sins are forgiven, and that she is accepted of God."

"Well," I answered—"why not? Don't you read in the church every day that 'He pardoneth and absolveth all those who truly repent and unfeignedly believe His holy Gospel'? and does not our Lord say, 'He that believeth on me, *hath* everlasting life, and shall never come into condemnation'?"

"'Tis true!" said he; "but yet"—

"I can't stop to talk to you about it now," I said; "my Lady will be waiting for me; but, Mr. Penrose, I don't believe our Lord intends his dear children shall walk through the world with a rope round their necks, as it were. He tells us to rejoice evermore, and that because our names are written in heaven!"

"You believe in the doctrine of final perseverance?" said he, turning back and walking with me.

"I know naught of theological terms," I answered him; "but when I feel God's grace enough for me to-day, why should I distress myself for fear I should not have it to-morrow, or next week, or next year? We are taught to ask daily bread for daily needs, and why not daily grace? I see no presumption in taking our Lord at His word."

"But how can you know that you love Him, or that your faith is sufficient?" he persisted, still going on by my side.

"As I know anything else," I answered. "How do I know that I am glad to get my letter? I don't need any deep self-examination to find that out, I trow!"

"Nor I!" said Mr. Penrose. It needs only to look at your face. But we will talk of this matter again."

And so, to my relief, he turned and left me, with a kind good morning. He is far more patient of contradiction or opposition than he used to be. He formerly seemed to resent my having any opinions of mine own in such matters. I hope he will not go teasing Dame Yeo with his notions, though, indeed, I believe the old woman is quite able to hold her own with him.

I only glanced at my letter, reserving that and the contents of the package for the time when I should be alone; but though I knew my Lady was waiting, I did steal a few minutes for a fervent thanksgiving.

When I went into the nursery, my Lady smiled, and said, in her usual kind way, but with a touch of gentle malice:

"You must have found your walk pleasant, Margaret?"

"I fear I have been gone too long, my Lady," I answered. "I went to Corby-End, and Madam detained me a little."

"Oh!" said my Lady, significantly. "Well, what is the news at Corby-End? Hath my cousin any tidings of her son?"

"Yes, my Lady," I answered. "Will Atkins is returned, and has brought a great package of letters to Madam, and some to my Lord, I believe, as well."

"Oh!" said my Lady, again; "and doubtless Master Walter is well. When does he mean to return?"

"In about a month," I told her.

"I wish Walter would come home!" said Betty, a little plaintively. "It is not nearly so nice going out riding and walking, when I know he is not here, and there is no use in expecting him. We used to meet him so often, didn't we, Margaret? Mamma, what are you laughing at, and why does Margaret blush so?"

"Never mind, Betty," answered my Lady, composing her face. "Little maidens should not ask too many questions."

Betty looked far from satisfied, but she never disputes her mother's commands.

When I had time to open Walter's package, I found it contained, among other keepsakes, a small thin volume of poems by Mr. John Milton, and a small but beautifully bound and printed prayer-book. "I know you have one already," Walter writes: "but it pleases my fancy to think of you using this book, which is besides of a convenient size for your pocket. I think you will like the poems. I hold not with Mr. Milton in all things, but he has more of the true poetic fire than any other man in this age."

Walter says public affairs are very discouraging. The King, wholly governed by his wife and his own arbitrary temper, vexing and oppressing the subjects with monopolies, and all other little provoking exactions. The Archbishop punishing with the utmost rigor all *innovations*, as he calls them, in religion, yet daily making more than any one else, and, as it is believed, urging on the king—Wentworth in Ireland pressing his scheme of *thorough*, and as many think favoring the Papists against the Protestants. I can see that Walter feels greatly discouraged, and fears some great disasters both to Church and State. He says there is a new sort of people risen up, who call themselves "Independents," and believe in a toleration of all men, except it may be Papists—and that they have some strong men among them. He says he does not believe the Archbishop to be altogether a bad man, but that he is weak and arbitrary—two things which he believes often go together—and very narrow-minded; and he says, what I do believe to be true, that foolish people often do more harm in the world than downright wicked people. He says, also, that the Archbishop's innovations are not usually in matters of any great importance, only in vestments, postures, decorations, and the like, which makes it the more provoking that they should be so pressed upon people as matters of conscience and religion. The two things which have made him the most unpopular, Walter thinks, are the reviving and promoting the book of Sunday Sports; and the forbidding preachers to handle certain points of doctrine, as predestination and the like, on which the Calvinists lay great stress: and that these two have alienated the minds and hearts of many who were well affected, nay, deeply attached to the Church. Then the growing luxury and laxity of the Court—for though the King is a grave and religious prince himself, he does not scruple to employ and forward men of the most openly bad lives, and of course that has its influence; and because the Puritans practise great strictness and purity of morals, the younger men of the Court party affect just the opposite; so that it is coming to be the mark of a fine gentleman to swear, cast dice, and drink, not to speak of worse matters. Truly the nation is in evil case.

Walter's letter was very long, and contained much beside politics. I must not forget to say that he sent me a watch—which is a toy I have always longed for. This one is incased in gold, and is smaller and prettier than any I have ever seen. Walter bought it of a French artisan, a very ingenious man, and one of the persecuted Protestants who came hither from France. It does seem cruel and shameful that they should not be allowed to find rest even here, but should have their worship and the education of their children interfered with.

October 7.

Madam Corbet sent up the letters for my Lord yesterday, and last night at supper time he spoke of them peevishly enough, saying that the world had run mad, and there was no peace in it for any honest, quiet gentleman, who desires nothing but to live at home and mind his own business.

"Here hath been Sir Thomas Fulton's chaplain telling me that David Lee holds a conventicle at his house, and urging me to prosecute him. But I wont do it!" said my Lord, with an oath, and striking the table with his hand, as his wont is when excited. "Old David is an honest fellow, and his family have been good friends to me and mine these hundreds of years, and I wont interfere with him for any parson of them all. Let him manage his family his own way—and sing psalms through his nose, if he likes. What do I care?"

"But you ought to care, and to act too, so long as he breaks the laws, brother!" said Lady Jemima, sharply. "Why else are you a magistrate and Lord of the Manor, save to execute the laws?"

"You think so, do you?" said my Lord, turning short round on her. "Suppose somebody chooses to bring up the laws, of which there are plenty, against Popish ornaments and books, and after spying into your closet, should come to me with a complaint against you. Should I be bound to execute the laws therein?"

"That's a very different matter!" answered Lady Jemima, looking a good deal discomfited. "The Archbishop sanctions those things."

"The Archbishop does a good many things which he would find it hard to answer, if he were brought before a court of law—as he may be, sometime or other," said my Lord. "Here is Walter writes me from London that the Puritan party is gaining strength every day, and the people cry out on all sides for a Parliament, and no wonder. It is twelve years since we had one, or nearly that. And, by the way, Wat himself had a narrow escape. He was set upon by highwaymen, not far from Salisbury, and came near coming by the worst. Had you heard of that, Margaret? You were down at Corby-End this morning, I think."

I answered quietly that I had heard the story.

"And why didn't you tell it, then?" demanded my Lord, with some impatience. "Think you nobody but yourself hath any right to news of Walter?"

"My Lady was not well this morning," I answered. "I thought the news might perhaps disturb her."

My Lord smoothed his brow. "You think of everything," said he. "You are a good girl, Margaret, and Wat might do worse, after all said and done," he added, as if speaking to himself.

I don't know what I should have done, but that poor Lady Jemima made a diversion by fainting away, in her place, almost scaring my Lord out of his wits.

"It will be nothing," I said, as I was loosing her boddice: "she is better already."

"Do you think it was the story about Wat that upset her?" asked my Lord, like a marplot, as he is.

"Not at all," said I (I fear it was a fib on my part). "She hath had these fits more than once lately. I think they come from going too long without eating. See, her color is coming back already."

The poor lady opened her eyes and gave me a look of gratitude and woe, which went to my heart. I do wish she would be friends with me. But in ten minutes she was as cold and austere as ever.

As I arranged her dress for her, I saw that she wore sackcloth next her skin, and a cross with sharp edges turned inward, which had left their mark on her tender bosom. Alas! poor lady, my heart bleeds for her!

CHAPTER X.

November 9.

SO many things have changed since I wrote last, that I hardly know where to begin. My Lady is safe, that is the great thing, and has a fine sturdy pair of twin boys, to every one's great delight. I think it is my luck to have to do with twins.

Then my engagement with Walter is openly acknowledged and sanctioned, too, by everybody concerned, and I am now treated quite as a daughter of the house, though I go on mine old way with Betty.

Lady Jemima hath been very sick, but is, I hope, in a way to recover. And we are at last the best friends in the world.

It all came about in this wise. My Lady had been ailing for a good many days, and kept her chamber for the most part. I had partly promised to ride to the revels at Langham with my Lord, Mr. Penrose and his sister, a very pretty and pleasant young lady, lately come out of Cornwall to visit him. I confess I looked forward to the jaunt with some pleasure, for I love seeing new places and people, and I have been very quiet since I came hither. But the evening before we were to set out, my Lady sent for me to her room I found her lying on the couch, with no other light but that from the fire, and she beckoned me to a low seat by her side.

"Margaret," said she, "is your heart very much set on going to these revels to-morrow?"

"No, my Lady," I answered: "not set upon it at all, if you wish me to stay at home."

"I fear I am very selfish in asking it," continued my dear Lady, taking my hand in hers, and stroking it with her slender fingers: "but, sweetheart, if the disappointment will not be too grievous, I should like to have you stay. I am not well, and I am very fanciful—and I have learned to depend very much upon you, my dear. Maybe I shall not ask much more of you in this world."

"My dearest Lady, don't say so," said I, kissing her hand, and hardly able to speak as quietly as I knew that I ought, for the lump that rose in my throat. "It will be no disappointment for me to stay at home, since you desire it. I shall be glad to do so."

"Mr. Penrose will be ready to say hard things of me, I fear," said my Lady.

"I don't think he will mind," I answered. "They are to join the party from Fulton Manor, you know, so Mrs. Kitty will not want for company or countenance."

"Do you really think he is looking in that direction?" asked my Lady.

"I told her that I did, and I was very glad, both for his sake and Mrs. Priscilla's."

"'Tis just as well, as things have fallen out," said my lady, sighing a little, methought; "but I gave Mr. Penrose credit for more constancy. Then, my dear, I will break this matter to my Lord to-night, and save you any trouble about it. And, Margaret, I have written a letter to my Lord in case of my death, in which I have explained your relations to Walter, and asked him, for my sake, to countenance them. I am sure he will do so in the end, but you know my Lord's hasty spirit, and you must not mind a little roughness just at first. 'Tis ever his way to say more than he means. I have also explained my wishes with regard to Betty, and have written a letter to her and one to Walter, which will all be found in my cabinet. And now, Margaret, if you can listen quietly, I want to speak to you of some other matters."

"I will try, my Lady," said I. And so I did, while she went over various matters respecting her laying out and burial, and the disposal of her clothes, together with the provision she wished to have made of mourning for the school children, and the old folks at the alms-houses.

"I have tried to talk over these matters with my Cousin Judith," concluded my Lady; "but she always breaks into tears, and that is ill for both of us. I have good hope that they will be unnecessary, but I shall not die the more for having them arranged and off my mind."

"I think not, surely, my Lady," I answered, as she seemed to expect me to speak. "On the contrary, your mind will be the easier for having them all settled. I never could understand the feelings that people have about such matters—making wills and the like. A man is none the more likely to die for having made his will, and settled his affairs, and if he does receive a sudden call, what a comfort to him to think that he has left everything in order for those he must leave behind."

By this time I had talked away the lump in my throat, and felt quite calm and composed; so I said to my Lady that I thought I had best take notes of what she had told me, that there need be no mistake. She agreeing thereto, I got lights and paper, and wrote down her desires as she dictated them to me, and then read them over to her.

"That is all clear and plain!" said my Lady; "and now for your own matters, Margaret. I believe I ought to release you from the promise you made to me, to remain with Betty for a year. As matters then were, it seemed best for both of you ; but the case is altered."

"I don't desire to be released, my Lady," I answered her. "I mean to keep my word with you. I have told Mr. Corbet so, and he agrees that I am right."

"Mr. Corbet is the most reasonable of men, and will have the most reasonable of wives," said my Lady, smiling somewhat sadly: "but that is no argument for his being imposed upon, or you either."

"Indeed, my Lady, I don't feel that I am being imposed upon," I said, eagerly. "I am very happy with you. I am very young to be married, and I am all the time learning what will make me the more worthy of my new position."

"Learning of Mrs. Judith to make tarts and conserves, and to order a household; and of Mrs. Brewster to clearstarch and work lace—and what of me, sweetheart?" asked my Lady.

"Everything good, madam," I said, kissing the hand she had laid on mine—"Truth, and kindness, and patience"—and here the lump came in my throat again, and I could say no more.

"Aye, patience! Learn patience, maiden. It will stand thee in good stead," said my Lady, with something nearer to bitterness than ever I heard from her before, and then she murmured some lines, which, as I remember, ran thus:

"Bring me a woman constant to her husband,
One that ne'er dreamed a joy above his pleasure;
And to that woman, when she hath done most,
Yet will I add an honor—a great patience."

"Do you know who writ those lines, Margaret?"

"Shakspeare, I should say, Madam, though I never read them," I answered.

"You are right; they are Shakspeare's. No one else could so have expressed that character of

Queen Catharine. People do not set much store by him now-a-days, but I cannot but think the time will come when he will be set far above those playwrights, who are now so much the fashion. You shall have the book and read the play for yourself. But never mind that now. Margaret, I have no special directions to give you regarding my poor child. I am sure you will manage her rightly and reasonably, and always be her friend. For her sake I am glad that you are like to be settled so near us. I might say more on this head, but that I feel an inward persuasion, almost amounting to a certainty, that Betty will not be long behind me, if I am taken away."

She paused a little, and then went on to speak of the child that was coming, saying: "If it should be a boy he will have friends, more than enough, but if a girl, I commend her to your love and care. I am sure you will care for her, Margaret."

I answered her as well as I could.

"You must not mind my Lord's humors," she continued. "He is brave, generous and kind-hearted, but he is naturally high-spirited, and having been used to living so much amidst dependents, he is naturally impatient of contradiction."

"Or of anything else but gross flattery and subserviency," I could not help thinking. And in truth 'tis hard to believe very much in the greatness of a man, who must be managed like a child, and who cannot hear the least word of dissent or contradiction, without scolding and fretting, till he makes himself a spectacle. I am glad Walter has been knocked about the world a little more, for I am sure I should lose all respect for him if he should treat me many times as my Lord treats my Lady, who has more sense in her glove than he ever had in his hat.

My Lady finished what she had to say to me, and my Lord coming in, I retired.

"So I find we are not to have your company to-morrow," said my Lord, meeting me afterward on the stairs. "'Tis very kind in you to stop with my Lady, and lose the pleasure of the day; but you shall fare none the worse, I promise you. Of course it is not to be expected that I should remain at home—(I did not see the "*of course*"— it would have seemed to me only natural, remembering my dear father's way at such times)—"but I am glad you will be with her, and I shall not forget it. You are a good girl, Margaret."

I courtesied, and said, "Thank you, my Lord."

"By the way, I hear that Wat Corbet is coming home soon," said he, detaining me on the stairs, as I was about to pass him. "Have you heard of it?"

"I know he expected to be at home about Hallowmass," I answered.

"You know a great deal about him, it seems to me," said my Lord, in rather a discontented tone. "However, an that come to pass which I hope for, he may marry whom he likes, for all me. You have always been a good girl, Meg, and fond of my Lady. You are not scheming to stand in her shoes, are you?"

"No, my Lord, that I am not!" I answered, rather hotly. "I hope my Lady may stand in her own shoes this many a day to come. As for scheming, I am scheming for nothing, and I see not why I should be accused of it!"

"Well, well, you need not be so tart!" said my Lord. (People like him always wonder how folks can be so tart.) "I only asked the question. I am sorry to miss your company, and so I dare say some other folks will be; but my Lady's fancies are to be considered, of course. Tell me what I shall bring Betty from the revels? Poor child, 'tis a hard case that all such things must pass by her, and she have none of the fun: but I suppose she would like a fairing."

I felt sure she would, and told him what I thought she would fancy, namely, a thread-case and scissor-case—for she is beginning to take great pleasure in needlework.

"I will remember," said he, taking out his tablets, and setting down what I had told him; "and what shall I give you?"

"I will leave that to your own taste, my Lord," I was saying, when Lady Jemima coming down the stairs, a little way, called out, "Brother, I wish to speak with you!" and I made my escape. But going down again presently, to carry some message which my Lady had given me to Mrs. Judith, I heard my Lord say to Lady Jemima, as he left her room:

"Well, well, we can do nothing now, my Lady is so set upon her. But if you are right, Jem!"— I hurried on and heard no more, but I felt sure that they were talking of me.

The next day dawned clear and bright, though there were signs which might portend a storm before its close. I did not go down to the early breakfast, for Betty had had a turn of pain in the night, and Mary had called me up to soothe her, and give her some quieting medicine, which she will take from no hand but mine and her mother's: so after I had given it her, I lay down beside her in the bed, and would not rise for fear of waking her. She waked herself when my Lady came in, and I rose and went to my room. Here I found Mrs. Judith, intent upon taking down and brushing the hangings, and performing I know not what other cleaning operations: so after I had dressed, I locked up all my small treasures in my cabinet, and putting my watch in my bosom, and in my pocket the little Prayer-book and the Thomas à Kempis which Walter had sent me, I went down to the chapel to say my prayers there. I found Lady Jemima before me, busied in decorating the altar with late flowers, which she arranged with a great deal of taste. She seemed to make an effort to be pleasant with me, I thought, for she bade me good morning, and then said, as I stopped to look at her work:

"I suppose your Puritan notions would condemn these decorations?"

"I have no Puritan notions that I know of," I answered: "and certainly not that one. I love flowers anywhere, and I don't know any place where they seem prettier or better bestowed than in church. I should not like to see artificial flowers in such a place, because they would look tawdry and unworthy; but the real flowers are quite another thing."

"I should not have expected to hear that from a friend and upholder of Mr. Prynne!" said Lady Jemima.

"Mr. Prynne was my father's friend and kinsman, and hath been kind to my mother since his death," I answered: "but he never was specially a friend of mine. On the contrary, I am afraid I had a mortal fear and dislike to the poor man, because he used to contradict and browbeat my father so."

"And yet your father was friendly with him!" she remarked.

"Yes, madam," I said. "My mother would be indignant sometimes, and then my father would laugh and say that he knew how to separate the husks of opinion and prejudice from the sound and sweet fruit of the man: but I must confess the husks ever stuck too much in my throat to let me relish the fruit. But I could not but grieve for his hard fate, when I remembered his kindness to the poor, and to my mother, above all. I should love a Turk if he were kind to my mother."

She made no answer to this, but turned to go

away, gathering up the rejected stalks and leaves of her flowers, in which I made bold to help her. She thanked me, but rather stiffly, and asked me what had brought me thither so early. I told her I had come to say my prayers, as Mrs. Judith was cleaning my room.

"That is well!" said she. "Do you pray for your enemies?"

"I should, if I had any, madam," I answered: "but I think I have none, or at least only one," I added, thinking of Felicia.

"I am that one, I suppose!" said she.

"No, madam," I answered her. "I was not thinking of you."

"Pray for me, nevertheless!" said she, her face growing pale and sharp, as if with some hidden pain, and with that she went quickly away. I could not but wonder at her words, but she is always unlike other people, so I did not think so much of it. I said my prayers, not forgetting to pray for the poor lady, and then, as my books were heavy to carry in my pocket, I bestowed them, as I thought, safely in a corner of my usual seat, little thinking what a scrape they were going to bring me into, and went about my business.

The weather was gloomy and lowering all day, but the sun shone out bright and clear about half an hour before its setting, and Betty, taking a fancy to go out, I wrapped her up and took her into the garden, on the west side of the house, which is warm and sheltered in the afternoon. Here she played about awhile, talking to Dick Gardener, who is a great ally of hers, and gathering a nosegay of late flowers for her mother; when, just as I was thinking that we must go in presently, I saw Lady Jemima coming down the steps toward me. As she drew near, I saw that her face was white with passion, and that she had my two books in her hand. She came close up to me, and holding them up before me, asked, in a voice which trembled with anger:

"Where did you get these books? Whose hand is this in the beginning?"

Then, before I could speak, she added: "Tell me no lies, wench! This is Walter Corbet's hand!"

I was cool in a minute. I saw that the time had come, and that I must hold mine own with her, and if possible keep her from disturbing my Lady.

"I do not mean to lie—why should I?" I said. "It is Walter Corbet's hand, and he gave me the books!"

"And you dare to tell me so!" said she, turning paler still, if that were possible. "You receive love tokens from Walter Corbet—you!"

She caught her breath, and stood looking at me with the utmost scorn and abhorrence in her face.

"We shall see what his mother will say to such treachery, my dainty mistress—'his beloved Margaret,' forsooth! I will tell her what an honor is in store for her, and what a fine intrigue her pure-minded son is carrying on under his cousin's roof!"

"You will tell her no news, and there is no intrigue in the case!" said I. "I am Walter Corbet's betrothed wife, with his mother's full knowledge and consent, and also with my Lady's!"

With that I stooped to pick up the books which she had cast on the ground at my feet, when, as ill-luck would have it, my watch and Walter's picture slipped from my bosom and fell on the grass, the picture face uppermost, of course. With a cry of wrath and anguish such as I never heard, she set her heel on the picture, and crushed it to atoms, and then turning to Betty, who had come up panting and full of amazement, she seized her by the arm, saying, in a stifled voice:

"Come away from this wretch—this viper! Come away, before she shall poison you!"

Then, as Betty hung back, and clung crying to me, scared by her aunt's violence: "Come with me, I say, or I will drag you away by force!"

"I wont!" screamed Betty, all her passionate temper aroused in turn; and, wrenching away her arm: "You are a viper yourself, and a dragon too, Aunt Jemima, and I hate you!"

"Yes, you have profited by your teaching!" said Lady Jemima, in the same strange, unnatural voice. "Come with me, I say!"

And with that she seized the child by the shoulder, and by a sudden wrench, pulling her away, she dragged her toward the house. I was horrified, knowing how easily she was hurt, and sprang to the rescue, and at the same moment Betty gave a shrill cry of agony, and called out, "Mamma! oh mamma! Aunt Jem is killing me!" Then looking up—oh, sight of horror!—I saw my Lady running down the stone steps of the terrace, and, catching her foot, fall headlong to the ground!

I forgot all else—even my child, at that sight, and I was by her side in a moment, raising her head in my lap.

Betty burst out crying—"Mamma is killed! Mamma is killed!" and threw herself on the ground by her side.

Lady Jemima stood as if turned to stone. I saw in a moment that my Lady still breathed, and presently she opened her eyes. By this time Dick Gardener and his assistants came running up, and I made Ambrose, who is a great, strong, handy fellow, take up my Lady and carry her to her room, while I ran before to call Mrs. Judith and Mrs. Brewster. By this time all the servants were alarmed, and came running into the hall to meet us. I sent Mary to bring in Betty and put her to bed, and the others on different errands, to get them out of the way, for somehow I seemed to have everything to do, and to think of everything at once. As for Lady Jemima, she had never moved from her place, and nobody seemed to think about her at all.

By the time we got my Lady to her room, she was quite herself, and gave directions about everything she wanted, bidding Brewster undress her, and telling me to go and see to Betty and bring word how she was; for she feared she had been hurt in the struggle. I found Betty crying and sobbing in Mary's arms, who was trying to coax her to be undressed, instead of going to her mother, as she was determined to do.

I now found the benefit of having reduced the child to obedience. She submitted, sorrowfully, but passively, when I told her that she could not go to her mother to-night, but if she wanted to please her she must be good and quiet and do as she was bid.

"I will try to be good!" said she, pitifully, as I began to unlace her boddice; "but oh, Margaret, Aunt Jem did hurt me so! I could not help crying out! You don't think it was my fault that mamma fell down-stairs, do you?"

I told her no—that she was not to blame in the least; and indeed I could not feel that she was.

"How is mamma? Is she dying?" asked Betty.

"O no!" I answered, as cheerfully as I could. "I think perhaps she will be quite well in the morning, if she is not disturbed to-night. She is troubled about you, and I want to carry back a good account of you."

Betty was all docility in a minute, and let me undress her and rub her back and shoulders.

"Does it hurt you, now?" I asked.

"Not so *very* much," she answered, with a strong emphasis on the "very." "Not so very much, when I am quite still. Tell mamma so, please."

"You shall go to bed now, and I will sit with

you while Mary brings your supper," said I. And I made her a sign to make haste, for I was on thorns to get back to my Lady.

When I had seen Betty comfortable, I went back again to my Lady's room. By this time it was quite dark—the wind was blowing, and the rain dashing against the windows, and it promised to be a wild night. I found Mrs. Judith had sent man and horse after the doctor and nurse: "For though my Lady seems quiet enough just now, my dear, we shall want help before morning, I am sure. I only wish my Lord had left us Roger, instead of Harry Andrews."

I wished so too, for Harry was young, and not over steady, and besides he was brother to Tom Andrews, which was enough to set me against him. I could not help wondering at my Lord, knowing as he did what was like to happen at any time, and said so."

"Oh, there's no use in expecting any sense in *men!*" said Mrs. Judith, with decision. "They are all alike in those matters, my dear. An ounce of trouble for themselves outweighs a pound for anybody else."

"Not with all men, I think!" said I, remembering my dear father. "What time ought Harry to be back?"

"By eight o'clock, at farthest."

"And when ought we to expect my Lord?" I asked. Mrs. Judith looked grave.

"Not to-night, I am afraid: or at least not till

late. They will sup with Sir Thomas Fulton, and most likely stay all night, as it is such a storm."

Eight o'clock came, and half-past eight, but no Harry, and no doctor. My Lady began to grow worse very fast, and by half-past nine she was in convulsions. Mrs. Brewster lost her head entirely, and could do nothing but cry; and Mrs. Judith was terribly flurried, and evidently quite at her wits' end.

"You see I have had so little experience!" said she to me, as she came out into the ante-chamber. I never had but one of my own, and my Lady always had her mother with her before. I would give my right hand if Mrs. Corbet were here—but how to bring her!"

"Surely she would come if she were sent for!" said I.

"Aye, but how to send. You see, my dear, this is All-Hallow's even, and I don't believe you could get one of the servants to go down to Corby-End for love nor money!"

"What, not for my Lady?" I exclaimed.

Mrs. Judith shook her head.

"Fear makes people selfish, my dear; and indeed, considering what hath been seen between here and there on All-Hallow's eve, I should not like it myself. Not but that I would go if I could."

"I will go down to the kitchen and see what can be done," said I, and I went. I found the maids, with old Thomas and David, who were the only men left at home, gathered closely round the fire, listening to some dreadful tale of ghosts and what not, which Anne was doling out to them: and one or two of them shrieked as I opened the door, as if I had been the White Dame herself. I told my errand, but was answered only by blank looks and a torrent of expostulation and assurance that no one would dare to go through the park this night, no not to have the whole of it, for fear of meeting the Halting Knight and a certain evil spirit which is supposed, at this time, to be mousing about the Abbey for any unlucky soul that ventures out after dark.

"And so you will let your good Lady die for lack of help!" said I, as soon as I could get a hearing.

"As to that, our lives are worth as much to us as my Lady's to her!" answered Anne, pertly enough; "and who knows what Madam Corbet might do, if she did come? I'll be bound she hath heard the news before this time. She doth not need earthly messengers, as honest folks do. Everybody knows that!"

"Everybody knows that you are an ungrateful fool, Anne Hollins," said old Thomas; "and if you do not lose your place for that same speech, it will not be my fault, I promise you. I would go in a minute, Mrs. Merton, but you know I can scarce put one foot before the other."

"And you, David!" said I. David only shrunk together and muttered something, but it was clear he would not go.

"Get me the lanthorn ready—I will go myself!" said I, at last. "I fear no evil when on a good errand, and hold myself safer out in this storm and under God's protection, than you are here round the fire. Remember stone walls cannot keep out spirits, and the Evil One himself is like enough to be busy among you—selfish cowards that you are!"

With that I left them, and running to mine own room, I put on my thick woolen gown, which mother would have had me leave at home, and in less time than I can write it, I was back in my Lady's room, telling Mrs. Judith of my purpose.

"God bless you, dear maid!" she exclaimed, kissing me and bursting into tears. "Go then, and good angels guard you!"

"And so you are really going!" said Dorothy, the fat cook, as she put the lanthorn into my hand: "and you, you idle, good for nought men, will let her go alone! I would go myself, but I should hinder more than help you!"

"I'm going with Mrs. Merton!" said Jacky, the little knife-boy, starting up from his corner, and buttoning up his doublet, while his pale face and staring eyes showed his fears were only less strong than his sense of duty. "I'm only a lad, but I am somebody, and she shan't go alone—so!"

"Good boy!" said Dorothy, as she tied her own kerchief over his ears to keep his cap on. "Thou shalt have a fine plum bun, I promise thee! There, go along, and God bless you both!"

As we went out into the night, the wind caught us, and we had much ado to keep our feet. It came not steadily, but in heavy gusts, laden with sharp, stinging rain, and roared fearfully in the great trees. It was not so very dark, for there was a moon, which shone out now and then through the flying clouds, but a wilder night sure no two young things were ever abroad in. I walked on as fast as I could, and Jacky trudged manfully by my side, not even blenching when we passed into the Abbey church-yard, which we must needs cross, as the shortest way to Corby-End. As we were in the midst thereof, the moon shone out suddenly, and an owl—I suppose it was an owl—gave an unearthly screech.

"Save us!" cried Jacky, pressing close to my side. "What's that?"

"Only an owl," said I, valorously. "Never mind him!" But I did not feel as brave as my words, by any means. However, we crossed the church-yard safely enough, and descended into the ravine.

Here it was very dark. The brook, already swollen with the rain, narrowed the path, so that we had to go one by one. There were strange sounds in the trees, and the passing gleams of the lanthorn made strange shapes on the rocks and bushes. I grew very impatient to reach the end, for, aside from all other fears, I knew the brook, which hath its rise in the high moor, sometimes swelled very suddenly, and made the track quite impassable. But the more haste the worse speed. In my hurry I stumbled and fell, putting out the light. Jacky burst out crying: "Oh, mistress, what shall we do now?"

"Push on as fast as we can," said I, affecting a courage I by no means felt. "Take hold of my gown, and make what haste you are able. Even as I spoke, something seemed to brush past me, so near to my face that I felt it, and again we heard the same wild scream which had greeted us in the church-yard. Stumbling and tripping, however, we hurried on, and at last came out at the little gate I have mentioned before in these memoirs. We were still in the thick woods, but then the path was plain, and at last—oh, welcome sight! we saw the lights in the windows of Corby-End!

Never did any one look more amazed than Madam Corbet, when I burst into her pretty, orderly room, all dripping, torn, and draggled as I was, and told my tale with breathless haste. Not till it was ended, did I see that Walter was at my side. Then all my strength seemed gone in a minute, and I should have fallen, but for his arms.

"I must go to my cousin instantly," said Madam, rising. "Walter, will you order my horse, and tell Will to get ready to ride? There is no time to lose!"

"I will myself go with you as far as the great house, and then ride on in search of the doctor," said Walter. "As for Margaret, she must abide here and go to bed."

"No, no!" I cried. "I must go back. Indeed I must! If Betty wake and misses me, no one will be able to manage her, and I shall be wanted, beside. I must go back directly!"

"I believe she is right!" said Madam, to my great joy. She would have me drink some hot wine, however, and indeed I was glad of it. I believe they made all the haste possible, but it seemed an age before we were ready to set out As for Jacky, he was left with the servants to be dried, warmed and feasted to his heart's content. I rode behind Walter, and Madam her own horse, and we were not long in reaching the house. When we were safely dismounted, Walter said he would ride on with Will and find the doctor.

"You will be drenched through!" said I.

"Nay, I have my horseman's coat, and I am not made of sugar nor salt, more than yourself, my dear love!" said he: "but, dear mother, do see that Margaret changes her clothes."

And with that he was gone. Many people would have thought it not a very sentimental greeting, after so long an absence: but I was well contented with it. I hurried to my room to dress myself, for indeed I was wet through, and I know it was but right that I should take due care of my own health. When I had done so, I looked in at my child. She was awake, and started up at my entrance.

"Mamma!" said she, breathlessly.

"She is likely to do well, I trust," I answered. "Your Cousin Corbet is come to stay with her. Try to go to sleep, my dear one."

"But you will come and tell me?" she said, holding my hand. "I don't want you to stay, because mamma might need you, but you will come and tell me. And I have tried to be good, haven't I, Mary?"

"Indeed you have, my dear, tender lamb—my sweet, precious young Lady!" said Mary, wiping her eyes: "I am sure an angel could not have behaved any better!"

I kissed her and again assured her that I would bring her the first news, and bade her pray for her mother; and then I left her and hurried back to my Lady's antechamber, where I met Lady Jemima coming out.

"Mrs. Corbet is with her," said she. "She will not endure me in her sight—and no wonder. I feel as if I had murdered her."

"You have!" I answered her, bitterly enough. I was wrong, but at that moment I did really feel that if my Lady died, Lady Jemima would be answerable for her death. Lady Jemima looked strangely at me for a moment, and then turned and fled swiftly to her own room.

Mrs. Judith opened the door in a few minutes to whisper to me that my Lady was already quieter, and seemed soothed and comforted by her cousin's presence, and to ask me to go down and see that some supper was prepared for my Lord, in case of his coming home, which I did. I found Dorothy had anticipated me, however, for she had made everything ready, and not only that, but she had some dainty broth keeping hot by the kitchen fire, which she begged me eat a part of, and carry the rest up to Mrs. Judith.

"I had not thought of wanting anything to eat, Dorothy," said I.

"No, I dare say not, nor Mrs. Judith neither," answered Dorothy, dryly. "You're not the kind that always thinks of your own insides, whatever happens; so much the more need that others should think for you."

I would not seem ungrateful for the good soul's care, so I drank a cup of broth, and indeed it did me a great deal of good. I had hardly got upstairs again when I heard a clatter of horses' hoofs, and my Lord's voice above the storm, directing Roger and Will about the horses. Mrs. Corbet at the same moment opened the door.

"Go you down to meet my Lord, dear heart!" said she. "Tell him Elizabeth is going on well, but do not let him come up. Everything depends on quietness, just now!"

I needed no second bidding, but ran down-stairs, and met my Lord at the door. He was coming in, after his usual jolly, careless fashion, evidently merry, yet not much the worse—but that he never is—for the wine he had drank at supper. He checked his whistle on seeing me.

"What, Margaret! What keeps you up so late?" Then, as I held up a warning finger, he seemed to divine the state of the case. "My Lady! Is she?"—

"She is in a way to do well, I trust and believe!" said I; "but she has been very ill, and Mrs. Corbet says all depends on quietness."

"The surgeon is here, I suppose?" said he, after a minute.

I told him how it was—that Harry had gone for him at first and did not return; and that, growing alarmed, Mrs. Judith had sent for Mrs. Corbet, about an hour ago.

"Aye, that was well!" said he. "But who went for her? I would have said there was not a wench about the place who would have gone down to Corby-End to-night on any errand whatever; and David is a greater coward than any of them."

"I went myself," said I.

"You!" exclaimed my Lord, putting his hand on my shoulder, and holding me off to look at me. "Meg! You never went down to Corby-End alone, this wild night!"

"Nay!" I answered. "I had Jacky the knife-boy for protector. We had a rough walk, but we met with no worse misadventure than slipping into the brook two or three times, and putting out our lanthorn. And I rode back and left Jacky to be petted by the maids down there!"

He caught me in his arms, kissing my forehead,

called me his brave maid, his good girl, and I know not what else, and swearing a great oath, as his fashion is, that I should marry whom I liked, and no one should hint a word against me. I got him quieted at last, and set down to his supper, and then stole away, promising to bring him news from time to time; but when I went down again, at the end of an hour, he was fast asleep and snoring on the settle, so I even let him sleep.

The night wore slowly away, and still the doctor did not come; but I dare say we were as well without him. Between five and six, just as the gray dawn began to show in faint streaks above the high moor there was a bustle in my Lady's room—and then—oh, sound of joy, which I well knew—the cry of a little babe. I sprang to my feet, but dared not go near the door.

Presently, after what seemed an age of suspense, Madam opened it, her dear fair face all flushed with joy!

"Good news, Margaret! we have two bouncing boys—and I believe the mother will do well, in spite of all! Go you and tell my Lord—you have well earned the right—but do not let him come up-stairs, just yet!"

I ran softly but quickly enough down-stairs to the hall, where I found my Lord awake, rubbing his eyes and shivering. He started up when he saw me.

"Good news, my Lord—the best of news," I

cried out. "Two nice lads—and my Lady is doing well!"

"What!" said he, staring, as if he had not taken in my words. I repeated them.

"But my wife—Elizabeth!" he said, paler than I ever could have believed possible. "How is she doing? Will she live?"

"I believe she will!" I said. "Madam thinks so, but she bids you not come up just yet!"

I shall ever like my Lord the better for what followed. The great strong, soldierly man fell on his knees, and, amid streaming tears and sobs which shook him like an infant, gave broken and heartfelt thanks to Heaven for his wife's deliverance.

I cried heartily, and the tears seemed to wash from my heart the bitterness and weight which had lain there all night, ever since Lady Jemima had trodden under foot Walter's picture.

"But the bearer of good news must be rewarded!" said my Lord, when he had calmed himself a little —(I saw with pleasure that he seemed no ways ashamed of his emotion). "What shall I do for you, Margaret?"

"If I might ask so much!" said I.

"Let me hear it!" said he. "It will be hard if you ask what I cannot grant."

"It is that you will go and carry Lady Betty the good news yourself, my Lord!" I said. "It will be better to her from your lips than from any other source, and it may prevent some jealous fancies, such as children sometimes have."

"You are always thinking of your bantling!" said he, evidently well pleased. "I bade you ask something for yourself."

At that moment the hall door opened and Walter entered, followed by the surgeon. Walter told me afterward that he had found Harry Andrews drunk at an alehouse near Biddeford, and that he had rode five miles beyond the town before he found the surgeon.

"Hallo, Wat!" cried my Lord, cheerily. "Doctor, you are a day after the fair. You have lost your chance of the title this time, Watty, my boy! Meg here and your lady mother have choused you out of it fairly, between them!"

"Thank God!" said Walter, fervently.

"Good! That's well said," returned my Lord; "and what is more, I believe you mean it, both you and Margaret! And that is more than I would say of some folks."

"I mean it, I know, and I am sure I can answer for Margaret!" said Walter.

"Aye, you are mighty ready to answer for Margaret," said my Lord. "You and Margaret have been a pair of sly-boots, I believe. However, all is well, and I am sure you will never find a better wife or a fairer, if you look the west country over; so here's God speed you with all my heart!" And he gave Walter a mighty shake of the hand and a slap on the shoulder, which might have staggered a giant. "However, I have promised to break the news to Bess, and I must keep my word."

He went up-stairs, and I followed, for I wanted to see how the child would take it. As my Lord opened the door, I saw that Betty was kneeling in the bed, with her hands clasped. She looked up with an eager glance, and a burning blush, when she saw her father.

"That's right, Bess, my girl!" said her father, coming to the bed, and taking her in his arms. "Thank God for giving you a pair of fine little brothers to take care of you!"

She clung round his neck. "Oh, papa, has my little brother come?"

"Aye, that has he, and brought another with him!" answered my Lord, cheerfully: "and what is better, dear mamma is doing well."

Betty seemed quite overwhelmed, and laid her head down on her father's shoulder. Presently she raised it again, and looked anxiously in his face.

"You wont wish I was dead *now*, will you, papa?" said she. "Indeed, I will try to be very good!"

"Wish you dead! No, child, of course not!" said my Lord, quite shocked. "How could you think of such a thing as that?"

"You said so that day in the church-yard, papa!" said Betty. "You know I could not help being crooked, and, indeed, I will try to learn all I can, so that I can help mamma and teach my little brothers!" she added, with wistful pathos.

"Bless the child!" said my Lord, kissing her with real tenderness, and hugging her in his arms,

"I never thought of such a thing! Why, Bess, you must not lay up every word I say as if it were gospel. What will you do when you are married, and have a husband of your own, if you make so much of every rough speech?"

"I never will be married!" said Betty, with decision. "I mean to live single all my life, as Margaret does!"

"But suppose Margaret gets married—then what will you do?" asked my Lord.

"I should not like it at all, and I won't have it!" said Betty. Then gravely, as if reconsidering the matter—"unless she will marry Walter, and live at Corby-end. That would be very nice, I think, don't you, papa?"

My Lord gave one of his great laughs, kissed her again, and calling her a wise little maid, put her down on the bed, and pulled out of his pocket I know not what expensive toys in the way of scissors, needle-cases, and the like, telling her that he had bought them for her yesterday. Then saying he must go and look after his guests, and giving my ear a parting pull, he went away, leaving Betty happier than any queen.

"What did Aunt Jemima say?" asked Betty, after she had found out that I had not seen the babes, and making me promise to take her to her mother as soon as possible.

"I don't know that she has heard yet," I answered, my conscience smiting me, as I remembered my own words to her the night before, and the look she had given me. "I will go now and tell her."

I tapped gently at Lady Jemima's door, but as no one answered, I ventured to open it and look in. Lady Jemima had not been to bed all night, and now crouched on the cold floor before the little altar in her closet, pale as death, and with eyes swollen with long and bitter weeping. She started up as I entered, but did not speak.

"Good news, madam!" I said, cheerfully. "The best of news!" And then I told her what had happened.

"Is not my sister dead, then!" she asked, in a strange, bewildered way: "I thought I had murdered her. You said so!"

"I was angry and said what was very wrong, and I beg your pardon," I answered. "My Lady is like to live, I hope and trust. Madam thinks she is doing well, and also the surgeon, who is come just in time to be too late."

She threw her arms round my neck, and burst into hysterical sobs and cries. I got her into her chair, and supporting her head, I soothed and quieted her as well as I could, till she was in some degree herself again.

"You heap coals of fire on my head, Margaret!" said she, when she could speak: "but you did not come here to triumph over me, did you?"

"God forbid!" said I, earnestly. "I came but to bring you the good news, and to ask your forgiveness for my wicked words last night."

"They were true words!" said Lady Jemima, hastily. "I had the spirit of a murderer, if not toward my sister, yet toward you. I could have killed you, Margaret!"

I did not ask her why. Poor Lady! I knew well enough how she felt I had injured her. I only said:

"Dear Lady Jemima, I never meant to harm you!"

"I know it!" said she, bitterly. "You never did harm me. If you had never come near the place it would have made no difference. It was my own insane vanity and passion. I have been a wicked woman, Margaret—a wicked hypocrite, condemning and judging others, when I was far worse than they: but mine eyes have been opened this night, and I have seen myself as I am!"

"I am not so sure of that!" I said.

She looked at me in surprise.

"When the Saviour put his hands on the blind man's eyes, and asked him if he saw aught, the man answered that he saw men as trees walking. He saw, it was true, but as yet nothing clearly. It needed a second touch before he saw things as they were. It may be so with you."

She shook her head sadly. "I can never trust myself again," she said.

"I would not try!" I answered her. "But you know whom you can trust—who will never fail those who seek Him. But, dear Lady Jemima, you are now in no fit state to judge of anything. You are wearied out with grief, and watching, and fasting, too, I dare say. Your hands are as cold as ice. Let me help you to bed, and get you some food, and when you have eaten and slept you will be much better fitted to see and feel rightly."

"Tell me one thing, Margaret," said she, taking my hands: "are you and Walter truly betrothed?"

"We are," I answered her; "and my Lord hath given his consent."

She made a movement, as if to draw her hand from mine, but refrained.

"And you will soon be married, I suppose!" she added, after a pause.

"I believe not," said I. "I promised my dear Lady before there was any likelihood of such good fortune befalling me, that I would not leave Lady Betty for a year, whatever happened; and I mean to keep my word, unless I have more reason than I see now for breaking it."

"How I have wronged you!" she said, sighing. "Margaret, there is hardly any evil that I have not thought of you."

"You were prejudiced against me by one whom you might well have believed," said I. "I know not why Felicia hath always been mine enemy, except that it seems a part of her nature to have to hate somebody."

"It was not that—not altogether!" said Lady Jemima. "It was"—

"You shall tell me another time," said I, venturing to interrupt her; "that is, if you see fit to honor me with your confidence. I really think you ought to go to bed now, and rest, that you may be ready to see my Lady when she asks for you, and to make the house pleasant for my Lord."

"I will do anything you tell me," she said, sadly.

"Dear Lady Jemima, I don't mean to dictate!" I began to say; but she stopped me.

"Yes, you shall dictate!" said she. "You shall command, and I will obey. It is fit that I should humble myself before you, aye, even in the dust—that I should be humbled in the eyes of all the world—if so I make any atonement for my sins."

I could not let this pass. It seemed to me such a dreary notion, and at the same time such a false one, that I felt I must speak.

"Dear madam, why should you think of making any such atonement?" I said. "Surely the one oblation of our Lord, once offered, is a sufficient atonement and satisfaction for the sins of the whole world, let alone yours and mine: and no suffering of ours, no voluntary humiliation or penance, will add anything to its virtue. Only cast all your care and sin on Him, and leave Him to lay upon you such crosses as He sees best: I don't think we need be afraid of having too much ease in this world, if we are willing to bear the burdens and do the tasks He provides for us. And if we go to work making burdens and tasks for ourselves—doing our own work—I am afraid we are in great danger of neglecting His."

I doubted how she would take my little sermon. She did not seem displeased, however, but said we would talk of it again. I helped her to undress, and got her to bed.

"I do not see how you can find any rest on such a bed!" I said, feeling how hard and uneven it was. "I wish you would let me make it up comfortably."

"Do as you will!" said she, wearily, leaning back in her chair. I looked out into the gallery, and seeing one of the maids, I bade her bring a matrass and quilt from an unused room near by, wherewith I made the bed as nicely as I could. The poor lady could not help a sigh of relief and satisfaction, as she lay down. Then I sent Dolly down for a manchet and a cup of cream, and persuaded Lady Jemima to eat a little. She promised me that she would lie still and try to sleep, and asked me to come in again after a while, kissing me at parting. As I shut the door, I heard her sobs burst forth, but I did not return, thinking that she would at last weep herself to sleep.

I found Betty up and dressed, and in due time took her in to see and kiss her mother. My dear Lady looked very lovely in her paleness, but Madam would not let her speak a word to any one, which was no more than right, of course, though Betty was inclined to murmur thereat, till Madam explained to her the reason; after which she seemed hardly to dare to breathe. She was sadly disappointed in the babes.

"They are so red and spotty—they are not nearly as pretty as kittens," said she, pouting a little: "I think they look more like the young rats Ambrose showed me."

My Lord nearly exploded into a laugh at this criticism, and my Lady smiled, but Mrs. Brewster was indignant.

I explained to Betty that all very young babes looked so, and that they would grow pretty in time.

"Will they?" she asked, wistfully. "When will they get their eyes open?"

This was too much for my Lord, who fled precipitately into the gallery. But, at that moment, one of the babies opened his eyes and showed that they were blue. I made Betty slip her finger into one of the little hands, which closed on it at once, and Betty was more than satisfied.

Since that time we have gone on very quietly. My Lady is not so strong as we could wish, but the doctor says it is only because she exerted herself too much just at first, and that a long rest will set all right again. The babies are all that any one could desire, stout, well-grown, and healthy. Betty sees new beauties and wonders in them every day, and would, if she were permitted, nurse them all day long. She does not show the least jealousy of them, but seems to rejoice in all the attention and admiration they receive. Only the other morning I found her taking Anne severely to task for something she had said. As I entered, she appealed to me in great excitement:

"Anne says my nose is broke, and that nobody will care for me any more," said she, half crying; "and it is not true, is it, Margaret? She says I shall be nobody, now that there is an heir, and"—

"Anne is a very bad girl to say such things!" I answered her; and then turning to the girl, I reproved her sharply; whereto she answered me at first saucily enough; but when I said I should speak to Mrs. Judith, she cooled down and begged my pardon. I have forbid her speaking to Betty hereafter, and have told her plainly that I shall complain to Mrs. Judith if she disobeys me, or if I hear any more of her pert speeches.

Lady Jemima continues very ill, with a kind of low fever, and her mind is worse than her body. From thinking herself all but a saint, with her penances and fastings, she has gone round to the opposite extreme, and now believes herself such a sinner that there can be no hope for her. It is painful to see how woe-begone and sorrowful she is. I spend as much time with her as I can, and try to cheer her up: and I really think she likes to have me with her. I have not encouraged her to talk to me of her feelings about Walter. I believe such things are almost always best kept to oneself, and I am afraid of her saying what she will be sorry for by and by: but I read to her, and tell her stories about the poor folks in the village and what happens in the family, and sometimes I sit by her in silence whole hours at a time, busy with my needle.

For myself, I can only say I am as happy as the day is long—happier than I ever believed anybody could be in this world. My engagement is now spoken of as a matter of course, and my Lord treats me as a daughter or younger sister, and will have me receive all tokens of outward respect, as one of the family. I think Mrs. Judith was a little shocked at first, but she is reconciled now, and is quite sure that all is for the best, especially since she has found out that my mother was a Seymour, and my father's mother a grandchild of my Lord Falkland. But setting that aside, I do think she loves me enough for my own sake not to grudge me any good fortune. Walter has written to mother and Richard, and also to Aunt Willson, which, he says truly, is only her due, since she has been so kind to me. I would love to be married at home, in my dear father's own church, but the journey is a long one, and I don't know how that will be. At any rate, Walter has promised that I shall go very soon to visit them all. I see him every day. My Lord begins to fret at the wedding being put off, and to say that Bess can do well enough without me: but I am quite content that matters should rest as they are for the present. I am sure I shall never be happier than I am now.

CHAPTER XI.

November 30.

MY journal is not very regularly kept, now-a days, I have so much to do and to think about.

Letters have come from home, and from Aunt Willson. They all write very kindly, and dear mother is greatly pleased. She says she is thankful to have seen and liked Walter, for she would hardly have felt like giving me to a stranger. Dick writes gravely, after his fashion, and Aunt Willson bluntly, after hers. She says she had a shrewd guess how matters were going when she saw Walter in London, and she believes I am about to do well.

"I have only one bit of advice to give thee, child," she says; "and that is, never, on any account, to speak to any human being, however near and dear, of thy husband's faults and short comings, nor let any one talk to you. I dare say you wonder that I should think such advice necessary, but 'tis a rock which has wrecked the happiness of many a married pair. Amend what thou canst, and what thou canst not amend, bear with patience and love, in God's name. For the rest I daresay you will do well enough. You were brought up as a gentlewoman, and you are young enough to mold your habits where they need molding. You will have a second mother in Madam Corbet, who is one of the chosen ones. I send you some matters for your fitting out, and likewise some money for your purse."

The "matters" turn out to be a great mail filled with beautiful stuffs and silks, such as I never thought to wear, with store of fine linen and laces, and a set of pearl jewels, good enough for a countess. But that I know that my aunt is rich, and that it is a pleasure for her to be giving, I should feel oppressed with her bounty. I have had beautiful presents from all the family.

I must not forget to say that Felicia is also going to be married to a rich merchant of London, a worthy man, Aunt Willson says, but a great Presbyterian, and very strict in all his notions. Aunt says he hath altogether converted Felicia to his own way of thinking, insomuch that she looks upon a Bishop as Antichrist in person, and believes that no prayer read from a book can possibly meet with any acceptance.

My new uncle sends me a fine shawl or mantle, of some kind of Eastern stuff, called crape, white and embroidered in heavy silk, with roses and other flowers, in quite a wonderful way; also a treatise by Mr. Baxter, a young Presbyterian divine, which I have not yet found time to look at. Felicia sends me nothing, save a civilly scornful note, in which she says she is glad I have played my cards so well, and that I am going to be *married*—the words underlined—to Mr. Corbet. For her own part she is content with her lot, and would rather be the wife of a godly, honest merchant, than of any hanger on of a great family. I did not show the note to Walter, for I knew it would vex him. For myself I care not for her venom, which hath lost its power to sting me; but I am sorry for her husband. She sends her respects to Lady Jemima, and bids me tell her that she (Felicia) has seen the error and darkness of her ways, and the wickedness of the scheme in which they had both been engaged, and hopes her Ladyship may have grace to repent the same. I was not going to tell Lady Jemima the message, but she heard I had received letters, and at last I showed her Felicia's.

"How I was deceived in her, as well as in myself!" said she, sighing deeply, as she returned me the letter. "My fine scheme has vanished into air, like the bubble it was."

"Perhaps it has vanished that something better may come in its place," said I.

She shook her head sadly. "Nay," said she, "I have learned more about myself since then."

She is better in health, but sadly out of spirits, and seems to find little comfort in anything. I do hope the Bishop will be able to set her right.

My Lady hath recovered faster than we could have expected, sits up all day, and has walked a little in the gallery, but does not yet get out or come to the table. The babes are all that any one can wish, and Betty now resents bitterly any criticism upon their good looks. I think she loves the blue-eyed babe, perhaps, the best of the two. Her own health has not been good since the shock of that day. She is again growing thin, and complains of the pain in her back and side once more. I cannot but fear that she received some injury in the struggle. She hath made up her quarrel with Aunt Jemima, and often sits by her bed and reads to her in the Bible, though she has to spell a good many words.

We are to have a distinguished guest in the course of two or three weeks, no less a person than Anthony Van Dyke, the great court painter. Walter knew him well both abroad and in London, and hearing he was to be in Exeter, invited him to paint his mother's portrait, to which she consented, on condition that Walter's and mine should be painted also. My Lord is much taken with the fancy of having my Lady and her children sit to him, and I hope the plan will be carried out; but it seems doubtful whether the great man can stay so long in this west country. Walter says he is a very fine gentleman, and is glad that the king gives him encouragement to stay in this country.

December 10.

The Bishop hath been with us nearly a week, holding his visitation, and especially inquiring into the condition of the moorland parishes, which he finds sad enough; no preaching save perhaps once or twice a year, no catechising, the young folk growing up like utter heathen, knowing no more of the word of God (so Walter says, who hath accompanied my Lord in most of his journeys), than so many Turks or Indians. They believe enough, however, in the devil and his servants, in witches, pixies, moormen, Jack Lanterns, night crows, and what not; and through fear of such like creatures live all their lives in most cruel bondage.

The Bishop is greatly exercised by this state of things, and hath a great many schemes for improving the condition of these poor folks, by sending them faithful preachers, and establishing schools among them. He hath already found a mistress for one of these schools, in the person of Mabel Winne, an excellent woman in the village, and daughter of a substantial farmer, who being single, and in a manner left alone by the death of all her friends, desires to devote her life to some such good work. Jane Atkins tells me that Mabel was for a long time head girl of the school, and a good scholar, though proud and high-spirited, but that having caused the maiming and final death of a friend, by pushing her down in a sudden fit of passion, the sad event so changed her that she hath ever since sought her pleasure in doing good offices among her poor neighbors, nursing the sick, and so forth. She seems just the person to carry out the Bishop's plan, especially as she is by no means poor, but hath enough to support her comfortably, in a simple way.

Lady Jemima hath had many talks with the Bishop, and I think is in a fair way of regaining her peace of mind. She seems for a day or two past quite cheerful, and at last, at my Lord's earnest entreaty, came down-stairs to supper. I was sorry, for I knew Walter would be there, and I dreaded their meeting; but it passed very nicely, she wishing him joy with a sweet smile, and saying most kind things of me; but, withal, I saw tears come into her eyes as she took her seat. I don't know whether Walter suspects aught or not: I am sure he shall never hear it from me.

After supper she told me that she was tired, and would withdraw. I went with her to her room, and when there she told me that she had been telling the Bishop about her scheme for a nunnery, and that he had put another plan in her head, namely, to turn her house near Exeter into a refuge for orphan girls from the city, where they might be trained to usefulness and piety, and fitted to earn an honest and comfortable living. "He says," she continued, "that I might always have six or eight such young maidens in my family, and he would have me live among them myself, and oversee them. Is not that a pretty castle in the air?" she added, sorrowfully smiling.

"Indeed, I think it a much prettier one than your nunnery," I answered, "and one much more easy to erect on firm ground."

"Aye," said she. "My sisterhood has turned out finely, with one sister marrying a priest, and another a Presbyterian." (For it is quite settled now that Mrs. Priscilla and Mr. Penrose are to make a match of it. I need not have been so distressed at breaking the poor man's heart. 'Tis something easier mended than Betty's china image.) "But I feel myself unfitted for such a work and responsibility, otherwise I would welcome the suggestion at once. As it is, I shall not put it away, but consider upon it, and consult my sister."

I do hope the plan will succeed. I am sure Lady Jemima will be better and happier in a house of her own, than she is here, and also that this house will be better without her. The desire for employment and for doing good, which here makes her only troublesome, will be well laid out on a family of her own.

December 10.

My dear child seems better again, and once more goes about the house, and looks after her fowls and other pets, and nurses her little brothers, though the latter not so much as she would like, ecause their weight makes her shoulder ache. Still I am very uneasy about her. She grows thin, and has a little cough, and two or three times she has had something like a fainting fit, save that her face turns brownish instead of pale. She is wonderful happy in her spirit, and all her old irritability seems entirely gone.

The great painter is come, and is at work on Walter's and his mother's pictures. He is a wonderful courtly gentleman, with a quick eye, which nothing escapes. He hath already expressed a wish to paint Betty, saying that she has one of the most lovely and touching faces he ever saw: to which my Lord and Lady gave their consent, and are mightily pleased, as is Betty herself. But Mary does not like it at all, and says she hopes there may be nothing wrong, but it stands to reason that the gentleman cannot put so much life into his pictures without taking it out of the people he paints; and that Betty has none to spare, she being weakly already. I think Mrs. Judith is much of the same mind, though she will not own it.

The matter is quite settled as to Lady Jemima's orphan-house. She is to be the head of the family, with a suitable establishment; and is to begin with six young girls, not of the very poorest, but from clergymen's families, and the like. This is by the Bishop's advice, who says that less is done for this class than for any other. One is to be the child of an artist, a great friend of Mr. Van Dyke's, and worse than an orphan, her mother having deserted her child, and the poor father, all but distracted, desires to go abroad, but has no one with whom to leave the poor young maid, who is only six years old. Mr. Van Dyke desires the privilege of paying her necessary expenses (the care and safety he gracefully says can never be paid for), and he hath given Lady Jemima a hundred pounds. It shows how really humbled dear Lady Jemima is, that she took the money without a demur. She is much more cheerful since she hath been engaged with this plan, and rejoices with trembling in the hope of present forgiveness and favor. She has long chats with Dame Yeo, and I think the old woman hath done her much good. Every one notices the difference in her, and even her face is changed. She does not see Walter often, and when she does, she meets him as a brother: but I can see it costs her a pang.

Ah me! It seems very hard that the happiness of one should cost the misery of another: but I believe what she says is true, and that Walter would never have thought of her, even if I had never come to the Court to live. She is two years older than he, for one thing, and a woman always seems older than a man at the same age; and then all their notions are so different. The only wonder to me is, how she should ever have fancied him.

December 20.

Betty's picture is nearly done, and is wondrously beautiful. Some of the family think it flattered, but I do not. It is only that Mr. Van Dyke has seized upon her most lovely expression, that which her face wears when she is saying her prayers, or nursing her little brothers, or looking upon something which pleases her—a sunset, or the like. Mr. Van Dyke himself thinks it the best picture he hath painted in these parts. When it was finished, Betty looked at it long and wistfully.

"Is it really like me?" she asked.

"Indeed it is," said I.

"I am glad of it," she said, and took another long look at the picture. "My little brothers will see it and know what I was like, and I think papa will love to look at it."

She has several times lately said things of this kind, which led me to think that she herself believes she will not live long. I cannot help feeling the same myself. Nobody ever sees a fault in her now —not a pettish word or look ever escapes her, and instead of thinking all the time of herself, as she used to do when I first came here, all her care is for other people : and she never loses a chance of pleasing and helping those around her. She is much interested in her aunt's scheme of the orphan-house, and has tried to work for it by hemming sheets and napkins, and the like, but she can sew and knit only for a few minutes at a time, because of the pain in her shoulder. I fear she will soon leave us. And yet why should I say fear? 'Twould be a blessed change for her, and I am sure she is ripe for it.

I have been to Exeter with my Lady Jemima, to see her house there, and help her choose matters for her housekeeping. The place is called, in the neighborhood, "Lady House," and was once a small convent of gray nuns. It is in good repair and mostly well furnished, and there is a gallery with cells on each side, which she will fit up as bed-rooms for her older girls. She will have a nursery for the young ones, and is looking about for a suitable nurse for them. I think she will take the oldest girl in Lady Rosamond's school, who is good and steady, and understands spinning and knitting, as well as all sorts of needlework, coarse and fine. We stayed at the palace, and I think Mrs. Hall, the Bishop's lady, has quite overcome in her mind her old prejudice against married clergymen. She was remarking to me on the beautiful order and peace of the household—the servants so well behaved and attentive, and so happy each in his or her own place—the maids trained so as they may make good wives and mothers, and carefully instructed in religion by Mrs. Hall herself; the children so well bred and restrained, yet withal so cheerful, and on such happy terms of respect and intimacy with both father and mother. I ventured to say to her:

"Do you think the Bishop would be a happier or a better man if he were condemned to a lonely, solitary life, with no home, and no wife or children to cheer him after his labors? And is he not better prepared to sympathise with both the joys and sorrows of his flock, from having experienced some of the same?"

"Maybe so!" said she, and then presently she sighed—a very deep, sorrowful sigh, methought.

I knew well enough what she was thinking of. She has three orphan maids from Exeter, and one for whom Walter specially made interest from Plymouth, the child of an old sea captain, lately dead of a fever, besides the little child from London, who is now at the Court, and sleeps in Lady Jemima's room. She is a very pretty, gentle little creature, full of play, and of wonder at all she sees, having never before been out of London. Betty has introduced her to the fowls and the cat and kittens, and hath also made over to her, her great linen baby, which I made when I first came here. Lady Jemima thinks there never was such another child made.

Christmas is close at hand, when we are to have great revels, as is the custom here. Mr. Van Dyke tells us a deal about the manner of keeping the holiday in the Low Countries, and of St. Nicholas (whom they call Santa Claus,) coming with gifts to put in the children's socks and shoes when they are asleep. Betty and the little Catharine are much interested, and wish the saint would come hither.

Last Christmas I was at home, and dear father preached in the church, and afterward superintended the giving away of the Christmas dole of bread and blankets, and a fine plum bun to each child in the school. I little thought then how matters would be changed with me before Christmas came round again.

My Lady now goes down-stairs, and hath even been out into the garden. She seems better in health, and more light-hearted that I have ever known her, and has lost much of the melancholy expression which used to mark her face. My Lord is even more devoted to her than ever. He is no more captious and disposed to quarrel with Walter, as he used to be, but makes him very welcome, and I think consults him a good deal upon business matters. He is a good deal perplexed and annoyed because the neighboring magistrates and gentry urge him to prosecute some of his tenants, who are Puritans, and seldom or never attend the parish church—a thing he is no ways disposed to do. David Lee, the farmer, of whom I spoke once before as having some of his neighbors meet for prayers in his house, has given up the farm on which he and his have lived for I don't know how long, and is going to the new plantations in America, along with John Starbuck, from the Mill Heads, whose brother is there already. David is brother to old Uncle Jan Lee, down at the Cove, and nearly as old a man, though not so infirm; but he has two stout sons, and three daughters, one of whom is betrothed to Ephraim Starbuck, and he says he values his religious liberty more than his home. My Lord is much grieved, and has tried to prevail on him to remain, promising him protection and countenance, but failing to move him, he has (so Walter says), dealt most liberally with him, and given him some valuable presents in the way of stock and tools. My Lord thinks the old man is throwing away his own life and those of his family; but Walter is more hopeful. He says the land over there is good, and the harbors excellent, and he believes the new colony may in time become a place of importance. He tells me the colonists have begun by establishing schools, and have even founded a college, which seems odd enough. What will they do with a college out there, among the savages?

CHAPTER XII.

January 3.

HOW ill have I treated this poor faithful journal of mine! And I fear 'tis like to fare even worse, in the future. I can hardly realize it, but such is the fact. I am going to be married the day after to-morrow; whereas I had not expected such an event before June, at the nearest; and my poor dear child, Lady Betty, is the good fairy who has brought all this about. But I will go back and tell my story in an orderly manner.

There was great bustle and interest in making ready for the holidays—more even than usual, for my Lord meant to celebrate the birth of his sons, by giving a good piece of beef, and a fine pudding to each one of the cottagers. He was to have had a feast for them at the Court, but on account of my Lady's health, and for some other reasons, that is put off till next summer. Then the school children were to be feasted at my Lady's expense, and a Christmas gift made to each, and all the maid servants were to have new gowns; all of which involved a good deal of work for some of us.

Most of the shopping fell upon Lady Jemima and myself, and we had a fine time going to Biddeford, and selecting gowns, ribbons, and the like; and I was surprised to see how much interest dear Lady Jemima took in the purchase. I could not have thought it was in her, to care so much for such a matter. She is a great deal more cheerful than I have ever seen her, and really grows pretty and plump, now that she has left off her fasting and sitting up of nights. Every one sees the change. I am sure she is very good to love me as she does. I don't believe I could do it, in her place.

Betty was very grave and thoughtful for two or three days before Christmas, and I wondered what was in her head. On Christmas-Eve, as she and I were sitting in my Lady's room—my Lady nursing one of the babes, and Betty holding the other, I was glad to sit still, for I was thoroughly tired, and the quiet was very grateful to me. We had been silent for some minutes, when Betty spoke:

"Mamma, why don't Margaret and Walter get married? I thought that was the next thing, when people were betrothed."

"And so it is, my dear one!" answered her mother; "but then you see Margaret has a little nursling whom she does not like to leave. What do you think you would do without her?"

"But she would not go so very far away. She would only be at Corby-End," said Betty. Then, after a little silence, "Mamma, I should like to see Margaret married."

"Why, so you shall, and be bridesmaid too, if you like," answered her mother. "Why not?"

"Then, mamma, I should like them to be married pretty soon," replied Betty; "because I don't believe I shall be here a great while longer."

This was the first time she had spoken so plainly, though she had hinted as much a good many times lately. My Lady started and looked anxiously at her.

"Why do you say that, my darling?" she asked; "don't you feel as well?"

"I don't know, mamma," said Betty. "I feel languid and weary, and there is a feeling *here*," (pressing her hand to her heart,) "which I never had before you were ill, and which tells me that I shall not live long."

"Dear child, that is only a fancy," said her mother, kissing her. "You must drive away such gloomy thoughts."

"They are not gloomy," said this strange child; "and they are not fancies, either. Something calls me away all the time, and at night, when I lie awake, I hear such strange, beautiful music in the air and among the trees. But I wont talk about it, if it makes you unhappy, dear mamma," she added, seeing the tears in her mother's eyes; "only, if you please, I should so much like to have Walter and Margaret married very soon. Please, wont you have it so?"

"We will see," answered her mother.

Betty was silent, but I could see she was turning

the matter over in her mind, as her fashion is; and when she went to bed she spoke of it again.

"Margaret, if you want to make me very happy, you will be married very soon. I am quite sure that I have only a little time to live now, and I do so want to see you married. Please do let me speak to papa about it."

What could I say? I saw how much in earnest she was, and I believed with herself, that she had not long to live, and that she might go from us in any of the fainting fits she had lately. She saw, I suppose, that I was moved, and urged me again, even with tears, to let her speak to my Lord.

"Don't cry!" said I, alarmed; "you shall do as you please, but you must not cry, or you will bring on one of your bad times again."

But the bad time came, in spite of me. She fainted, and it was more than ten minutes before we could bring her round. I began to think she had gone for good, but she breathed again at last, her breath coming in most painful gasps and sobs. She is weaker after every one of these fits, and longer in recovering herself. When she mentioned the subject again, I told her she should do as she liked, and at last she went to sleep, quite content and happy. I did not leave her save to go to my room and put on my wrapper. As I went out into the gallery, I met Mr. Van Dyke, with his hands full of toys and sweetmeats.

"See here, Mistress Merton," said he. "Cannot

we put these into the shoes of my little lady and Catharine, and so give them a pleasant surprise, and let them think the good Saint Nicholas has been to visit them?"

I was well pleased with the fancy, and we went to my Lady Jemima's room, where the little Catharine sleeps. Lady Jemima entered into the sport and we filled the little socks and shoes with sugar-plums and toys. Then I went back and lay down by Betty, whom I did not mean to leave that night.

Early in the morning, long before dawn, we were roused by the schoolboys, and the young men and maids from the village, coming to sing carols under the window. Mrs. Judith and her maids were up early, as it was, and they were called into the hall and regaled with cakes and spiced ale. Soon the whole household was astir, and Betty would get up and be dressed with the rest, to meet the family at breakfast. I did not oppose her, for she seemed strong and bright for her, and besides I did not believe that anything would make much difference. There is that in her face nowadays that I have seen too often to mistake its meaning. She was very merry this morning, and much delighted at finding the St. Nicholas gifts in her shoes.

"I know how Saint Nicholas looks, Margaret!" said she. "He hath fine dark eyes, and curling hair, and a peaked beard, and he paints beautiful pictures."

So I saw that she had guessed the riddle at once. Little Catharine, however, was not so quick in her apprehension, but I believe thinks, to this hour, that St. Nicholas paid her a visit, and only regrets that she was not awake to see him.

Betty had made a couple of fine handkerchiefs for Christmas gifts to her father and mother, doing the open hems very nicely, with a little of my help; and after prayers she had the pleasure of giving them, and seeing them admired to her heart's content.

"And please you, my Lord, I have to beg for a Christmas box!" she said, with a little formal courtesy. "You know you promised me one."

"Why, so I did, Boss, and what shall it be?' said my Lord, well pleased.

"Let me whisper in your ear, papa," said she.

He bent his stately head down to her—he is very indulgent to her, nowadays—and then, as she whispered eagerly to him, he stared, laughed heartily, and bade her ask Walter, since he was the person most concerned.

"I think he will be willing, don't you, papa?" said Betty: "he is always so kind and obliging."

My Lord roared with laughter again, and said he did not doubt he would be willing, since it was to oblige his cousin. And so I hardly know how, 'twas all settled in an hour that we were to be married on Twelfth Day, and so go home to Corby-End.

It grieves me that I must be married away from

mother, but there is no help for it, and Walter promises to take me home for a visit so soon as the spring opens.

The Christmas revels went off very nicely. We all went to church, my Lord and Lady, and all—and my Lord stayed to the sacrament—a thing I never knew him do before. The church was beautifully adorned with ivy and holly, and such late flowers as the mild season often spares till Christmas. Everybody was dressed in their best, and all were exchanging good wishes and Christmas words. I could not help shedding some tears as I remembered last Christmas, when I was at home, and dear father was alive and well: but for all that I felt wonderfully tranquil and happy. Old Uncle Jan Lee was at church, and so I was glad to see were his brother and all his family. My Lord would take no denial, but would have them all up at the Court for their Christmas dinner—Will Atkins and his wife, and all—so we had a great gathering, and a very merry one, but all sober and decorous enough. Betty lay down and had a nap after dinner, and so was ready to see the revels in the evening, when we had the Christmas murmurs—Lord Christmas, Dame Mince Pie and all the rest, with a fine copy of verses from the schoolmaster, in which he compared our poor babes to Castor and Pollux, and I know not what other heathen gods. I fear he was rather scandalized by our levity, for no one could help laughing, but my Lord thanked him and made him a handsome present, so he was consoled.

Mr. Penrose was not with us, he keeping his Christmas at Sir Thomas Fulton's. And so ended our Christmas day.

Since then I have lived in a kind of dream, recalled to this lower world, however, about once an hour, by Mrs. Brewster, who wants me to try on something, or to give my judgment on some solemn matter of trimming or pattern. But I am sure I shall never know what to do with so many fine clothes as they are preparing for me. It is very silly in me, I dare say, but I cannot help wishing I were not so poor. If my poor dear father's ship had come home, now!

January 5.

I have to-day had the greatest—yes, the very greatest surprise of my life, greater even than that of finding myself on the eve of marriage to a great gentleman like Walter. I was hearing Betty's Latin lesson, which she will still keep up, though she has dropped most of her other lessons these short days, when Mrs. Judith herself came up, and informed me that a gentleman was inquiring for me and was awaiting me in the little parlor.

"A gentleman to see me—you must surely be mistaken, Mrs. Judith!" said I.

"Indeed I am not!" she asserted, with a merry twinkle in her eye. "'Tis a gallant young gentleman as I wish to see, and he asks for Mrs.

Margaret Merton. So go you down and see him."

I arranged my dress and went down-stairs, wondering who it could possibly be, and thinking over all the gentlemen I had ever known, which were not many. Somehow it never came into my head to think of Dick, and yet when I opened the door of the little parlor, there he was, looking as composed and grave in his sober riding suit, as if he had but just come over from Chester to spend Sunday at home.

I don't know what I said or did at first, save that I cried, laughed, and talked all at once, till suddenly a thought came over me, which made me cry out: "Oh, Dick! you have brought me no ill news, have you?"

"No, no! very far from that," he answered me, cheerfully. "Why, Meg! how you have grown, and how handsome you are! The gentleman who met me in the hall, and to whom I made myself known, tells me that I am just in time, for that you are to be married to-morrow. How is that? I thought the great event was to be put off till spring."

I explained that the time had been shortened to gratify my little lady, who was in delicate health, and who was bent on seeing the wedding.

"Aye, doubtless it was a great sacrifice!" said he, in his old way.

"But Dick," said I, "what wind has blown you

here? I am sure something must have happened more than common."

"A good wind, though a most unexpected one," he answered. "The last one I ever thought of, I am sure. Meg, my father's ship has come home, safe and sound, and with a wonderful rich freight. My father's poor venture of three hundred odd pounds is magnified tenfold, and more. Mr. Gunning tells me that our fair share of the cargo comes to five thousand pounds, and he is quite willing to advance us the money upon it."

I could only sit and stare stupidly at him for a moment. Then I burst out crying, and sobbed: "Oh, if my poor father had but lived to see it!"

"He will not miss it where he is," answered Richard, gravely. "But is it not wonderful?"

"Wonderful, indeed," said I. 'Tis like a chapter of romance. I can hardly believe it."

"Nor could I, till I saw the ship herself, and went on board of her, for you must know I have been in Bristol; and a fair and great city it is. I have had a wearisome journey."

And here came in one of the men with a great tray of refreshments, sent by Mrs. Judith; and while Richard was eating, came in first my Lady, who made my brother welcome with her usual grace and courtesy; and then Walter and my Lord, and the lawyer from Biddeford, who is here now, and there was a deal of talk about business before I could get Dick to myself again. But I did finally, and carried him off for a walk by ourselves in the chase, and he told me all about home matters. How my mother took the news, and how she loves the cottage too well to leave it, but will add somewhat thereto, as she can do with great convenience. How all our old neighbors rejoiced in our good fortune, specially Dame Crump, who is still alive, and who has always prophesied that the ship would come home sometime. How Mr. Carey makes himself loved by all, both rich and poor, save that he and Sir Peter Beaumont do not well agree. Finally, and best of all, how Dick himself is now to carry out the darling wish of his heart, and go to Cambridge, to begin his studies as soon as possible.

And so ends the day before my wedding day, with all the content possible; and as I look back at the last year, and see how wonderfully I have been preserved and helped, what friends I have found on every side, and how the plans of mine enemies have been frustrated and brought to naught, my heart overflows with thankfulness and joy, and I feel like consecrating myself anew and more entirely than ever to Him who is the Father of the Fatherless and the God of the widow.

Here ends all of my journal which I have seen fit to transcribe for my daughters to read when I am gone, as I feel that I soon shall be, to join my honored parents and my dear Lady.

My married life hath not been wholly without clouds, as what life is? In the civil wars which began soon after, my husband took part with Parliament, and afterward served under the Protector, while my Lord was on the other side: yet did that circumstance never wholly divide the families, and my husband was able to be of great service to my Lord in protecting his property from sequestration. But Walter was never satisfied with all the actions of Parliament, and was wont to say that in many things they showed themselves as oppressive and regardless of the laws and liberties of the land as ever the king and his party had been. Yet did he adhere to Cromwell, as being the only hope of the nation; and truly he made the English name respected as it hath never been respected since. He made the Dutch, now so saucy, know their place, and the French likewise, and he interfered for the poor Vaudois to some purpose.

Poor Lady Betty survived till Easter, gradually growing weaker, but suffering little, and able to keep up till the last. On Easter Sunday she received the Sacrament, at her own earnest request, Mr. Penrose having given her preparatory instruction. It being a fine warm day, she rode to the parish church, sat out the whole service, and seemed none the worse; but the next morning, when Mary went to call her, she was dead, having, as it seemed, passed away without ever waking up. We all grieved for her, and I think none more than my Lord, to whom she had become very dear of late; but we could not but feel that it was well with the child.

My Lady survived her daughter some four years. After a decent time my Lord married again to a very good woman, a widow lady with two daughters. She was a very good wife to my Lord, and a kind mother to his sons, but she was never to be compared to my own dear Lady.

Lady Jemima lives in her own house, with her family of orphan maids about her, and is much loved and respected. Little Catharine—now a fine tall young lady, is still with her, but she has changed the rest of the family many times over, and always for their advantage. She is indeed a most excellent lady.

Felicia is still alive; a sour, discontented woman, rich, but feeling poor, and always imagining that somebody is leagueing to rob her or impose upon her. Her first fall in life I do think was when her husband positively refused to let her put in any claim to my father's estate, saying that he was rich enough already, and that she ought to be ashamed to ask for a penny, seeing she had been brought up at my father's expense. Felicia scolded and sulked, but he was firm, and for once she met with her match.

Mr. Fowler is dead now, and poor Felicia lives alone, having quarrelled with all her husband's relations, and not being able to find a waiting gentlewoman who will stay with her more than a month at a time. She came to see me when I was last in London, and entertained me with a catalogue of her sorrows, not the least of which was that my Aunt Willson, who died at a great age, divided her large fortune equally between Felicia and my father's children. She says she is the most unhappy woman in the world, and I dare say she is right.

Richard went abroad just at the beginning of the trouble, as tutor to a young nobleman, and did not return till the restoration, when he took orders, and is now a useful, unambitious parish-priest in Chester. I don't think he will ever be a bishop, as I used to dream, and I don't believe he wishes it; but there is some hope that he will have my father's living at Saintswell, and dwell in the dear old house where we were all born.

www.ingramcontent.com/pod-product-compliance
Lightning Source LLC
Chambersburg PA
CBHW020220240426
43672CB00006B/369